A Dictionary of Electronic and Computer Music Technology

A Dictionary of Electronic and

Computer Music Technology

Instruments, Terms, Techniques

Richard Dobson

Oxford   New York
OXFORD UNIVERSITY PRESS
1992

Oxford University Press, Walton Street, Oxford OX2 6DP
Oxford New York Toronto
Delhi Bombay Calcutta Madras Karachi
Petaling Jaya Singapore Hong Kong Tokyo
Nairobi Dar es Salaam Cape Town
Melbourne Auckland

and associated companies in
Berlin Ibadan

Oxford is a trade mark of Oxford University Press

Published in the United States
by Oxford University Press, New York

© Richard Dobson 1992

British Library Cataloguing in Publication Data
Data available

Library of Congress Cataloging in Publication Data
Data available

ISBN 0–19–311344–9

Set by Columns Design and Production Services Ltd.
Printed in Great Britain by Bookcraft (Bath) Ltd.,
Midsomer Norton

To my Parents

Contents

Introduction

While there are certain difficulties that may be faced in compiling any dictionary, concerning in particular what information should be left out, a dictionary of electronic musical instruments presents some possibly unique challenges. The immediate problem derives from the fact that, especially today, instruments have so many technical features in common. This compares with the substantial independence of acoustic instruments; one may write about a flute, for example, without needing to refer to any other instrument. By contrast, it is hardly possible to discuss any modern electronic instrument without explaining how sounds are generated and controlled, especially in relation to digital technology, which is noted for its ability to blur distinctions. The similarities between instruments such as the sampler, the synthesizer, the sequencer, and the signal processor are substantial (they are all particular applications of computer technology), such that these instruments cannot be discussed in mutual isolation. This was already true before 1982, but the introduction of MIDI has (quite literally) linked disparate instruments even more inseparably.

The second problem is that the pace of technological development has led to a rapid 'turnover' of instruments. During the preparation of this dictionary a number of potentially noteworthy instruments have been introduced, with attendant pomp and circumstance, only to disappear within a few years. In certain areas of the market, it is understood that new models are introduced at least annually, and others discontinued. The problem of what to include becomes as vexing as that of what to exclude. Any dictionary of instruments which relied on references to particular models would become rapidly out of date.

A third problem relates to the fact that a great deal of technical information needs to be introduced and explained. The approach adopted in this book is to provide comprehensive entries not so much on individual instruments but on common principles and techniques. For example, the subject of the synthesizer is dealt with in two complementary entries, the first dealing with the basic principles of synthesis, the second dealing with the different ways in which those techniques might be implemented in a real instrument. Specific products may then be referred to as examples of a particular approach. This is likely to be more useful in the long term than myriad references to individual instruments which may be obsolete, or 'of historical interest', with a year of publication.

The dictionary can thus be used both as a reference and as a tutorial text. In addition to the entries on synthesis, there are substantial background entries on acoustics, the computer, and electronic components, which (though fully referenced from other entries) are perhaps worth reading as preliminaries, for those readers new to these subjects.

In compiling this dictionary, I have placed the emphasis firmly on commercial instruments, and the principles underlying them, rather than on those largely confined to research and academic institutions. In many cases historical information has been sacrificed in favour of more expansive technical material. In particular, little attempt has been made to cover the history of electronic music; readers with an interest in this area are encouraged to read Peter Manning's book *Electronic and Computer Music* (Oxford, 1985). Nevertheless, much historical information on instruments is included, most especially on the electric guitar, but also on companies and individuals whose work has been central to the development of electronic instruments and their music.

Finally, acknowledgements are due especially to Dr Anthony Baines, without whose encouragement and scholarly guidance this book could not have been written, to Dr Peter Manning of Durham University, who read early drafts of much of the material and whose suggestions have been invaluable in helping me to clarify my approach to the subject, and to the staff at O.U.P. whose encouragement, advice, and patience have contributed so much to the final form of the book.

A

Accordion

Electronic tone generation was first incorporated into the piano accordion by the Italian company Farfisa in 1962 (though facilities for simple amplification had been available for several years), with a view to giving accordionists facilities similar to those of the electronic *organ. Although some purely electronic instruments have been produced, the most popular instruments are those which combine electronics with a traditional acoustic accordion. Other companies to develop electronic accordions include Hohner and Elka, both established manufacturers of electronic organs. Of the three, Elka were the first to introduce a *MIDI-equipped accordion (the 411 Musette, 1985), enabling players to combine acoustic accordion sounds with a wide range of synthesized and *sampled sounds and automatic accompaniment facilities. Most MIDI accordions allow the use of separate MIDI channels for treble, bass, and chords. Kits are also available to add MIDI functions to any acoustic accordion.

Acoustics

The science of acoustics deals on the one hand with the physics of sound and vibration (and therefore of musical instruments), and on the other with the transmission and behaviour of sound in space (e.g. a concert-hall or a loudspeaker cabinet). In both cases a distinction is made between the objective properties and behaviour of sound as measured by technical apparatus and the sound as subjectively perceived by the listener. Studies of the cognitive and physiological responses to sound are generally collected under the title of 'psycho-acoustics'. From here the subject can branch out even further to encompass issues of general psychology, music education, and music therapy.

Such an extensive and complex subject cannot be given a comprehensive treatment here; the paragraphs below outline those areas of the subject which relate directly to the design, operation, and use of electronic instruments and *signal processors, and serve to introduce and explain the principal technical terms.

1. The Physical Properties of Sound

(a) Pitch

Acoustic musical instruments produce sounds by excitation of an elastic medium. This may be a solid material such as a string or metal bar, or an enclosed volume of air (e.g. in a wind instrument). In some cases the excitation is continuous (a bowed string or an organ-pipe), in others impulsive (a struck drumhead, or a plucked string), in which case the vibrations decay as the energy is transferred to the air and any elastic components (such as a sound-box) physically linked to the vibrating medium. The elasticity and physical proportions of the medium itself are also clearly of great importance—a hard thin metal sheet (e.g. a cymbal) will vibrate for several seconds, whereas a simple block of equal mass may hardly vibrate at all (one would be more aware of the impact noise). While in a musical context the normal medium for the transmission and reception of sound is the air, sound can travel through almost any material (e.g. water, wood, metal, etc.) often with greater speed and efficiency.

Elasticity in a medium (whether air or a solid) is a measure of the tension and stiffness within it. The simplest demonstration of this is the difference between a slack and a taut string, but it applies also to thin sections of wood (the tension and stiffness deriving from several factors including the grain, any applied varnish, and moisture content, as well as the shape) and metal plates, which often need to be hammered and/or heat-treated to develop the internal tensile stresses necessary for a musically satisfying sound.

To be perceived as having a definite pitch, a sound of sufficient intensity (i.e. above the 'threshold of hearing'; see DECIBEL) must possess a regular period of vibration (frequency) within the audible range, which is between approximately 16 Hz (*Hertz) and 20 kHz (i.e. 20,000 Hz), the latter being about five octaves above the high E on the treble staff—the open string of the violin.

An alternative measure of period is the wavelength of the sound—the distance travelled to complete one cycle. This measurement requires a knowledge of the speed of sound in air—this depends on the temperature and humidity, but for dry air at room temperature (20°C) is approximately 334 metres per second. Thus a pitch of 334 Hz would have a wavelength of approximately 1 metre. This presumes that the sound source and the listener are stationary; if the sound source is approaching the listener the perceived pitch rises (the Doppler effect) in proportion to the speed of travel (for a musical application of the Doppler effect see LESLIE).

The ear's response to pitch is logarithmic; it hears not the absolute (arithmetic) difference in pitch (measured in Hertz) but the relative (geometric) difference, measured as a ratio. Thus, the interval of an octave corresponds to a ratio of 2:1. Similarly, all musical intervals, whether belonging to a recognized scale or not, can be described by a numerical ratio, or approximated by sums of a ratio quantity. For example, a common measurement of interval is the cent, corresponding to a 1,200th of an octave ($= 2^{1/1,200}$), or a 100th of an equally tempered semitone (see TUNING AND TEMPERAMENT).

(b) Overtones

The theoretical foundations for the study of vibration were developed by the French mathematician Jean Baptiste Joseph Fourier (1768–1830). He established that any periodic wave can be represented as a sum of harmonically related sinusoids (e.g. a sine wave; for a detailed description of this and other related waves see WAVEFORM, *also* ANALYSIS). In this sense, the sine wave is the only truly 'pure' tone. The only 'instrument' acknowledged to produce a virtually pure sine wave (i.e. a pure 'sinusoidal' waveform) is the tuning fork. (For an interesting alternative theory of sound inspired by quantum physics see SYNTHESIS II 3(*f*).)

All pitched musical instruments generate more or less complex periodic waves which are made up of a number of (simultaneously vibrating) sinusoidal waves, each at a different frequency. Each individual frequency component is thus termed a 'mode of vibration' or a 'partial'. The partial with the lowest frequency is termed the 'fundamental' (corresponding in most cases to the perceived pitch of the tone), and the remainder are known either as 'partials' or as 'overtones'.

If the frequencies of the overtones are all integer multiples of the fundamental frequency, the overtones are described as 'harmonic partials' or, more simply, 'harmonics'. Overtones not in this harmonic relationship (for example, in the case of many bell sounds) are termed 'inharmonic partials' and the tone as a whole 'inharmonic'.

(c) The Harmonic Series

To return to the Fourier model of a complex periodic wave, it is clearly possible to define a wave composed of each ascending harmonic partial—literally, a 'harmonic series'. For example, taking an arbitrary fundamental frequency (or 'first harmonic') of 100 Hz, successive partials would be at 200 Hz, 300 Hz, 400 Hz, and so on, in theory for ever (i.e. an infinite series), though, as indicated above, components above 20 kHz are not generally regarded as significant in the context of human hearing.

The musically most important feature of the series is that the ratio of the frequencies of adjacent partials begins at 2 (the octave) and converges towards 1 (without ever actually reaching that value). Since a musical interval is defined by the ratio of the two frequencies, this means that the musical interval between successive partials progressively decreases. Thus, using the above example, the interval 200 Hz–100 Hz is an octave (ratio 2:1), while that between 400 Hz and 300 Hz is a perfect fourth (ratio 4:3).

This series is most frequently described in relation to brass instruments, which achieve a full chromatic compass of several octaves by obtaining harmonics from a limited number of deep fundamental pitches. However (and most relevant to the present study), the series is also of primary importance in the context of a single tone, as the relative intensities of different partials (which together comprise the 'spectrum' of the tone, which may be determined by *analysis) determine the perceived timbre of the note.

2. Auditory Responses

(a) Dynamic Sensitivity to Pitch

In relating the measured spectrum of a sound to the perceived timbre, it is important to be aware of the 'non-linear' dynamic response of the ear to vibration, especially at low to moderate sound levels. The ear is most sensitive to frequencies in the range 3,000 Hz to 4,000 Hz, which corresponds closely to the frequencies of the upper vocal formants (see below). The sensitivity falls away towards the upper and lower extremes of the audible range, the ear being the least sensitive to frequencies below about 200 Hz. These differences are far less marked at dynamic levels above

90 dB or so. This is why music recordings played at unnaturally low dynamic levels (e.g. on a domestic hi-fi system) sound less than true to the original—hence the 'loudness' control often fitted to amplifiers, serving to boost the bass frequencies at low listening levels.

In order for measurements of intensity to correspond as closely as possible to the response of the ear, professional sound-level meters use a system of 'weighting'. Three standards are in regular use, giving different primarily low-frequency compensations: the 'A' weighting closely matches the response of the ear, the 'C' weighting gives a much more objective reading of the power in a sound, with the 'B' weighting intermediate between 'A' and 'C'. In the recording industry, several weighting formulae are used, for example to define the subjective level of *noise present in a signal.

The ear's sensitivity to pitch is such that it can discriminate differences of as little as three cents. It is, however, much less sensitive to differences of intensity. For designers of *digital *synthesizers this means that the processing required to achieve a smooth portamento, for example, requires a high degree of arithmetical precision, whereas dynamic *envelopes can be managed with relatively crude approximations.

(b) Combination Effects: Beats and Difference Tones

If two sinusoidal tones have exactly the same pitch, they will be heard as one. Should the pitch of the second be raised slightly, the result would be heard as a regular variation in amplitude as the waveforms alternately reinforce and cancel each other (see Fig. 1). The effect is known as 'beating', the frequency of the beating corresponding to the arithmetic difference between the two tones. Thus two tones at 440 Hz and 445 Hz will beat five times a second. The effect is familiar from the sound of an out-of-tune piano.

While the difference in pitch is below 15 Hz or so, the result will be heard essentially as a single tone with beats (like a rapid vibrato). Beyond that point, the tone begins to break up, being heard as a roughness in the sound until two separate consonant tones are distinguished. This transition from a single beating tone to two distinct tones is termed the 'critical bandwidth', and for sinusoidal tones is, depending on register, roughly between a minor second and a minor third, beyond which any interval will be perceived as consonant.

Tests have demonstrated that even skilled musicians have difficulty in tuning familiar musical intervals correctly using only sine waves. It has been established that the ear's perception of the consonance of two complex tones derives from that of the harmonics of those tones. In a 'dissonant' interval such as a second or a seventh, it is likely that some harmonics of the first will lie within a critical bandwidth of those of the second. This correlates

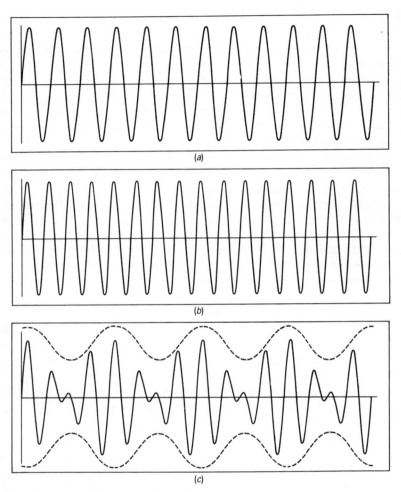

Fig. 1. BEATS AND DIFFERENCE TONES. Addition of sine waves at 300 Hz (*a*) and 400 Hz (*b*) gives audible difference tone (shown as dotted line) at 100 Hz (*c*).

with common experience; such an interval sounds markedly more dissonant played by two trumpets, for example, than when played by two flutes.

Related to the phenomenon of beats is that of the difference tone heard when two pitches sound together above a certain dynamic level. The ear hears the difference in pitch as an added low tone of that pitch. For example, if two tones of 1,000 Hz and 1,200 Hz are sounded together (the effect is naturally clearer with high-pitched tones), a 'fundamental' difference tone of 200 Hz will be heard as well. An important consequence (familiar to orchestral wind and brass players) of this effect is that an equally tempered interval played thus will generate a dissonant difference tone.

3. The Formation of Musical Sounds

(a) Resonance

The phenomenon of resonance will be familiar to most readers. The air, carrying vibrations at a given frequency, can directly excite an elastic medium as described above into 'sympathetic vibration' or resonance if the frequency corresponds to the 'natural frequency' of the medium. The simplest example is of adjacent strings tuned to the same pitch. If the first is set into vibration, the second string will vibrate in sympathy as energy is transferred to it through the air.

The physicist Hermann von Helmholtz (1821–94), whose treatise On the Sensations of Tone is acknowledged as the first 'modern' study of acoustics and the phenomena of hearing, used sets of tuned hollow glass spheres (now known as 'Helmholtz' or 'cavity' resonators) to identify the components of a complex tone. The enclosed volume of air inside each sphere had a single natural frequency and would vibrate in sympathy with a partial of the same frequency. Helmholtz was thus able to document the frequency and intensity of each partial of the sound, whether harmonic or inharmonic. The modern electronic spectrum analyser does the same thing with a high degree of numerical precision, but the basic principle (the resonator is, in effect, an acoustic band-pass *filter) is much the same.

(b) Vocal and Instrumental Formants

The human vocal tract can be described as a series of cavity resonators, of complex and variable shape and volume, which modify the spectrum of the vibrations of the vocal cords. This modification is to a great extent independent of the pitch of those vibrations; thus a given vowel sound (determined by particular combinations of vocal resonances or 'formants') is recognizable over a wide range of pitches.

Such formant regions are characteristic not only of the voice, but of many musical instruments. For example, the body of the violin has a complex shape which thus vibrates in a complex way reinforcing some frequencies while suppressing others; the air enclosed within the instrument vibrates in an equally complex manner. As a result, the relatively simple vibrations of the strings themselves are modified by the material and shape of the body, coupled with that of the enclosed air, into a rich timbre distinguished by multiple formant regions.

4. Reverberation

The natural acoustic of a room or concert-hall derives from the many ways in which a sound is reflected, and thus delayed, before it reaches our ears. The stereophonic perception of a sound source depends not only on the relative strength of the sound reaching each ear, but also, more importantly, on the slight difference in the times at which the sound reaches each ear (the 'precedence effect') and the relative strength of the direct signal and sound reflected off surfaces. This phenomenon is most apparent at the higher frequencies, where the wavelength of the sound is shorter than the distance between the ears.

Reverberation consists of a large number of overlapping quasi-random echoes, the rate of build-up and density of which are determined by the nature of the enclosing acoustic space. This comprises a number of reflecting surfaces, such as walls, floor, ceiling, etc., enclosing a volume of air. These factors, together with the precise geometry of the space, determine the length and character of the reverberation.

To the casual listener the most significant parameter is the reverberation time. This is defined to be the time taken for the reverberation to decay by 60 dB (see DECIBEL)—in effect, to just above the threshold of hearing. In a large hall, a reverberation time of around two seconds is regarded as ideal; this is, however, too long for speech, which needs a time below one second to be heard clearly. The reverberation time is affected in complex ways not only by the volume of the acoustic space, but also by the nature and orientation of the reflecting surfaces—including, for example, the presence of an audience as well as the walls, floor, and ceiling.

The degree to which a surface reflects or absorbs sound depends on its hardness. The 'absorption coefficient' of a surface is a measure of the degree to which a surface absorbs, and thus does not reflect, sounds over the audio range. Most surfaces absorb high frequencies more efficiently than low frequencies. Also for large volumes of air the absorption or attenuation of high frequencies by the air itself (affected by such factors as temperature and humidity) becomes significant.

Thus generally the high frequencies will decay more rapidly than the low frequencies. The softer the material, the greater the difference in the absorption coefficient across the audio range. Hence for marble or tiled walls the coefficient is virtually constant—typically 0.01 at 125 Hz and 0.02 at 4 kHz. For a heavy carpet, on the other hand, the value at 125 Hz is 0.02, but rises to 0.65 at 4 kHz.

Conversely, small, partly enclosed spaces, such as alcoves, balconies, and even the space between rows of seats, can act as Helmholtz resonators and, so to speak, 'trap' or absorb low frequencies. This phenomenon is exploited in the design of recording studio control rooms, which will incorporate carefully tuned 'bass traps' to avoid undesired resonances.

The quality of the reverberation is to a great extent determined by the spread of reflections or 'diffusion' of the reflected sound. The more irregular the reflecting surface the greater the diffusion. Since, however, the energy of the incident sound is also diffused, the reverberation time is reduced. An extreme example of this is the anechoic chamber, in which all the surfaces are so irregular that reflections are eliminated.

In a well-diffused acoustic the first echoes or 'early reflections' merge rapidly and smoothly into the mass of the reverberation (which typically consists of between 1,000 and 3,000 echoes per second), and the character of the sound does not differ too much from one point to another. It is for this reason that the surfaces of modern concert-halls are not only out of parallel (to avoid 'flutter echo' and local 'standing waves' at a particular frequency), but often broken up by irregularly oriented panels of different sizes.

Address

The term used to signify the number of a memory location in a *digital *computer. More generally, the term is applied to the process of communication between the computer and peripherals such as printers or disk drives, whose 'addresses' are often seen by the computer as memory locations.

After-Touch

A much valued facility in an electronic keyboard, particularly the *synthesizer, whereby extra pressure on a key after it has been struck is converted into an electrical signal which can be used to alter some aspect of the sound, for example by making it louder or by adding vibrato. The most sophisticated keyboards allow independent after-touch for each key; a less expensive alternative is a simple 'global' after-touch which affects all notes equally. After-touch data can be transmitted by *MIDI. See *also* VELOCITY SENSITIVITY.

Aliasing

See ANALOGUE TO DIGITAL CONVERSION.

All-Pass Filter

See FILTER, REVERB 3.

Amplitude

One of the parameters used to describe the intensity of a sound (or any *analogue signal) in terms of its *waveform. At the simplest level, the term is used to signify the volume of the sound as a whole, i.e. the average height of the waveform if it were to be represented graphically. A complete *analysis of the sound usually requires a measurement of the amplitude of the various frequency components (see ACOUSTICS 1) which make up the sound.

There is no single formal unit of measurement of amplitude. Depending on the context, either voltage (for an absolute measurement) or *decibel (dB) units (for a comparative measurement) may be used.

Amplitude Modulation

See MODULATION.

Analogue

In the context of electronics, the term is used to signify any conventional electrical signal which is an 'analogue' of some other signal. The output from a microphone, for example, is an analogue of the sound-wave acting on the microphone. More particularly it is used in contradistinction to *'digital' as a description of electronic circuit function. Thus an analogue circuit (e.g. an amplifier or an analogue *synthesizer) handles continuous (analogue) signals, while a digital circuit handles electrical signals consisting of two alternate voltage levels which represent logic levels, which in turn can represent numbers.

Analogue to Digital Conversion

The process by which an *analogue electrical signal (e.g. from a micro-phone) is converted (by an 'analogue to digital converter' or ADC) into *digital *binary numbers for processing by a *computer. Each number represents the voltage level (*amplitude) of the input signal 'sampled' by the ADC over a very short period of time (hence 'instantaneous amplitude'). The number of these samples taken in one second is known as the 'sampling rate'. The faster the sample rate, the higher the maximum frequency which can be recorded. The greater the number of *bits in the number representing each sample, the more accurately the digital data matches the shape of the input *waveform. Both parameters determine the accuracy with which the reverse process, digital to analogue conversion, re-creates the original signal.

Fig. I is a simplified block diagram of the whole ADC–DAC process, with representations of the forms the signal takes between input and output. It can be seen that the raw output from the DAC is a stepped waveform; the steps have the effect of adding unwanted high-frequency *distortion components to the signal, usually referred to as 'quantization *noise'. A special low-pass *filter is needed to remove these high frequencies and restore the smooth profile of the original signal. A matching filter is required at the input to remove frequencies above the limit of the ADC that may be present in the input signal.

The cut-off frequencies of these filters are related to the sampling rate by a factor known as the 'Nyquist limit'. This dictates that the sampling rate must be no less than twice the highest frequency to be recorded. For example, if an audio signal contains frequencies up to the recognized limit of human hearing, i.e. 20 kHz, the sampling rate must be at least 40 kHz. Should the sampling rate be lower than that, the high frequencies are misread as low-frequency components, creating a form of distortion known as 'aliasing'. The filters employed are thus commonly referred to as 'anti-alias' filters.

In practice, since filters approach their cut-off frequency not instan-

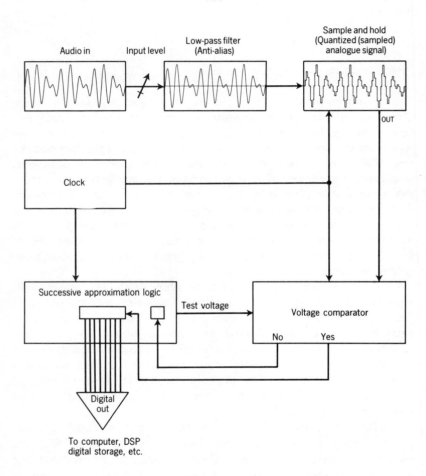

Fig. 1. ANALOGUE TO DIGITAL CONVERSION.

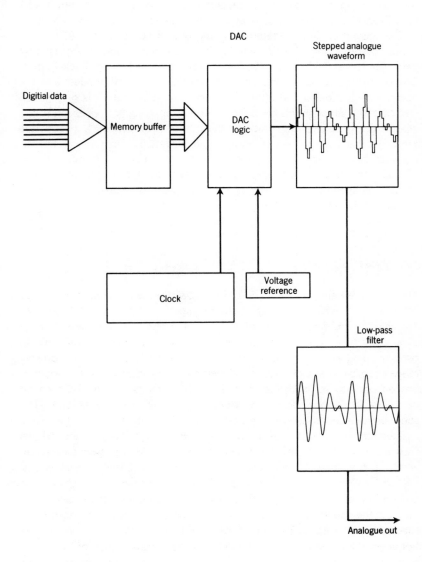

taneously but gradually, the sampling rate needs to be somewhat higher than the Nyquist limit. For example, the sampling rate of a compact disk is 44.1 kHz. Even this is regarded by many audio engineers as too low.

The second parameter determining the overall fidelity of the ADC is, as indicated above, the 'word length' in bits of the digital output. An eight-bit word (or *byte) can resolve 256 voltage levels, which for high-fidelity noise-free processing is insufficient. The difference between the loudest and the quietest recordable sounds (the 'signal-to-noise (S/N) ratio') is only 45 dB (see DECIBEL), although this can be improved by applying *compression to the input and a matching *expansion to the output ('companding'), a technique similar to that used to reduce noise on analogue tape recorders. A twelve-bit word can resolve 4,096 voltage levels and can offer an S/N ratio of over 70 dB, comparable with high-quality analogue tape recording, while conversion at the compact disk standard of sixteen-bit words achieves an S/N ratio of 96 dB.

Analysis, Signal

The measurement of the various individual frequency components (see ACOUSTICS 1), which make up a sound, most importantly with regard to *amplitude. The simplest form of analysis is the display of the *waveform (a 'time-domain representation') of the sound on a cathode ray tube (CRT) oscilloscope (see COMPONENTS 7(a)). A more sophisticated and certainly more important form of analysis is *spectrum analysis, in which the sound is broken up into its individual frequency components, which can then be displayed in graphic form (a 'frequency-domain representation'). The spectrum of a sound is closely related to the subjective *timbre of the sound.

Spectrum analysis can be performed with both *analogue and *digital techniques. In the former, the sound to be analysed is passed through an array of band-pass *filters. Each passes a narrow band of frequencies, typically within the range of one-third of an octave. Although precise numerical measurements are difficult to obtain, there are advantages to this method; the sound can be analysed continuously, allowing any changes in the spectrum with respect to time to be noted. The presence of undesirable frequency components can also be detected. Spectrum analysis of this kind is often used to test the *acoustics of recording studio control rooms. Should the room be found to amplify a particular range of frequencies more than others (thus adding undesirable colouration to the sound), a graphic *equalizer inserted in the signal path can be used to reduce those frequencies before the signal reaches the loudspeakers.

Digital spectrum analysis permits very precise numerical measurements. The technique involves, firstly, digitizing or *sampling a short section or 'analysis window' (ideally a single cycle) of the waveform, by means of *analogue to digital conversion. The resulting data is then processed by a complex mathematical program called a fast Fourier transform (FFT), which produces a list of each sinusoidal frequency component together with its *amplitude and *phase. The process is thus also termed Fourier analysis. The 'inverse Fourier transform' can be used to convert this list, perhaps after other processing, back into a waveform (see also SYNTHESIS II).

Due to the many thousands of calculations involved for each transform, a continuous analysis such as is available with analogue techniques is not possible unless an expensive, high-speed *signal-processing *computer is used. Because the FFT assumes that the waveform to be analysed is periodic and unchanging, it can give confusing results when applied to a non-periodic waveform (e.g. a waveform with a high noise content). There is a trade-off to be made between the conflicting demands of high-frequency resolution, requiring a long analysis window, and the tracking of transient detail, requiring a short window. This conflict can be resolved to a great extent by using overlapping windows, as in the 'phase vocoder' (see SYNTHESIS II 3(f)).

Where it is desired to observe the change in spectrum over time (by taking successive or even overlapping FFTs), all the resulting frequency/ amplitude plots can be combined into a single three-dimensional display on a high-resolution computer monitor. Such displays were important features of the first computer-based synthesizers such as the *Fairlight and the *Synclavier.

Apple

An American company founded by Steve Wozniak for the design and manufacture of one of the first self-contained personal *computers, known as the Apple II, introduced in 1978. This used the MOS Technology microprocessor (see COMPONENTS 6) the 6502, also used in the Commodore 'PET' first marketed at about the same time, as well as in many subsequent microcomputers. The Apple II proved very successful for both scientific and business applications. By virtue of its built-in expansion ports (spare internal sockets for additional circuit boards) it could easily be adapted for specialized applications, and many independent companies developed music *synthesis systems based on it. Of these the most important was the Alpha Syntauri digital *synthesizer—a combined hardware/software system offering additive synthesis, polyphonic outputs, and many other facilities, including an *interface for a music keyboard.

Following the development of sixteen- and thirty-two-*bit micro-processors, Apple introduced first the 'Lisa' computer (1983), featuring sophisticated graphics-based system software, and subsequently the highly successful 'Macintosh' (1984), which offered similar facilities at less expense. These machines marked Apple's adoption of the MC68000 processor chip from Motorola, a chip more powerful (with thirty-two-bit internal processing) than the INTEL 8088 used in most business-oriented personal computers of the time. The 68000 was later used in the *Atari 'ST' and the *Commodore 'Amiga'. The Macintosh is the most favoured computer in the USA for professional music applications. In the UK and Europe its comparatively high price has confined its use to the upper end of the market, the Atari ST being the more popular computer for music applications. Unlike the ST, the Macintosh does not have built-in *MIDI ports. The Macintosh is also widely used in desk-top publishing applications.

ARP

A series of electronic *synthesizers designed by Alan R. Pearlman, who established the ARP name in 1970 as a division of Tonus Inc. The first instrument, the Model 2500, followed in the tradition of the modular studio systems pioneered by *Moog and *Buchla, but later models were designed to meet the demands of the rapidly expanding commercial market. The portable Model 2600 (1971) retained certain features of modular design, such as the use of patch cords to make connections between modules, but included internal preset connections for the most popular configurations and built-in monitor amplifiers and speakers. The 'Odyssey', introduced in the same year, was a direct competitor to the Moog 'Minimoog', and introduced a feature that was to be retained on several later instruments, in the form of three touch-sensitive rubber pads for the control of pitch-bend and vibrato.

The 'Omni' (1975) combined the functions of a synthesizer with preset string ensemble sounds and a separate bass synthesizer which could be assigned to the lower register of the electronically 'split' keyboard. The 'Quadra' (1980) made use of microprocessor technology (see COMPONENTS

6) to include user-programmable patch memories and a *sequencer. It contained four separate 'instruments': a bass synthesizer, a string ensemble, a polyphonic 'synthesizer' (the sounds being processed through a single voltage-controlled amplifier and *filter), and a duophonic 'lead' synthesizer.

The 'Avatar', a *guitar synthesizer introduced in 1978, proved so costly to the company that, despite the fact that a survey made in 1980 showed that ARP had a leading 40 per cent share of the market, it was forced to cease trading in 1981. In development at the time, the 'Chroma', an advanced digitally controlled polyphonic synthesizer which included an interface for an external *computer, was taken up by CBS and marketed by their Rhodes division.

Arpeggiator

An 'easy-play' facility found on many electronic *organs, *synthesizers, and 'home keyboards' for the automatic generation of arpeggios, either from a single bass note, or from a held chord. A superior arpeggiator permits a variety of styles, such as up, down, up and down, and so on.

Atari ST

A *digital *computer made by Atari Corp. of Sunnyvale, California. Introduced in 1985, it was the first of its kind to include built-in *MIDI ports, and was thus rapidly adopted by musicians working with MIDI-equipped instruments. A wide range of high-quality MIDI software is available for the ST, enabling it to be used not only as a *sequencer but also as an editor or programmer for *samplers and *synthesizers, and, indeed, to be used directly as a digital synthesizer, with soundfiles being transferred to a sampler over MIDI. The ST uses the powerful MC68000 microprocessor (see COMPONENTS 6) developed by Motorola and used also in the *Apple 'Macintosh', the *Commodore 'Amiga', and others.

Attack

On a musical instrument, the very beginning of the note—how rapidly the tone reaches maximum intensity. The overall shape of an instrumental note is sometimes referred to as its *envelope. Three basic phases are defined—the attack, the steady-state or 'sustain' stage, and the decay. In a *synthesizer, the attack is thus the first element of the dynamic envelope applied to the tone by the envelope generator (see SYNTHESIS II 2 (e)). The attack of many musical instruments often possesses complex *timbral characteristics (see ACOUSTICS I, ANALYSIS) and is in many cases what gives that instrument its distinctive character. Putting it another way, if a recording of a note is edited to remove the attack portion, it often becomes very difficult to identify the instrument concerned.

B

Bandwidth

The difference between the lowest and highest frequencies handled by an electronic circuit. The 'audio bandwidth', for example, is the range of frequencies within the audible range (see ACOUSTICS 1) processed by an audio system such as a hi-fi amplifier. It is usually measured by taking the points at which the frequency response is 3 dB (see DECIBEL) below maximum. The measurement is of particular importance as a description of the operation of a *filter.

Baud Rate

A measure of the speed of serial transmission of *binary data (i.e. one *bit at a time), for example from a *computer to a printer, or between *MIDI instruments, in bits per second. It is important to note that, in calculating the overall rate of data transmission, it is not sufficient to divide the baud rate by 8 to determine the rate in *bytes, since extra control bits (typically two) are usually added to each byte transmitted as part of the transmission protocol.

BBC Microcomputer

A personal *computer developed by the British manufacturer Acorn for a computer literacy project promoted by the British Broadcasting Corporation in consultation with education groups such as the National Extension College. The project centred around a series of television programmes on computing linked to a home study course. The computer, referred to invariably as 'the BBC Micro', was marketed from 1982. It featured a specially developed 'structured' BASIC interpreter which included the facility to write embedded assembler code, high-resolution colour graphics, internal sound generator, and four channels of *analogue to digital conversion. Later, a second processor option was introduced offering faster processing and extended memory.

The computer later became an officially approved system for use in schools, and a substantial range of software and peripheral hardware was developed by independent manufacturers, covering business, educational, scientific, and musical applications.

Beat Frequency Oscillator

See OSCILLATOR.

Beats

See ACOUSTICS 2(b).

Binary

A system of counting (to 'base 2') that uses only the two digits 0 and 1. Counting in binary uses the same principles of 'place-value' familiar from counting in decimal, with the difference that the digit columns progress leftwards in powers of two. Thus the number 2 in decimal is '10' in binary, 4 is '100', 9 is '1001', and so on. Binary counting is the basis of *digital electronic circuits, most importantly the digital *computer. See also Appendix 1.

Bit

Short for *Binary digIT, the smallest working unit of data in a *digital *computer. It represents a single 'logic state', either 'on' or 'off', represented by the binary digits 1 and 0. Larger numbers are represented by strings of bits called 'words'; a common word length is eight bits, known as a *byte. The size of the word a computer is able to use is regarded as an important measure of its power. Thus one speaks of an 'eight-bit' computer as being less powerful than a 'sixteen-bit' computer. This is, however, a simplification;

many applications do not need the power of sixteen-bit processing, which can be cumbersome and wasteful. In a musical context, however, the word length is directly proportional to the fidelity of the processing (e.g. in a *sampler or a digital *synthesizer). See *also* ANALOGUE TO DIGITAL CONVERSION.

Breath Controller

See SYNTHESIZER 5, WIND SYNTHESIZERS and CONTROLLERS.

Buchla

A pioneering series of electronic *synthesizers designed by Donald F. Buchla (b. 1937), and manufactured in Berkeley, California from 1964. Like the *Moog synthesizers designed at the same time they used the principle of voltage control (see SYNTHESIS II 2) to link a number of separate synthesis and control modules. A close collaborator in the development of the system as a whole was the composer Morton Subotnick, working firstly at the San Francisco Tape Music Center, for which the Buchla modules were originally designed. In 1966 Subotnick moved to New York University, where he established a new studio based on the Buchla system, and where he completed several pieces for tape and acoustic instruments.

A unique feature of the Buchla system was the use of capacitative touch plates for performance control, rather than a conventional keyboard, and the early use of hybrid *digital and *analogue electronics. Buchla was responsible for much of the pioneering work on the design and use of *sequencers and *computer control. The Series 100 modules (1962–70) and the Series 200 (1971 onwards, collectively known as the 'Electric Music Box') were entirely analogue, but in 1975 Buchla introduced a series of digital control modules, based on an eight-*bit microprocessor (see COMPONENTS 5). The Model 300A processor employed a cassette recorder for program and data storage and a video monitor for display. A special music composition language called 'Patch IV' was provided for interactive communication between the musician and the synthesizer. Other digital modules included the Model 360 digital *oscillator bank, and the 364 function generator, which enabled up to sixteen control voltages to be processed simultaneously.

In 1980 this technology was employed in Buchla's most 'conventional' instrument, the non-modular 'Touché'. This used a more modern sixteen-bit computer and, exceptionally, a conventional five-octave polyphonic key-board. This did not, however, signify the end of the touch plate keyboard, which was used in the Model 400 (also non-modular) introduced in 1982.

In the Buchla system, control and audio signals were kept separate, unlike, for example, the Moog system. In this respect Buchla ran somewhat counter to the preferences of the rock and commercial market; as a studio system, however, the Buchla synthesizers offered considerable flexibility together with opportunities to explore otherwise inaccessible (at the time) digital synthesis techniques such as FM (*frequency modulation; but see, especially, SYNTHESIS II 3(c)).

Buffer

1. Memory

In a *digital *computer, a special area of memory set aside to store data being transferred from one storage area to another. For example, data can be sent to a printer much faster than it can be printed, so the data is stored in a buffer memory in the printer itself. The computer can then continue with some other process until the contents of the buffer have been printed. A similar buffer memory is used by a computer to store characters entered on a keyboard (which may not actually be read by the computer until some other process has completed), *MIDI data from a *synthesizer, and so on.

2. Amplifier

In both digital and *analogue electronic circuits, a signal emerging from one circuit may be too weak to feed the input to a second circuit correctly. In this case a buffer amplifier is included to raise the signal to the necessary level. Buffer amplifiers are also used to ensure that the circuit *impedances are correctly matched between different stages. Buffers may operate on voltage or on current.

Byte

In a *digital *computer, a *binary word of eight *bits. It can represent numbers from 0 to 255, which in turn can represent anything from the characters on a typewriter keyboard to computer instructions and data. Bytes are counted normally in units, then popularly in simple thousands and millions—thus 1,024 (2^{10}) bytes is counted as 1 Kbyte, 1,048,576 (2^{20}) as 1 Mbyte.

C

Capacitance

See COMPONENTS 2.

Cent

See TUNING AND TEMPERAMENT, *also* ACOUSTICS 1.

Chorus

An electronic treatment, associated chiefly with the *synthesizer and the electric *guitar, applied to a signal to give the impression of a multitude of voices. See, especially, DELAY LINE 2, *also* SIGNAL PROCESSOR.

Clavinet

An electric *piano manufactured by Hohner and introduced in the early 1960s. The name derives from the action, which is based on that of a clavichord. When a key is pressed, a short metal string is pressed on to an anvil, causing the string to vibrate. The vibration is detected by electro-magnetic pick-ups and converted into an electrical signal.

The first models included built-in amplification, but by the time of the introduction of the D6 model (1971), regarded by many players as the classic version, this had been dispensed with; most players preferred to put the output from the instrument through effects units of their choice (see SIGNAL PROCESSOR) and then feed the result into an amplifier.

Four rocker switches are provided which select different tone colours. A further two switches select either or both treble and bass pick-ups, in or out of *phase, in a manner very similar to that used on the electric *guitar. A mechanical damper bar is also included for a more muted sound. The five-octave keyboard, thanks to its electromechanical action, is touch-sensitive—the harder the key is struck, the louder the note (see VELOCITY SENSITIVITY). The bright percussive character of the sound is ideally suited to a 'funky' style of playing, and at the time of the instrument's introduction proved to be a popular alternative to the sound of the electronic *organ.

The instrument remained in production until the early 1980s, when *synthesizers began to replace electromechanical instruments. The sound of the Clavinet has remained fashionable, while being relatively easy to synthesize, and is regarded as a necessary inclusion in a synthesizer's repertoire of preset sounds.

Comb Filter

See DELAY LINE 2, FILTER, REVERB 3.

Commodore

One of the first manufacturers of affordable personal *digital *computers using the new microprocessor chips (see COMPONENTS 6(a)). The 'PET' computer appeared in 1979, using the same microprocessor chip (the MOS Technology 6502) used in the *Apple II, which appeared at the same time. Later models such as the C64 (1982) proved very popular as inexpensive vehicles for *MIDI software. Commodore's latest computer, the 'Amiga' (1987), is of great interest to musicians as it includes both powerful graphics and sound-synthesis facilities. The lack of built-in MIDI ports has meant that professional MIDI software has taken longer to appear. The Amiga uses the same sixteen-bit microprocessor (the Motorola MC68000) used in the Apple 'Macintosh' and in the *Atari 'ST'. Unlike the latter, the Amiga can run several programs concurrently, a facility normally associated with more expensive 'professional' computers.

Compander

A *signal processor which applies the combined functions of *compression and *expansion to the *dynamic range of a signal.

Components, Electronic

Electronic components fall into a number of categories or families, not necessarily mutually exclusive, reflecting not only their physical construction and electrical characteristics but also their applications—the circuits in which they may be used. A common cause for confusion is the distinction between the designations *'analogue' and *'digital' often, though misleadingly, applied to components. These terms apply properly to the design and operation of circuits, and by implication to the signals processed by those circuits.

However, recent technological advances which have made it possible for large numbers of components, especially resistors, diodes, and transistors, to be fabricated on a single silicon chip, have given rise to the usage of the term 'digital' to describe such 'integrated circuits', to distinguish them from similar chips which are designed to handle analogue signals. When used individually (i.e. by being directly soldered to a circuit board), components such as resistors, capacitors, and so on are referred to as 'discrete' components (see sections 1–5 below). Thus a digital circuit may be made of discrete components (as were the first computers, for example) or of integrated circuits. To add to the possibilities for confusion, both discrete and integrated circuits can combine analogue and digital functions—for example, an *analogue to digital converter.

1. Resistors, Resistance, and Ohm's Law

The resistor is usually the most numerous component type in an electronic circuit. As its name suggests, the purpose of a resistor is to limit the flow of electric current through a circuit. There is a precise and predictable relationship (known as 'Ohm's law') between the current through the resistor, the voltage across it, and the value of the resistor itself, measured in ohms: the resistance in ohms is equal to the voltage in volts divided by the current in amperes. Given any two values, the third can be calculated.

Resistors are made to an enormous range of values—large values are indicated by the usual abbreviations for thousands (k) and millions (M). Very low values (i.e. less than 1 ohm) are often expressed in terms of the reciprocal of resistance (1/R), termed 'conductance'.

Fixed-value resistors are usually very small components (a few millimetres long—the larger the resistor, the greater the power it can handle). Variable resistors, also known as 'potentiometers', exist in a variety of sizes from the miniature (for mounting on circuit boards) to the large panel-mounting types.

Rotary potentiometers are familiar through their use as tone and volume controls. The linear potentiometer or 'fader' is most familiar from its use in studio mixing desks, which benefit from the much finer degrees of adjustment obtained from the linear construction.

As used above, the term 'linear' refers to the physical design of the potentiometer. The term is also used to describe the electrical characteristic of the component. A linear potentiometer exhibits a fixed (i.e. linear) rate of change of resistance from minimum to maximum. The alternative is a logarithmic potentiometer, in which the rate of change of resistance varies in a logarithmic ratio to the movement of the sliding contact. When used for volume controls, this enables the control to match the response of the human ear (see ACOUSTICS 2).

2. Capacitors and Capacitance

A resistor affects alternating (AC) and direct (DC) currents equally, but a capacitor behaves very differently. It consists of two metal plates close together but not in direct contact. They are separated by an insulator termed the 'dielectric', which may be air, or material such as paper, plastic, mica, or ceramic. When a DC current is applied to the terminals of a capacitor a static charge builds up between the plates, opposing the flow of current. In an ideal capacitor the charge will remain indefinitely until it is discharged by shorting the terminals together. The rate at which the capacitor charges and discharges can be controlled by means of a resistor, thus altering the 'time constant' of the circuit.

In DC circuits the capacitor functions as a combination of a reservoir and a sort of shock absorber. A large capacitor can store several thousand volts and can cause severe damage and injury if carelessly discharged. 'Smoothing' capacitors absorb the fluctuations in voltage in a mains power supply so that a stable DC voltage is supplied to the target circuit.

When an AC current is applied to the capacitor it charges and discharges continuously, thus presenting a resistance to the current, but not blocking it as it does a DC current. This resistance is termed the 'reactance' of the capacitor, and is similarly measured in ohms. The capacitor presents very little opposition to high-frequency AC signals, but increasing reactance as the frequency falls, until as explained above it completely blocks a DC current.

This frequency-dependent response (adjustable, as noted above, by means of an associated resistor) makes the capacitor very useful in the design of *oscillator and *filter circuits. A 'coupling' capacitor can be used to prevent any undesirable DC present in a signal from affecting a further circuit;

similarly it can be used to shunt any undesirable frequency components to ground.

A static charge will tend to build up between any conductive surfaces which are not in direct contact, but very close. Much of the skill in practical circuit design consists in preventing 'stray' capacitance from building up where it is not wanted. It exists even in multicore signal cables; a cheap microphone cable, for example, may possess sufficient capacitance to seriously degrade the signal quality, especially if it is very long.

The unit of capacitance is the farad. A one-farad capacitor is very large indeed—most capacitors are measured in thousandths (microfarads—µF) or millionths (picofarads—pF) of a farad. The physical size of a capacitor reflects its capacity as well as its power rating. Both fixed and variable types are available. The most familiar use of a variable capacitor is for the tuning control on a radio receiver.

The phenomenon of capacitance also lies behind the operation of touch-operated switches, high-voltage discharges for photographic flash-guns, interference suppressors, and capacitor microphones.

3. Coils (Inductors) and Inductance

Electromagnetic effects arise wherever a current passes along a wire. A magnetic current ('flux') is created which revolves around the wire clockwise in the direction of current flow. The wire thus radiates electromagnetically—this is the basis of radio transmitting aerials. The reverse process also occurs. A magnetic field impinging on a conductor induces a current in the conductor. The effect is greatly intensified if the wire is wound into a coil. Applying a direct current to a coil produces an electromagnet whose strength is proportional to the current. The electromagnet is the basis of devices such as the relay, the doorbell, and the electric motor.

The most important electromagnetic effects are those associated with AC signals. While the current through a conductor remains constant in one direction (i.e. direct) the magnetic flux is in effect static. If the current is increased, the magnetic flux increases in such a way as to oppose the increase in current.

Thus the reactance of the coil increases with frequency—this is therefore the opposite to the behaviour of a capacitor. The combination of a capacitor and an inductor results in a circuit which has a minimum reactance at a frequency depending on the values of both components. This frequency is the resonant frequency of the circuit. Such circuits are used in the early tuning stages of radio and television receivers. Variable inductors can be made by using a threaded core which can be adjusted to alter the magnetic characteristics of the inductor. They are used in such 'tuned circuits' to facilitate alignment. Once the correct setting is found the cores are usually sealed with wax to prevent any disturbance. They are not used for front-panel controls, for which variable resistors and capacitors are more practical.

Like the capacitor, the inductor can be combined with a resistor (or indeed all three components can be combined) to create oscillator and filter circuits. One disadvantage of the inductor is that for use in audio circuits it needs to be physically quite large, so is not favoured for use in modern electronic instruments.

The most familiar musical applications of electromagnetism and induction are in transducers such as microphones, pick-ups for the electric *guitar, gramophone pick-up cartridges, and loudspeakers. In the first three cases, physical movement causes a current to be induced in a coil. In the last a current is applied to a coil to cause physical movement.

4. Semiconductors

A semiconductor is a component whose resistance can be altered, firstly at the time of manufacture, and secondly in a circuit by application of a control current. Depending on these and other factors, a semiconductor can be used as a switch or as an amplifier, in which a small current controls a much larger one.

(a) Semiconductor Principles

The starting-point for a semiconductor is an insulator. The first generation of semiconductors used materials such as germanium, but this has been almost entirely superseded by common silicon. This is a crystalline mineral in abundant supply in the form of sand. In order to give the raw silicon a semiconducting characteristic it has to be 'doped' by the addition of selected minerals such as phosphorus or boron. Doped silicon can be made to be either electron-rich ('n' type) or electron-deficient ('p' type—often said to have 'holes'). Once doped, the new material will conduct, under certain circumstances. The fundamental principle of semiconductor technology is to join pieces of each type together to form a 'junction'.

(b) The Diode

A single p-n junction is the basis of the semiconductor diode. A current can flow only in one direction (the direction of 'forward bias') through such a junction. Current in the reverse direction (reverse bias) is blocked. The diode is the principal means of converting an AC voltage (e.g. from the mains supply) to a DC voltage, in a process called rectification. The process may be explained as follows. Supposing that a small battery is connected across the diode—the positive terminal of the battery being connected to the positive terminal (the 'anode') of the diode. The opposite, negative, terminal is called the cathode. Since opposite poles attract, the free electrons in the n-type half of the diode will be drawn through the p-type half to the battery—thus current flows. Reversing the connections prevents any flow since the electrons are now attracted directly to the positive terminal, away from the junction.

Although in the former case current flows, there is still a small resistance to current flow, with the peculiar characteristic that the voltage drop across the diode is approximately 0.6 volts. The diode will not conduct until this threshold is reached.

It is possible to force the diode to conduct in the reverse direction. This happens suddenly, once the reverse voltage has reached a certain level. Normally, the sudden current surge would be fatal for the diode, but a special 'Zener' diode is available designed for just this situation, and used as a voltage regulator.

When forward-biased, the junction emits a small amount of electro-magnetic energy in the form of light. Diodes are available which exploit this phenomenon. Known as 'light-emitting diodes' (LEDs), they are widely used as miniature indicator lamps. The most common colour is red (including infra-red), but yellow, orange, and green LEDs are also available. The most recent development has been the 'laser diode', the most familiar application of which is in the compact disk player.

(c) The Junction Transistor

The junction transistor consists of two junctions in the form of a sandwich, either n-p-n or p-n-p. While the majority of modern circuits use n-p-n transistors, both are in common use. There is a direct electrical connection to each element. The central element (i.e. p in the case of an n-p-n transistor) is called the 'base'; the outer elements are called respectively the 'collector' and the 'emitter'.

The transistor can function both as a switch and as an amplifier, depending on the voltage (termed the 'bias' voltage) applied to the base. If, in an n-p-n transistor, the base bias is negative (i.e. near or equal to the emitter), the transistor behaves like an 'n-n' junction, and no current flows. If the bias voltage is made positive, the transistor behaves like a forward-biased diode and current flows. In between these extremes, a small change in base current is converted into a corresponding but much larger collector–emitter current—amplification takes place. The transistor is thus the 'active' component in a circuit, and can be used not only as a simple switch or amplifier, but also as the basis of a wide range of *filter and *oscillator circuits.

(d) The Field-Effect Transistor (FET)

Since the development of the first transistor in 1948, many powerful variations have been devised, many taking advantage of advances in manufacturing technique to make smaller and multi-junction devices.

Of these, the field-effect transistor is the most important. There are two basic types—the 'junction FET' (J-FET) and the 'metal-oxide semiconductor FET' (MOSFET). Although quite similar to the junction transistor in construction (the essential difference being that the central element of the sandwich is more like a clamp round a single core or 'channel'), the J-FET has significant new properties. The input resistance is very high (several Mohms), so that the J-FET has little or no effect on the circuit feeding it. Also, hardly any input current is required to operate the FET. J-FETs are ideal for small-signal amplification and high-frequency applications. Like bipolar transistors, J-FETs are available in both n-channel and p-channel versions.

The most important of the newer transistor types is the MOSFET, which may be thought of as an enhanced J-FET. The input resistance is so high as to be virtually infinite. It can switch extremely fast, and is easy to make. Most integrated circuits (see section 6 below) use MOSFETs. In addition, 'power MOSFETs' have been developed that can handle very large currents. They are popular in professional audio power amplifiers as they are almost in-destructible—a short circuit of the output, for example, which would destroy an ordinary transistor, merely causes the output current to fall gradually to a minimum level—the MOSFET in effect turns itself off until the output conditions return to normal.

(e) Other Semiconductor Types

Other types the reader may encounter include the 'unijunction' transistor, which is not really a transistor at all, but a diode with two cathodes. It is used as a voltage-controlled switch and does not amplify. There is a further family of semiconductors known as 'thyristors' specifically designed for switching functions. These are multi-junction semiconductors, and fall into two groups.

The 'silicon-controlled rectifier' (SCR) has three junctions, and is similar to two diodes in series. Once switched on, it will remain on even if the gate control current is removed. As with all thyristors, the SCR enables a small current to control a much larger one. The 'triac' is in effect two SCRs connected in parallel. There are four junctions (e.g. *n-p-n-p-n*) plus a further gate junction. The triac is able to switch both DC and AC, up to currents of 40 amps and up to 1,000 volts. SCRs can handle even higher power, and are used to control motors, theatre lights, and other high-power appliances.

In addition to the light-emitting diode there are several other types of component which either generate or detect light. There are light-sensitive versions of all the semiconductor types described above. Of these, probably the most well known is the 'solar cell', which is in effect a *p-n* junction with a very large surface area. A single cell will generate about half a volt in bright sunlight. The 'opto-isolator' consists of a light-emitting diode and a light-sensitive diode or transistor in a single package, used as its name suggests to enable a signal to be passed to a circuit without any actual electrical connection. An opto-isolator is used by *MIDI to ensure that *synthesizers and other similar instruments are electrically isolated from each other.

5. The Valve or Vacuum Tube

The thermionic valve dates from 1906, when the triode was patented by Lee de Forest. It consists of a heated cathode which emits electrons which are collected by a positively charged anode. This in itself constitutes a diode—the introduction of a third electrode (the 'grid') enables the passage of electrons at a high potential to be controlled by a smaller potential applied to the grid, thus producing amplification. Electrons only flow efficiently through a vacuum, so the electrodes together with a heating element are enclosed in a glass vacuum tube, the latter being the common name in the USA.

The first valves were the size of light bulbs—indeed the vacuum light bulb was the starting-point for the development of valves—and needed a similar high voltage. Two voltages were needed—a 'high-tension' (HT) supply for the electrodes and a low-tension (LT) supply for the heater element. Valve equipment was bulky and very hot. Miniaturization managed to reduce the size of valves to the extent that portable radio receivers and transmitters were possible—but often the power-pack weighed as much as the radio itself. The enormous size of the first computers can be understood when it is appreciated that each gate (switching element) required a valve, and that a complete computer required thousands of gates.

In recent years, the valve, though eclipsed by the transistor in almost all areas of electronics, has made something of a come-back both in hi-fi amplifiers and in amplifiers for use with an electric guitar, where the 'authentic' valve coloration of the original designs is regarded as superior to the theoretically superior performance of transistors.

6. Integrated Circuits

The integrated circuit (IC) is a small wafer of silicon on which has been etched a number of diodes, transistors, and resistors—using photographic masks to create the necessary n and p-doped areas and the connecting tracks. Inductors and capacitors depend on their physical size for their electrical properties and cannot readily be integrated. Gold wires connected to contact pads are brought out to terminal pins for mounting on printed circuit boards. The whole assembly is encapsulated in resin. There is no possibility of repairing an IC—if it fails it has to be replaced. The more expensive ICs are usually mounted into sockets for easy fitting and replacement. This does, however, add to the manufacturing costs.

There are several advantages to integrating circuits in this way. The most obvious is that of miniaturization. This has had the greatest impact on the design of computers, which depend almost entirely on semiconducting components. A second benefit is that of speed. As the connections between components become smaller, the circuit can function at higher and higher frequencies, enabling very high data-processing speeds. Heat dissipation has become an increasingly significant obstacle as more and more components are crammed into smaller and smaller spaces. Intensive research is currently being directed towards 'superconducting' materials which at extremely low temperatures exhibit no resistance and thus generate no heat. The objective is a superconductor that will operate at room temperature.

A further virtue of integration is that components possess very closely matched electrical characteristics, an important criterion in, for example, the design of amplifiers. Many ICs consist not of a circuit but simply of a number of independent, but closely matched, transistors. In many types of circuit thermal stability is important, and can be achieved relatively easily by the use of integrated circuits.

(a) Digital ICs

It would be impossible to list all the types of digital IC that are now available. They do, however, fall into certain broad groups, which are summarized below. (For additional information and technical explanations see COMPUTER 4.) 'Logic' ICs deal with relatively simple tasks. As their name suggests, they apply logic functions to a digital signal, and are usually named after that function. Chips will contain a number of independent 'AND gates', for example. More complex logic ICs provide the simpler processing operations such as adding *binary numbers, counting, and switching.

'Memory' ICs store information. They consist of arrays of transistor gates which can be independently switched ON or OFF. The status of each gate can subsequently be read, i.e. passed to another part of the circuit.

'Converter' ICs change data from one format to another. A 'BCD' converter, for example, converts a binary representation of a decimal number (binary-coded decimal) into the true binary equivalent. For example, the BCD code for 15 is 00010101 (0001– – – – = 1 decimal, – – – –0101 = 5 decimal)—the binary code for 15 is 1111. See also ANALOGUE TO DIGITAL CONVERSION.

'Microprocessor' ICs combine many thousands of logic, arithmetic, switching, and memory circuits on a single wafer of silicon, forming virtually a complete computer in a single package. Additional components are of course still needed to interface the microprocessor with the outside world.

As the technology has advanced, achieving densities of hundreds of thousands of transistors in a single chip, new designations have arisen, reflecting the increased size. Chips may be made in 'LSI' (large-scale integration) or even 'VLSI' (very large-scale integration). Such ICs use silicon wafers one centimetre square or more, rather than the few millimetres square of the first ICs. The limit to the size of a chip is the purity of the wafer (as well as that of the manufacturing process). The larger the chip, the greater the wastage (and therefore cost) if flaws develop during manufacture.

(b) Linear (Analogue) ICs

A linear circuit deals with smoothly varying signals. Amplifiers and oscillators are the most common linear circuits, and both have been targets for integration. The single most important amplifier IC is the 'operational amplifier' ('op-amp'), so called because it was originally designed for scientific and arithmetical operations. It amplifies the difference between two signals, which can be either DC or AC. The op-amp is extremely versatile, and can be used in the design of not only amplifiers (both pre- and power amplifiers) but also timers, voltage regulators, and function generators (oscillators). It is used even when space is not a consideration, to exploit the special advantages of integration (see above). Many ICs have been developed for the musical instrument industry, ranging from the specialized voltage-controlled oscillator, filter, and amplifier circuits needed for sound *synthesis to a complete 'electronic organ on a chip'.

7. Display Components

(a) Vacuum Tube Displays

The 'cathode ray tube' (CRT) used in television sets and computer displays is a variant of the vacuum tube as described above. A heated cathode (electron gun) emits a beam of electrons which strike a positively charged electroluminescent coating on the inside of the tube. Instead of a grid, a pair of plates deflect the beam according to the potential applied to them to create the desired image on the screen. A colour CRT uses three electron guns, one for each of the primary colours, red, green, and blue (RGB).

The resolution of the CRT—the amount of detail it can resolve within a given area—is important. The CRT in a domestic television is rated medium resolution at best. Professional graphics terminals can resolve over 1,000 points on both axes. A typical resolution for a high-resolution personal computer monitor is 640 by 400 points. Many domestic TV sets provide a video (composite signal) or 'RGB input' for the direct connection of computers, to get the best possible resolution on the screen.

(b) Other Display Components

There are two basic categories of display, 'alphanumeric' and 'linear'. The former includes such things as mechanical counters for tape recorders and seven-segment displays (used most familiarly on the first pocket calculators). These can be further divided into displays that emit light, and those such as the modern liquid crystal display (LCD) that reflect light. The latter is often a problem on instruments such as synthesizers which may be used on a darkened stage—the LCD display cannot be seen unless the manufacturer has provided for it to be lit from behind ('back-lit display').

The most important linear display is the moving-coil meter, which is used to give a display of any continuously changing signal. The 'peak programme meter' (PPM) is a specialized m/c meter used in recording studios to monitor the sound level. By indicating the absolute peak level of the signal (which ordinary meters cannot do), they enable the engineer to ensure that, for example, the signal does not overload the tape recorder and so cause distortion. Being a mechanical device, the m/c meter is expensive and fragile.

A cheaper and often just as effective alternative is a stepped display, which might use either light-emitting diodes or an LCD.

The 'cathode ray oscilloscope' is a further variant of the vacuum tube. It is used to create a visual display of the *waveform of the input signal applied to the deflexion plates. It is (with the possible exception of a multi-meter) the single most important item of test equipment for the electronics engineer. The 'storage' oscilloscope allows a fast or transient signal to be frozen on the screen for analysis. In the case of the digital storage oscilloscope, the signal is stored digitally in memory, thus permitting different types of signal *analysis to be used. The 'logic analyser' is used to study the very fast signals in digital circuits. It is important that the timing of such signals is correct—the logic analyser allows sixteen or more signals to be displayed simultaneously.

Composer's Desktop Project

A desk-top *computer-based *digital *synthesis system developed by the York-based non-profit-making co-operative of the same name. The system is based around the *Atari 'ST' computer, and uses a hard disk to store digital files created by *sampling *analogue sounds or by means of a variety of synthesis and *signal-processing programs. The system offers access to powerful synthesis and composition programs such as CSOUND (written by Barry Vercoe and based on his program MUSIC 11; see COMPUTER 3) normally only available in the large American and European studios.

Sound is input and output via a Sony PCM converter (see ANALOGUE TO DIGITAL CONVERSION), the communication between the converter and the hard disk being controlled and *buffered by a CDP-designed *interface called the 'SoundSTreamer'. The PCM can also be used with or without the computer to record digitized sound on videotape at the compact disk standard.

Compression

An important *signal-processing technique used (often in conjunction with *expansion) in studio recording equipment such as mixing desks and *noise reduction systems. A compressor scales the *dynamic range of a sound signal so that both the quietest and the loudest sounds can be recorded or otherwise treated without either losing the quiet sounds under the system *noise, or causing *distortion through excessive signal levels overloading recorders or other equipment. It acts by progressively reducing the level of loud sounds to below some preset threshold, which depends on the dynamic range of the recording medium, or on the particular special effect required.

Percussive sounds, such as those of drums and bass guitars, lend themselves especially to compression. On the other hand, it is regularly applied to vocal tracks both as an effect and also to help the voice stand out in a mix. It is important to distinguish between this process and the action of a *limiter, which simply prevents a signal from exceeding a specified dynamic level.

Computer

I. Low-Level Languages

(a) Internal

The primary building block of a digital computer (indeed, of any digital circuit) is the electronic switch, or 'logic gate'. The processing power of the computer derives from the complex way in which many thousands of such gates are interconnected. A switch can be either ON or OFF—either current flows or it does not. If the state of a second switch depends on that of the first, it can be said to make a decision based on that state. It is this ability to decide, at high speed, between one action and another that is the basis of computing.

The 'language' of switches is, strictly speaking, the only one understood by a digital circuit. It is, however, possible to use one language to write another that is easier for humans to understand. Computer languages are said to be at a particular 'level'. A 'low-level' language is as close as possible to the internal language of the computer; a 'high-level' language is one which is as close as possible to that of speech, enabling somebody to use the computer without any need to know its internal language. A wide variety of languages have been developed to suit the requirements of particular applications.

All languages and the programs written in them are described as 'software' to distinguish them from the 'hardware' of the computer itself—the electronic components and mechanical parts. The term 'firmware' has been adopted to refer to the grey area between the two—for example, the software built into a processing or memory chip at the time of manufacture.

Software is further divided into two categories: 'system' and 'applications'. System software (which may in fact be firmware) is concerned with the internal management of the computer—reading and writing data to and from memory, displaying or printing the results, and supervising the operation of peripheral equipment. The most common data storage medium is the magnetic disk, and all computers so equipped require a Disk Operating System, usually referred to by the acronym DOS. An applications program such as a language compiler (see section 2 below) will simply 'call' system software functions (e.g. commands to print characters to the screen) and pass the data to that function. Viewed another way, the system software insulates, so to speak, the compiler from the internal machine-specific details. The advantage of this is that programs written in that language are 'portable': they can run on any system for which that language is available.

(b) Binary Code

Gates are named according to the decision they make. The most common gates are shown in Fig. 1(a). Fig. 1(b) illustrates the action of an AND gate. If inputs 1 AND 2 are ON, the lamp will light. The OFF state can be thought of as representing the number 0, and the ON state as the number 1. Only these two numbers are possible, thus this is a *binary system of counting.

Gates are so designed that a short electrical pulse is all that is required to turn the lamp on or off. Thus, successive pulses can turn the lamp repeatedly on or off. It can be arranged that the switching off of one lamp causes a second lamp to light—this in turn can control a third. Fig. 1(c) lists the sequence of ONs and OFFs, and shows that with three lamps it is possible to count from 0 to 7 before the cycle repeats. It also shows how the binary number corresponds to the familiar decimal number. Taken together, the three lamps comprise a binary 'word', each lamp making up one *'bit' of that word. There are, therefore, eight possible 'words' in a three-bit binary counting system. The addition of a further bit doubles the number of possible words. Numbers in computing systems (for example, the number of available 'presets' in a *synthesizer) are almost invariably powers of 2; 64, for example, is 2^6.

Many computers use a word of eight bits, known as a *byte. The largest number that can be represented is 11111111—255 in decimal ($= 256$ available numbers—0 is a valid number; $256 = 2^8$). Numbers have to represent both instructions and data. A typical instruction might be 'add the next two numbers and store the result'. In this instruction, which may itself comprise one or more bytes, the computer assumes that the next two numbers are data and treats them accordingly. If the programmer has made a mistake, for example by forgetting the second data byte and writing his next

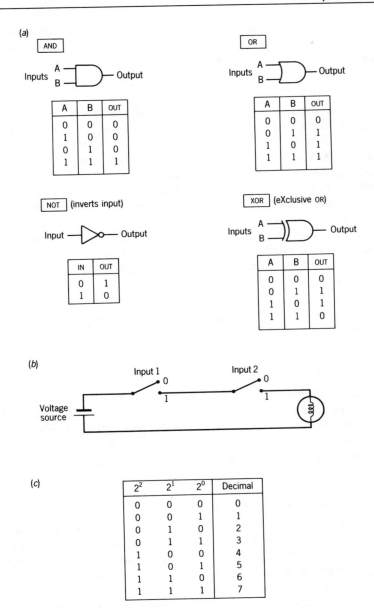

Fig. I. BINARY LOGIC. (a) Principal gates: symbols and truth tables; (b) Electrical model of AND gate; (c) Binary counter. See also Appendix I.

intended instruction byte instead, the computer has no way of knowing. It gets seriously confused, reading data as instructions and instructions as data—it 'crashes'. It is said that there is a 'bug' in the program.

(c) Machine Code

Binary numbers are not the easiest to read, and it is easy to see how mistakes can be made when writing a program consisting of rows of 1s and 0s. It would seem that a better system would be to enter the numbers in decimal. (Indeed, the very first computer, the 'Eniac', built by Mauchly and Eckert at the University of Pennsylvania between 1943 and 1946, was built, uniquely, to calculate directly in base 10.) However, given that a computer counts most efficiently in powers of 2, some compromise is inevitable, at least at this low level of programming, so that the codes entered by the programmer can be converted to binary as efficiently as possible, and can also reflect the internal 'word size' of the computer. In the early days of computing, 'octal' (i.e. counting to base 8, using only the digits 0 to 7) was used, but this was soon superseded by 'hexadecimal'—counting to base 16. This requires the use not only of the decimal digits 0 to 9 but also of the letters A to F, the latter representing decimal 15. Thus the largest eight-bit number (255 in decimal) becomes 'FF' in hexadecimal. Appendix 1 gives some conversion tables for binary, hexadecimal, and decimal numbers.

(d) ASCII Codes

Hexadecimal numbers can be entered into a computer by means of a simple sixteen-key pad, but in most general-purpose computers a full QWERTY typewriter keyboard is used. The universally agreed standard for encoding a keyboard is ASCII—American Standard Code for Information Interchange. This embraces not only the alphabetic and numeric symbols but also all the usual punctuation marks and control keys.

(e) Machine Code and Assembler

At the lowest level of programming, instructions are entered as a sequence of hexadecimal numbers for direct translation into the binary 'machine code' of the processor. Machine code programming requires detailed knowledge of the numbers corresponding to each processor command. Since a modern microprocessor (see section 4 below) may have a repertoire of over a thousand instructions, each with its own unique (possibly multi-byte) code, the potential for errors is substantial.

To make these codes easier to write and understand, short mnemonics are used to represent the instruction codes. For example, microprocessor (the Motorola 6809) the instruction 'load 1 with the following number' is 86 in hexadecimal. The mr [number]'—much easier to understand. An 'assembler' program not only converts these mnemonics to the correct machine code but also includes a variety of useful programming facilities, such as the ability to use names or 'labels' instead of numbers for variables, constants, and other data. Thus, instead of writing 'LDA $0F' (where the $ symbol means 'hexadecimal number') the programmer can write 'LDA keynum', which is much more meaningful.

The assembler also allows textual comments to be incorporated into the program listing as a further aid to comprehension. Despite all these facilities the programmer still needs detailed technical knowledge both of the particular microprocessor used and of the particular hardware configuration. The advantage of assembler programming over programming in higher-level languages is that by programming at machine level programs can be optimized for speed. This is of considerable importance in a musical application where timing is often critical.

2. High-Level Languages: Interpreters and Compilers

High-level languages allow plain English commands such as 'PRINT', 'LOAD', 'IF .. then', and so forth to be entered. Little or no detailed knowledge of the microprocessor is needed. The most popular high-level language on personal computers is BASIC—Beginners' All-purpose Symbolic Instruction Code, developed in 1964 at Dartmouth College, Connecticut, by John Kemeny and Thomas Kurtz. This is an 'interactive' language—commands can be entered directly into the computer for instant results. It is also, usually, an 'interpreted' language. Once the program has been entered, it can be run simply by typing in 'RUN', whereupon the program will be converted to machine code and executed a line at a time. Any syntax errors cause the run to be halted and are reported to the display screen.

The alternative to a interpreted language is a language 'compiler'. Historically, this is the earlier type of program. The text of a program is converted (i.e. compiled) as a whole to a program in machine code, which is then run. As a rule, compiled programs run much faster than the equivalent in an interpreted language such as BASIC. Further, compilers include a wide range of facilities for 'structured programming' as well as for occasional low-level work, and are thus suitable for writing large programs, which may be anything from system and applications software to other languages. The most common compiled languages are FORTRAN (the earliest, developed between 1953 and 1957 by John Backus of IBM, and designed for scientific and mathematical applications), ALGOL, PASCAL, MODULA-2, COBOL (for commercial and business applications), and C, a versatile 'mid-level' language in which the powerful operating system 'UNIX' is written.

3. Music Languages and Computer Synthesis

(a) Early Development of Computer Synthesis

The first experiments in computer sound *synthesis were conducted by Max Mathews at Bell Telephone Laboratories in the late 1950s. The computers were by IBM and relied initially on valve technology. With the introduction of transistor-based circuitry (see COMPONENTS 4) in the IBM 7094 Mathews was able to complete MUSIC III, the first comprehensive synthesis program. This inaugurated an intensive period of development both at Bell and at Princeton, culminating in MUSIC IV at Bell and an improved version, MUSIC IVB, at Princeton.

In the mid-1960s the next major technological development, integrated circuits (large numbers of transistors in one chip), heralded the next generation of computers, notably the IBM 360. The MUSIC programs were rewritten in FORTRAN, Mathews completing MUSIC V in FORTRAN in 1968. In the same year Barry Vercoe at Princeton introduced a fast version of MUSIC IVB in assembler for the IBM 360. He later moved to Massachusetts Institute of Technology (MIT) and in 1973 developed MUSIC 11 for the PDP 11 computer from Digital Equipment Corporation (DEC). The use of this relatively small and affordable minicomputer made digital music synthesis available to a wider community of musicians and researchers.

MUSIC 11 remained the principal tool for computer music research and composition for some eleven years, until Vercoe developed CSOUND in the mid-1980s. Written in C, it will run on any computer running the UNIX operating system and, with the necessary hardware extensions, on any personal computer that can run the language. Most notably it has been included in software for the *Composer's Desktop Project (CDP) developed at York University.

On a more modest scale, synthesis systems have been developed for some personal computers, notably the *Apple II. The British company Hybrid Technology introduced in 1984 the Music 500 digital synthesizer, which consisted of a small box of electronics attached to a *BBC Microcomputer. The package included a specially developed music composition language called AMPLE, itself derived from a popular and very compact mid-level language called FORTH.

(b) Computer Control of Analogue Equipment

The major obstacle confronting anybody developing software and hardware for digital sound synthesis is the sheer speed of the processing required, especially for real-time sound generation. Consequently, much attention has been devoted to the development of software for the control of external *analogue synthesis electronics. In 1970 Max Mathews introduced GROOVE—Generated Real-time Output Operations on Voltage-controlled Equipment—running on a Honeywell DDP-224 computer. As with any hybrid system, special interface hardware is required to link the digital electronics of the computer with the analogue electronics of the synthesis hardware. This limits the portability of the system, and GROOVE remained a single fixed installation.

Between 1962 and 1970 Peter Zinovieff developed in London a highly versatile, if complex, hybrid system. It started as a conventional analogue installation, but the need for some means of control soon became evident. A *sequencer developed between 1966 and 1968 proved too impractical, and eventually the analogue electronics were controlled by two PDP 8 minicomputers running MUSYS III, a software package written by Peter Grogono. Unlike the GROOVE system, the MUSYS system incorporated equipment that was marketed commercially through Zinovieff's company *EMS. The MUSYS system itself, although it attracted a number of composers including Harrison Birtwistle and Hans Werner Henze, was unable to support itself financially as a private enterprise and was finally dismantled in 1979.

(c) Modern Research: IRCAM

Research into computer music was thus confined largely to the above-mentioned institutions, and to a few universities, such as those at Stockholm and Utrecht. The composer Pierre Boulez was concerned about the general lack of communication between musicians and technicians, which he recognized was inhibiting the progress of musically significant research. Through his position of considerable influence in his home country he was able in 1970 to persuade the French government that there was a need for a major institution dedicated to such research. The result was the Institut de Recherche et Coordination Acoustique/Musique (IRCAM), which was opened as part of the Beaubourg project (based at the Centre Pompidou) in 1977.

IRCAM was originally divided into four departments, led by Jean-Claude Risset (computers), Luciano Berio (electronics), Vinko Globokar (instruments and voice), and Michel Decoust (pedagogy). Gerald Bennett was responsible for the so-called 'diagonal' communication between these departments. The departure of these and others in 1979 caused Boulez to restructure IRCAM into two main committees, scientific and artistic, and four departments encompassing research, pedagogy, production, and information. The changes encouraged a spirit of co-operation between departments, and between visiting composers and resident researchers. One further consequence has been an increase in co-operation between commercial organizations (such as Yamaha) and IRCAM.

Most important, in the context of the present article, has been the development by Peppino diGiugno of a series of real-time digital sound processors, beginning with the 4A in 1975 and continuing at roughly two-year intervals with the 4B, the 4C, and finally the 4X in 1980–1. This immensely powerful machine can realize up to 1,024 *oscillators or 450 *filters in real-time, with a maximum sample rate of 512 kHz. A wide range of synthesis and digital *signal-processing techniques can be implemented. The machine is manufactured by Sogitec and is available commercially through a French company TNA (Techniques Numériques Avancées) in a variety of configurations.

4. Hardware

(a) The CPU

The terms 'CPU' and 'microprocessor' are nowadays broadly synonymous. Both are used to signify the single-chip computer at the heart of the system. The chip is identified by its manufacturer's number. For example, the CPU chip used in the *Apple II, the *Commodore 'PET' and C64, and the *BBC Micro is the MOS Technology 6502; in the Apple 'Macintosh', *Atari 'ST' and Commodore 'Amiga' it is the Motorola 68000. As a rough rule of thumb, the larger the number, the more modern the chip.

The essential functions of the CPU include arithmetic operations (for demanding applications a maths 'co-processor' may additionally be used), reading and writing to and from memory (which includes moving data around in the memory), manipulation of individual bits within a byte, and, most importantly of all, logic and conditional operations (decisions based on the comparison between two numbers).

The speed of a CPU is determined by a precise crystal-controlled clock, each clock cycle stepping the CPU to the next instruction. Some of the more complex instructions require several clock cycles. The first microprocessor chips used clocks running at about 1 MHz (see HERTZ). The latest designs, despite considerable increases in complexity, can run at speeds in excess of 20 MHz.

The CPU also provides for interruptions. An electrical pulse to the appropriate connection causes the CPU to stop executing the current program and jump to a particular place in memory where a special Interrupt program is stored. When this has been executed the CPU returns automatically to where it left the original program. Most CPUs allow several levels of Interrupt—one Interrupt can interrupt another. Interrupts are of considerable importance to the designer of a music computer, since exact timing is essential, in, for example, the recording of *MIDI data or data from an *analogue to digital converter.

(b) Internal Memory

The entire world of a CPU consists of memory locations. These can, first of all, be in special memory chips permanently mounted within the computer. As new technology and mass production techniques have developed, the cost of memory chips has fallen dramatically while the capacity of a single chip has increased. Even inexpensive home computers can now store in excess of one megabyte (see BYTE) of data within the computer. In order to write to or read from memory it has to be 'addressed'; the address, needless to say, is a number (see below).

Memory chips are of two basic types. Random-access memory (RAM) can be both read from and written to, and constitutes the main working memory of the computer. The data in RAM is usually lost when the computer is switched off. Read-only memory (ROM), on the other hand, retains its data permanently, and is used for programs and data (firmware) that need to reside permanently in the computer, such as low-level operating systems (e.g. a 'machine code monitor'), small interpreted languages such as BASIC, or any dedicated program controlling a synthesizer or a sequencer.

Other forms of memory chip are also available. The most important of these is the erasable programmable read-only memory (EPROM), which as its name suggests can be filled with data by the programmer, who can then 'burn in' that data with a high voltage so that the data is permanent. It can, however, be erased at some future date, usually by exposure to ultraviolet light. For small quantities it is much cheaper than producing a true ROM.

One of the chief musical uses of EPROMs is the programming and storage of sound-sample data.

(c) External Memory

For long-term storage of programs and data the preferred medium is the magnetic disk. The principle is similar to that of recording tape, except that the data is recorded on concentric rings or 'tracks' divided up into 'sectors'. The exact way this is done varies from one computer to another. Disks have to be prepared by the computer before they can be used, in a process called 'formatting'. As well as marking out the tracks and sectors, the computer tests the disk to ensure there are no faults, and creates a section of the disk to be used for a directory, which is used to identify where each file of data is on the disk.

In personal computers, where normally the storage requirements are relatively modest, 'floppy' disks are used; these range from 8 inches to $5\frac{1}{4}$ inches (the mini-floppy) and, more recently, the $3\frac{1}{2}$-inch micro-floppy, widely used not only in personal computers by also in many digital musical instruments, such as the synthesizer and the *sampler. The storage capacity of a floppy disk depends not only on its physical size but also on the density with which the data can be recorded (single-, double-, and quadruple-density disks are available) and on whether one or both sides of the disk can be used. Storage capacity can thus range from under 100 kilobytes to several megabytes.

For very large amounts of data a hard disk is used. This consists of (usually) a number of stacked rigid disks permanently sealed within the casing (as distinct from floppy disks, which can be inserted and removed at will), and offers storage capacities, depending again on size, of several hundred megabytes. Hard disks are essential for the digital recording of anything but the shortest musical passages. Systems based on removable hard-disk cartridges are also available.

Magnetic tape is still used in some applications. Tape may be used to 'back up' data on hard disks to protect against a catastrophic loss of data should a fault arise in the hard disk. Magnetic tape is also used in recording studios not only in the familiar analogue form but also in the form of digital mastering tape. Cassette tape was used by early 'hobbyist' personal computers for data storage, despite the long time it takes to locate, read, and write data. Digital data storage systems have also been developed (e.g. by Sony) based on videotape.

Much research is still being conducted into alternative forms of data storage, in the quest for both higher speeds and greater capacities. The use of optical disks for rapid-access ROM is already established, and the technical problems in developing a read-and-write optical disk are likely to be resolved very quickly. 1988 saw the introduction of digital audio tape (DAT)—accompanied by protests from the publishers of compact disks that the new medium could be used to make flawless pirate copies of copyright material, objections that can be applied equally well to read–write optical disks.

5. Communication

The high speed of a CPU derives not only from the speed of the clock but also from the ability to transfer all the bits in a data word simultaneously between the CPU and memory. A signal path is provided for each bit, the paths as a whole being referred to as a 'bus'. In a small CPU the data bus may be eight bits wide (i.e. one byte), and the address bus (which selects the memory location in which to store a word of data) will be sixteen bits wide, allowing it to address sixty-four kilobytes of memory.

Since in the same CPU certain important memory locations within the chip, called registers, will be sixteen bits long, data to and from these registers has to be transferred in two stages, thus reducing the speed with which the CPU can process data. Such a CPU, with an eight-bit data bus, is categorized as an 'eight-bit processor'. Thus a more modern CPU such as the Motorola 68000 with a sixteen-bit data bus could be categorized as a sixteen-bit processor (the uncertainty is due to the fact that the CPU registers are thirty-two bits wide, so that it can justifiably be termed a thirty-two-bit processor). The address bus is correspondingly expanded—with twenty-four bits the processor can address sixteen megabytes of memory. A large memory capacity enables several programs to reside in memory, possibly sharing data or even running concurrently ('multi-tasking'). A large memory is also necessary for the storage of digitized sound.

The buses described above communicate in 'parallel'—there is a signal line for each bit. External devices such as disk drives and cassette recorders cannot record data in this way, but only one bit at a time. This is defined as 'serial' transmission—MIDI data, for example, is transmitted serially. There are numerous specialized serial transmission systems, for example for sending data down a telephone line. The only serial transmission standard of importance to most users of personal computers is the RS232 standard, provided on most computers to communicate with remote terminals and with printers. In the latter case a parallel communication standard ('Centronics') is also common.

The computer communicates with the outside world through 'ports'—for example, it will include an RS232 port and a parallel port. It will usually also provide a larger expansion port for the connection of more specialized equipment. Alternatively, a number of expansion slots may be provided inside the box. Expansion ports give access to all the data, address, and control lines to the CPU. Other common ports include those for a disk drive (or on a small system a port for a cassette recorder) and a visual display unit (VDU).

It is important to distinguish between a port and an *interface. The latter term, strictly speaking, refers to the electronics and in some cases the software required to create a given port; the word 'port' refers strictly to the physical outlet. In practice, the terms tend to be used rather freely, giving occasional cause for confusion. To illustrate the distinction, a MIDI interface may include one, two, or three ports (i.e. IN, OUT, and THRU).

Convolution

See FILTER 2.

Cross-talk

In a multi-channel sound system (including stereo), the leakage of sound from one channel on to others. This may occur in an amplifier if the stereo channels are not efficiently isolated (i.e. if the 'channel separation' is not good), or between adjacent tracks on a tape recorder, in which case the cause is usually faulty alignment of the record or playback heads.

Cut-Off Frequency

The frequency at which a low- or high-pass *filter has reduced the signal level by 3 dB (see DECIBEL). See also BANDWIDTH.

D

Dartmouth

See SYNCLAVIER.

Decay

In the dynamic *envelope of an instrumental sound, the fall in intensity after the initial *attack (e.g. of a plucked string). In *acoustics, the decrease in intensity of a sound characteristic of a reverberant room. See, especially, SYNTHESIS II 2(e): envelope generator.

Decibel

The decibel (dB) is used in acoustic and electrical engineering as the standard measure of the ratio of two intensities. Where one of these intensities is a 'reference', i.e. a fixed intensity with which the intensity under examination is compared, that intensity is defined as:

$$x = 10 \log_{10} P_1/P_2 \text{ dB}$$

(i.e. $x =$ the ratio in dB of the two intensities P_1 and P_2).

The logarithmic nature of the decibel is convenient for measurements of loudness, as the ear's own response is broadly logarithmic in character.

This formula needs to be modified where voltages or currents are being measured—these are usually measured as the square of the corresponding power ratio. The formula thus becomes:

$$x = 20 \log_{10} V_1/V_2$$

where x is as above; V_1, V_2 are voltages. Thus a doubling of power is measured as an increase of 3 dB, whereas a doubling of voltage is measured as an increase of 6 dB.

It can be seen that it is mathematically impractical to define 'pure' silence as a reference (i.e. to enter a value of 0 as numerator or denominator). Silence is defined as the 'threshold of hearing' and is physically defined as

$0 \text{ dB} = 0.000204$ dynes per cm^2.

Using this reference, the intensities in dB of commonly experienced sounds can be measured:

Threshold of pain	130
Pneumatic drill	110
Orchestra, *ff*	80–90
Loud conversation	60–70
Office noise	50–60
Whispers	10–20
Flute or violin, *pp*	5–10

Sound engineers choose as their 0 dB reference level the nominal maximum output or 'line' level. This level varies somewhat between professional and semi-professional equipment. Common values for 0 dB (sometimes indicated as 0 VU—volume units) are 1 volt and 0.775 volts.

The human ear is not equally sensitive to all frequencies (see ACOUSTICS 2). It is a common practice to 'weight' the dB value to reflect this. For example, the signal-to-*noise ratio (a parameter of the highest importance in audio systems) of a recording system might be nominally 65 dB; the 'weighted' value may be anything from 3 to 15 dB better. The greatest difference between the two values is usually found in the technical description of *noise reduction systems, which are designed to reduce the noise especially at frequencies to which we are most sensitive.

Delay

See ACOUSTICS 4; *also* DELAY LINE, SIGNAL PROCESSOR.

Delay Line

In the context of electronic *signal processing, delay techniques are the basis

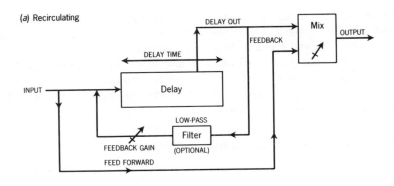

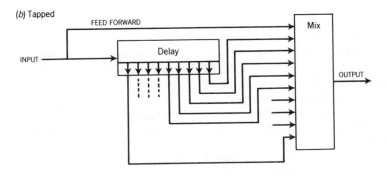

Fig. 1. DELAY LINES. (a) Recirculating; (b) Tapped.

of a wide range of musical effects, ranging from simple echoes to complex *timbral transformations. The principal factors determining the nature of the effect are the delay time and the number of repetitions of the delayed signal. The input signal is usually referred to as the 'direct' signal, and the path carrying the delayed signal is termed the 'delay line'; the latter term is, however, widely used to refer to a delay system as a whole.

There are two basic types of delay line (see Fig. 1). The 'recirculating' delay line uses a 'feedback loop' to feed the delayed output back into the input; the resulting mix of original and delayed signal is thus further delayed, fed back, mixed and delayed, and so on. If there is no drop in signal level through the delay line, the process may continue indefinitely (and at worst the signal will increase until the system is overloaded) even after the original signal is removed.

The 'tapped' delay line mixes a number of separately delayed ('tapped') signals with the direct-signal output. In either case, the possibility exists to apply a further process, such as filtering, to the delayed signal while still in the delay line. Similarly, it is also possible to combine the two techniques, for example by feeding back one or more taps to the input (see FEEDBACK).

Delay times above about 50 milliseconds tend to be perceived as distinct echoes; below that threshold the repeats merge, the effect being to alter the timbre and 'density' of the sound.

1. Delay Techniques and Systems

Delay lines require some means of storing the signal. This can be electromechanical (e.g. by a tape recorder), or by *analogue or *digital electronics.

(a) Mechanical Tape Delay

Tape delay exploits the physical distance between the recording and playback heads. This distance, together with the tape speed, determines the delay time. In a recirculating tape delay the signal to be delayed is recorded; the delayed signal from the playback head is output with the direct signal and is also returned to the record head to continue the process. A tape loop (a short length of tape joined end to end) can be used to allow the system to run indefinitely.

A simple recirculating delay can thus be set up on any tape recorder with separate record and playback heads; a tapped delay line requires a playback head for each delay tap. Specialized machines using up to twelve playback heads were designed in the 1950s for use in experimental studios, most notably that set up by RTF (Radiodiffusion-Télévision Française) in 1951 for the pioneer of musique concrète, Pierre Schaeffer. A later refinement added adjustable tape heads for fine tuning of the delay time.

For very long delay times, composers of electro-acoustic music have used separate machines for recording and playback, the tape passing around a variety of external guides before being taken up by the playback machine. Delays of several minutes have been realized this way.

For short delay times a delay system based on a tape loop can be made very compact. This was the method employed in the commercially produced WEM 'Copicat', a portable unit which used up to five playback heads.

A problem common to all tape-based delay systems is that of accumulated noise created by the continued rerecording of the delayed signal, especially when long repeated echo effects are required—the signal eventually becomes completely masked by the tape hiss. Tape delay has now been almost completely superseded by fully electronic systems.

(b) The Analogue Delay Line

The main component of the analogue delay line is the so-called 'bucket-brigade' chip containing a long chain of capacitors (see COMPONENTS 2), each of which stores the signal for a short time before passing it to the next. The practical upper limit to the delay time is between 300 and 600 ms, with a lower limit around 20 ms. At the time of their introduction, in the mid-1970s, the relatively low *distortion and noise levels made them clearly superior to tape-based systems. In turn, analogue circuitry has itself largely given way to digital, and is now only used where low cost is a prime consideration and the relatively poor frequency response can be tolerated.

(c) The Digital Delay Line (DDL)

A digital delay line works by digitizing (sampling) the incoming signal (see ANALOGUE TO DIGITAL CONVERSION) and storing the resulting data in memory. The maximum delay time depends both on the amount of memory and on the sampling rate. To reduce costs, either or both these factors may be limited. Halving the sampling rate doubles the possible delay time. A typical 'budget' DDL may have a maximum sampling rate as low as 20 kHz, and a delay time of perhaps 800 ms.

The resolution of the sampling process (i.e. the number of *bits in each 'word' used to represent each sample) is another potential area for economy. Eight-bit sampling is regarded as the minimum for an acceptable audio quality, but for professional applications at least twelve-bit words are required. The ideal is to sample at the compact disk standard—sixteen-bit precision at a sample rate of 44.1 kHz.

There are several technical and musical advantages to the DDL over the analogue delay line. Firstly, the audio quality is (for all but the cheapest DDLs) superior in terms of both distortion and system noise. Secondly, a wide range of delay times is available, from very short (e.g. less than 1 ms) to the limit of the available memory. Equally important is the ability to modulate the delay time (usually by a low-frequency *oscillator), which is essential for phasing, flanging, and chorus effects.

2. Delay-Based Effects

(a) Chorus

Based on the use of several parallel delay lines, each with a random variation of delay time centred around 30–40 ms, the chorus effect is used, as its name suggests, to create the impression of multiple sound sources from a 'solo' input. It is particularly valuable in enriching the sometimes rather lifeless sounds of a single-oscillator *synthesizer, especially those sounds designed to imitate orchestral strings. For guitarists, one of the classic uses of chorus (usually in the form of a small foot-pedal-operated unit) is in imitating the sound of a twelve-string *guitar with the usual six-string instrument. Chorus is frequently built into synthesizers and electronic *organs.

(b) Phasing and Flanging

These reputedly originated in the recording studio, and seek to reproduce the effect that arises when the speed of one of two tape recorders simultaneously playing back the same signal is altered. When the delay time of about 0.5 ms is slowly modulated, the changing *phase relationship (i.e. the shift of one *waveform relative to another) between the two signals causes a number of frequency bands to be alternately cut and boosted.

The result of phasing is a 'whooshing' *filter-like effect, not unlike that of a number of *wah-wah pedals linked together, each affecting a different part of the *spectrum. In a graphical display of the spectrum, the effect appears as a shifting comb, each 'prong' corresponding to a resonance peak—hence the technical name 'comb filtering' applied to the use of this range of delay times (see also REVERB 3).

Flanging is essentially a more pronounced form of phasing, deriving from a longer delay time of between 10 and 20 ms. Whereas the phaser might create a comb filter with perhaps four or five resonant peaks, the flanger may produce between ten and 100 peaks, depending on the delay time.

Both effects work best on a signal rich in harmonics (see ACOUSTICS 1)—a requirement which the electric *guitar, for example, easily meets. The purer sound of an instrument such as the flute would be much less affected.

(c) Double Tracking

Beyond about 50 ms, delay effects lose their filtering action and begin to be heard as distinct echoes. 'Double tracking' is the term used to describe the effect where the delayed signal is just discernible, as if a second player were doubling the first; the addition of a small amount of delay time *modulation serves to simulate the small temporal deviations that most human performers commit when nominally playing in unison.

(d) Pitch Shifting

A pitch shifter attempts to achieve a real-time transposition of the input signal by reading out the samples at a higher or lower rate, so that a second, ideally identical parallel voice can be added to the original solo voice. For an upwards transposition extra samples have to be inserted; for a downwards transposition samples have to be removed. Needless to say, the processing required to achieve this is complex and may not cope with all types of signal; the accidents which occur when the pitch shifter fails to generate a clean transposition are known as 'glitches'. As a rule, small transpositions are easier than large ones, and indeed an important application is to 'detune' very slightly an input signal rather as synthesists detune oscillators to create a fatter sound. One of the earliest pitch shifters was the 'Harmoniser' from Eventide; although strictly speaking a proprietary trade name, 'harmoniser' has since entered into popular usage to apply to all pitch shifters.

The most sophisticated pitch shifters can not only track the input signal cleanly over a wide range of transpositions, but can also perform 'intelligent' transpositions so that, for example, thirds will be either major or minor according to the specified musical scale. Such facilities, however, tend to be the province of specialized instruments rather than general-purpose DDLs, which mostly confine themselves, when they implement the facility at all, to the slight detuning described above.

3. Controls and Facilities

Delay effects are not necessarily to be used continuously. Long delay times can be used to add occasional echo effects, or to build up rhythmical ostinato patterns as a foundation for other material. Most DDLs include a facility to switch the delayed signal in or out by means of a foot pedal, and to 'freeze' a composite sound so that, while it continues to repeat, no more of the input signal enters the delay line. More rarely, a pedal (or some external control voltage) can be used to modulate the delay time while playing. Other essential controls are those which set the delay time, which may be done either via a numeric display or by switched ranges, and those which set the relative mix of direct and delayed signal and the amount of feedback.

The late 1980s saw the appearance of the 'multi-effects' unit, which takes advantage of the fact that the sound data once in memory can be processed in many different ways. Thus in addition to the delay-based effects described above, the same machine can be used as a general *digital signal processor to perform filtering and reverb functions, and with *MIDI control can even be used as a *sampler. As processing speeds have increased, it is now usual for such multi-effects units to perform several functions simultaneously. Like the modern *synthesizer, a DDL can be programmed, and pre-programmed settings recalled at the touch of a button or by receipt of a MIDI Programme Change command. Budget DDLs offer a range of preset effects with reduced facilities for programming. Synthesizers and samplers themselves now often include a wide range of signal-processing functions.

Digital

1. Representation of Data

A branch of electronics which represents information in a numerical format based on *binary numbers, which can be processed by a *computer. An *analogue (continuously varying) signal, such as a musical tone, can be represented as a series of binary numbers, each of which represents the *amplitude of the signal at successive moments in time. The process of encoding a musical signal into a digital format is called 'digitizing', or more usually *analogue to digital conversion. The reverse process can be used to restore the data to analogue form. Digital techniques can also be used to create and process sounds in 'real time'—see SYNTHESIS II 3; also SIGNAL PROCESSOR. The compact disk is now a familiar domestic example of the audio application of digital technology.

2. Digital Control and Communication

Digital switches can operate at high speed, and can be sequenced automatically, so that one command can trigger several subsequent actions. Conventional analogue equipment, such as tape recorders, may be digitally controlled, not only for the convenience of the operator, but also to prevent operational errors, or mechanical damage to the tape.

An important digital control system is that used for communication between electronic instruments, the Musical Instrument Digital Interface—*MIDI. The majority of modern electronic instruments employ digital electronics either in part or entirely; see e.g. DELAY LINE, REVERB, SAMPLER, SEQUENCER.

Digital Signal Processor (DSP)

A term usually reserved for specialized *digital circuitry (e.g. a DSP chip) designed to perform *signal-processing functions in real time. In fact, any digital *computer can perform digital signal processing; however, the calculations are often computationally demanding and most general-purpose computers are too slow to work in real time. True DSP processors are designed with a special 'parallel' architecture which enables several functions to be performed simultaneously. The most common DSP calculation is a combined multiply-and-add, which in a general-purpose computer would require several separate instructions; DSP chips perform the whole process in a single instruction (indeed, in a single clock cycle). High processing speeds are still required; processing at compact disk standard requires the generation of 44,100 output values (samples) per second for a single channel. A typical DSP chip can process over 200 instructions for each sample. Digital sound *synthesis is a special case of digital signal processing, and most modern *synthesizers and *samplers, as well as effects units such as the digital *delay line and *reverb processor, are based on proprietary DSP chips.

Diode

See COMPONENTS 4.

Distortion

In an electronic sound system, distortion occurs when the signal at the output does not exactly correspond to the input signal. Technically speaking, there is a non-linearity in the transfer characteristic. Distortion is measured by reference to a sine wave (see WAVEFORM). Any distortion appears as an additional harmonic (see ACOUSTICS 1) in the output signal—hence the general term 'harmonic distortion'. Some subtle forms of distortion do not show up under simple sine wave testing. The use of a square wave (a particularly stringent test) can reveal not only general harmonic distortion, but also transient distortion and poor frequency response. In this test the output waveform is viewed on an oscilloscope (see COMPONENTS 7 (b)); other tests use specialized distortion analysers.

Distortion can occur in a variety of ways. The circuit itself may be unsophisticated or badly designed. A good (hi-fi) amplifier may be driven into distortion if the input signal is too strong. This results in a clipped waveform at the output which can in some cases cause severe damage to loudspeakers. On the other hand, the overdriving of an amplifier is a much loved technique of many players of the electric *guitar (see OVERDRIVE).

Distortion is a particular hazard when recording music on to magnetic tape; microphones and loudspeakers can also distort the signal. Sometimes the distortion is not found objectionable—in these cases the more favourable term 'colouration' is used instead.

Although modern *digital recording techniques have been hailed by many as the ultimate solution to problems of distortion and *noise, in fact digital distortion is very real, and noticeably unpleasant, introducing a hard, gritty quality into the sound. Many engineers feel that the best *analogue equipment easily surpasses the quality of reproduction of compact disks. On the other hand there is little doubt that digital recording is in principle a great improvement on magnetic tape, the most noticeable benefit being the absence of tape hiss and a consequent increase in *dynamic range.

Distortion is measured as a percentage. A value of 0.1 per cent is regarded as a minimum for high-fidelity reproduction; professional equipment is required to have distortion figures less than a tenth of that figure. By comparison, the average domestic portable radio may introduce distortion as high as 10 per cent and the telephone as much as 50 per cent or more. Strictly speaking, a poor frequency response (e.g. a reduced *bandwidth) is a form of distortion, but it is always quoted as a separate parameter.

Doppler Effect

See ACOUSTICS 1, *also* LESLIE.

Drum Machine

This is a generic name for a broad range of electronic instruments which combine functions of the *synthesizer and the *sequencer in a way specially adapted to the generation of polyphonic *percussion patterns such as are used in rock, pop, and dance music. Depending on the degree of programmability, such an instrument will be described as either a drum machine or a 'rhythm machine', the latter term signifying an instrument allowing relatively little programming or, in the case of a 'preset rhythm machine', none at all.

I. The Rhythm Machine

Percussion patterns in rock and pop music are characterized by the use of deep levels of repetition. At the first level, a rhythmic pattern of up to sixteen semiquavers (sixteenth-notes) is constantly repeated. This basic pattern will be made up of interlocking rhythms from bass drum, snare drum, hi-hat, and suspended cymbal (which might simply be given as 'closed' and 'open' hi-hat), and one or more tom-toms. Other sounds which might be used include handclaps, cowbell, claves, and any number of Latin American instruments.

At the second level, this single bar pattern may be replaced by a more elaborate 'fill' pattern every eighth bar, to reflect the normal eight-bar phrasing of most songs.

A simple 'rhythm machine' will usually provide a range of pre-programmed rhythms, each of which will have an optional 'fill' pattern. The majority of these patterns will be in a 4/4 time signature, resolved to sixteen semiquavers. This would be described as a 'sixteen-step' pattern. A 'twelve-step' pattern, by contrast, would refer to a 4/4 bar of triplets. More advanced rhythm machines allow the rhythms for each instrument to be programmed, but the repetition pattern is still fixed by the machine.

The tempo range will equal or even exceed those available on electronic metronomes, embracing speeds between 40 and 280 beats per minute.

Such rhythm machines are a standard feature in electronic *organs and 'personal keyboards' designed for home use, where the need is for a simple automatic rhythmic accompaniment appropriate to the music style that is to be played. They can also be bought as self-contained instruments, some no larger than pocket calculators, and are used by amateur home recordists, and by composers developing songs, to provide an automatic rhythmic backing to the music.

2. The Drum Machine

True drum machines not only allow the precise programming of individual instruments' rhythms, but also allow the programmer to determine the sequence of repetitions of a large number of patterns, so that considerable rhythmical variety is available within a song. Programming and editing facilities are much as would be found on a sequencer, such as the ability to record a rhythm in 'real time' (by tapping keys on the instrument itself, or from a remote keyboard), edit individual notes of a rhythm, enter a pattern in 'step time', and automatically 'quantize' uneven rhythms to a specified resolution.

The modern drum machine, like the sequencer, can resolve very fine divisions of the beat (96 beats to a crotchet/quarter-note is a typical resolution) and can thus perform complex rhythmic patterns which human drummers could not be expected to accomplish.

Important though these programming facilities are, the success of a drum machine depends ultimately on the quality and quantity of its sounds. The modern drum machine dates back to 1978 when the California-based Linn Electronics introduced their LM1 Drum Computer, followed soon afterward by the 'Linndrum', featuring twelve high-quality digitized (sampled) percussion sounds (see DIGITAL; *also* ANALOGUE TO DIGITAL CONVERSION, SAMPLER). Since then, all drum machines aspiring to professional status have contained sampled sounds of both *acoustic and synthetic origins.

As the technology has progressed, drum machines have included more and more sounds, expanded programming facilities, and improved audio quality (the latter deriving not only from higher-quality digitization but also from the use of advanced recording techniques). The incorporation of *MIDI control, which can be both by or from the drum machine, gives it access to synthesizer voices. Alternatively, a MIDI keyboard (or any other MIDI controller, such as a *guitar controller or *drum pad) can be used to trigger the drum machine.

A modern drum machine will include not only the standard 'kit' sounds but a host of Latin American and 'ethnic' instruments, and even many that would seem inappropriate, such as sustained brass, wind, and string sounds, together with a host of effects such as vocal exclamations, gunshots, thunderclaps, and orchestral 'stabs'. Many models can read from memory cards or cartridges to replace or augment the resident sounds.

3. The Sampling Drum Machine

This is a standard drum machine with the added facility to digitize (sample) sounds directly. The SP12 (1985) from E-mu Systems (designers of the highly successful 'Emulator' and 'Emax' series of sampling keyboards) was the first sampling drum machine to reach the market, and was followed by, among others, a remarkably cheap model from Casio, the 'RZ1', a year later. An interesting example of the blurring distinctions between drum machine, sampler, and sequencer was the 'Studio 440' (1986) by Sequential Circuits, which combined all three functions in one 'workstation'.

4. MIDI Control

The 'NOTE ON/OFF' commands in MIDI are derived from the operation of a keyboard. NOTE ON corresponds to the depressing of a key, and NOTE OFF to the release. When used with percussive sounds of predominantly short duration, this manual separation is rarely convenient. The standard procedure in a drum machine is for the NOTE OFF command to be sent automatically immediately after NOTE ON. Drum machines receiving messages from a keyboard or sequencer will supply NOTE OFF commands internally, and will often function quite happily if NOTE ON commands only are transmitted. This convention needs to be borne in mind when the drum machine is used to trigger a keyboard-based synthesizer; some sounds may only function as expected if NOTE ON and OFF messages are clearly separated in time, as they would be if played from the keyboard. Some modern drum machines allow the time between NOTE ON and OFF to be set by the player—this is usually indicated as a *'decay' or 'gate' parameter.

Secondly, it is important to note that each instrument in a drum machine is assigned a MIDI note number. These normally correspond to the lowest notes of a standard five-octave keyboard. However, as the number of instruments in a drum machine has risen (to over 100 on some models) this simple convention is inadequate. Such drum machines will usually allow the programmer to set the MIDI note number for each instrument as he wishes; this is often extended (by means of MIDI channel assignments) to allow the use of a keyboard to play transposed versions of a given sound, a facility not available from the drum machine console. The control facilities of a synthesizer keyboard, such as pitch-bend (see SYNTHESIS II 3(f)) and *velocity sensitivity, can also be used via MIDI to add further nuance to a drum machine's sounds. A MIDI sequencer can be used to similar advantage.

Drum Pad

1. Design and Operation

A synthetic playing surface (similar to those used in drummers' practice pads) to which is fixed a transducer (which might, for example, be a simple contact microphone) which responds to the impact of a drumstick by creating an electrical pulse which can then be used to trigger an electronically generated (e.g. by a *synthesizer or *sampler) percussion sound. Since the drum pad itself has no need of an acoustically resonant shell, it can be made physically compact. Miniature pads (some designed for playing with fingers rather than sticks) are fitted to a number of popular electronic 'home keyboards' (see ORGAN 3), while full-size pads are designed for professional drummers, either in conjunction with, or instead of, an acoustic drum kit.

Modern professional pads are the product of sophisticated technological developments which make it possible not only for the output signal to reflect the intensity of the stroke (in itself not a particularly difficult task), but also for different regions of the playing surface to emit independent signals, i.e. to trigger different sounds. The playing surface itself has been the subject of much research by specialist manufacturers, who have sought to combine ruggedness with sensitivity, and a 'feel' as close to that of an acoustic drum as possible.

2. History and Development

(a) Up to 1980

As explained above, the principle of the drum pad is very simple—indeed the 'electronic drum' has for long been a popular project for electronics hobbyists. The appearance of commercial products has depended both on the availability of synthesizers able to create high-quality sounds, and on the willingness of established manufacturers to add to their range new experimental products which would appeal to the rock and pop market, with which electronic percussion is primarily associated.

The synthesizers available in the late 1960s (see e.g. MOOG, BUCHLA, ARP) used *analogue circuits which were, at least by modern standards, not suited to the creation of drum sounds sufficiently powerful to threaten the acoustic kit. Despite the presence, for example, in the Moog catalogue of a module which could convert the signal from a transducer into a suitable control voltage, there is little evidence of widespread use of synthesizers in this way. At this time even a monophonic synthesizer was expensive, and few groups were prepared to tie up such an instrument solely for the performance of synthetic drum sounds.

Of the independent designs marketed during the 1970s, the SYNARE series produced by Star Instruments of Connecticut represents probably the most concerted effort to promote the use of electronic drums. Each 'drum' was self-contained, with electronics adapted to the production of a particular sound. In addition to bass drum and tom-tom modules (the latter offering in fact quite versatile synthesis and control facilities), the range included, unusually, a timpani module. This was in essence a bass drum module with the addition of a foot-pedal-controlled pitch sweep.

The commercial breakthrough took place, in the event, not in America but in England. The musician and electronics engineer Dave Simmons developed circuits specifically for percussion synthesis including, for example, a variable 'stick click' component. The 'SDS3' (1978) used drum pads designed specially by the Premier Drum Co. This was soon followed by the much more powerful SDS5, which in its maximum configuration offered seven analogue synthesis modules, and which was triggered by Simmons's own highly distinctive hexagonal pads. The system was in demand especially for its powerful tom-tom sound, and the visual impact of the new pad shape proved an equally important factor in the success of the system. Significantly, publicity material for the SDS5 showed a drum kit made up of Simmons pads and acoustic cymbals, an open acknowledgement of the great difficulty in synthesizing cymbal sounds.

(b) The 1980s and the MIDI Revolution

The commercial development of digital sound sampling and, later, the introduction of MIDI opened up much wider possibilities for the remote control of electronic percussion sounds. Drum pads could be used to play not only synthetic sounds, but also samples of real instruments. Furthermore, thanks to the versatility of MIDI control, a single drum pad could trigger a number of different sounds either sequentially (by using different regions of the pad surface) or together—the MIDI code derived from the pad can be made to trigger almost any number of simultaneous 'notes', each corresponding to a different instrumental sound. Modern refinements include a facility to damp the sound on the pad itself with the hand or the stick, thus making available to the drummer not only percussive sounds but also the sustained instrumental sounds that were otherwise the exclusive province of the keyboard player.

Drum pads are now sold by many companies prominent in the manufacture of synthesizers, notably Yamaha, Casio, Akai, and Roland. In addition to standard full-size pads, a number of multi-pad units are available, such as the Roland 'Octapad', which carries eight hand-sized pads in a single box, and used typically as a supplement to a normal kit (e.g. for playing effects) or as a convenient system for the idiomatic real-time programming of a drum machine.

Dynamic Range

The range of dynamics (i.e. from quietest to loudest) of a sound, or which can be handled by an electronic sound system. Since the dynamic range is a ratio it is normally expressed in *decibels. If the dynamic range of a sound exceeds that of a recording medium, the quietest sounds will be covered by the system *noise, while the loudest sounds will overload the system and cause *distortion. There is a subtle but important difference between dynamic range as understood by a musician and by an engineer. For example, the musician might suggest that a harpsichord has a limited dynamic range (understood as a range of nuance), whereas the engineer will compare the intensity of the instrument's *attack with silence, and find that the dynamic range is very wide. See also ACOUSTICS 2, for a consideration of the ear's response to sound.

E

E-Bow

A small hand-held string driver for the electric *guitar, invented by the American Greg Heet and introduced at the National Association of Music Merchants' (NAMM) show in 1976. Never widely marketed, it was used by a select handful of rock guitarists. Its function was to achieve sustain by applying an electromagnetic field to the chosen string, so keeping it vibrating. Grooves on the underbody kept the device in proper alignment with the string. A revival of interest in the E-Bow from guitarists such as The Edge of U2 has prompted Heet to resume production, and to embark on some new products, including a model that will work on all six strings. The effect of the E-Bow is best understood by analogy with the action of a violin bow (from which it takes its name)—effects include soft (slow) *attacks, sustained harmonics, swells, and 'spiccato'.

Electronium

A monophonic electronic *organ designed by René Seybold in 1948 and manufactured by Hohner. It existed in two versions. The first (looking very like an accordion) had a forty-one-note keyboard which through transpositions could be played over a six-octave range, with sixteen stops; the second was intended for use with a piano and offered twenty stops over a three-octave range. It was used by Karlheinz Stockhausen in several works, specifically in *Prozession* (1967), and optionally in several others, including *Kurzwellen, Spiral,* and *Hymnen*. In performance by Stockhausen's own performance group it was played by Harald Boje.

EMS

A company established in 1969 at Putney, London, by the composer Peter Zinovieff for the design and manufacture of electronic *synthesizers and related equipment. Zinovieff had been running a private electronic studio since 1962, and established the commercial project with the collaboration of the electronics engineer David Cockerell, in response to encouragement from a number of composers, performers, and the Society for the Promotion of New Music, who were frustrated at the lack of facilities in the UK at that time for composers interested in electronic music. The factory itself was located in Wareham, Dorset.

The first EMS synthesizer was also the most successful. The VCS3 (1969), also known as the 'Putney', was the first low-cost synthesizer to be available in the UK and was adopted by a large number of music departments in universities and colleges as well as by individuals. It used a matrix patch board for interconnection between modules; these included three voltage-controlled oscillators (see SYNTHESIS II 2), one acting as a low-frequency oscillator, whose frequencies could be set directly from the front panel by precise vernier controls, as well as by the optional keyboard controller. As well as the expected *filter, *ring modulator, and *noise and *envelope generators, the VCS3 included a built-in spring *reverb system and a joystick controller linked to the patch panel. Signal inputs were provided to allow the processing of external sounds—the instrument was used in this way by Stockhausen for the first performance of Ylem (1972). A briefcase version, the 'Synthi-AKS', was introduced in 1977, and included a *sequencer and a capacitative touch keyboard (see COMPONENTS 2).

In contrast to the VCS3, the 'Synthi 100' was arguably the largest commercially produced voltage-controlled synthesizer ever made in a single console. Functionally it was equivalent to four VCS3s, but with the addition of two five-octave keyboards, two 60 by 60 matrix patch boards, a dual-beam oscilloscope, *digital frequency counter, and a 256-stage digital sequencer, the first of its kind to be developed. Also newly developed for the Synthi 100 was a pitch to voltage converter, which enabled the sound of an acoustic instrument to control any voltage-controlled circuit. The sequencer and the P/V converter were later released as separate products. Twenty-five Synthi 100 systems were sold, to customers as diverse as the BBC (who bought the first to be built) and the rock musician Pete Townsend.

Other products of the mid-1960s included the 'Synthi Hi-Fli' (1973) *guitar processor and two *vocoders. The Model 5000 (1976) was a sophisticated and expensive computer-controllable vocoder and speech synthesizer, but the Model 2000 (1977) was a simple low-cost instrument that, like the guitar processor, reflected a desire to reach beyond the specialized electronic studio market to the rock and commercial market. Most representative of this strategy was the 'Polysynthi' (1979). This was what might be described as an 'ensemble synthesizer'. It was fully polyphonic (i.e. any number of notes could be played simultaneously), but the sound was passed through a single voltage-controlled filter and amplifier chain, with the addition of an analogue *delay line for echo, chorus, and flanging effects. The instrument was, however, not a commercial success.

In 1979 EMS was liquidated, the factory and title being bought by Datanomics, a local Wareham company. The new owner continued to market the existing designs and invested considerable sums into new prototypes, including a digitally programmable version of the VCS3. Though exhibited at the Frankfurt Music Fair in 1981 the instrument never went into production. In 1983 the EMS title and design rights were offered to Robin Wood, an engineer who had worked for EMS since 1970. Lacking the necessary capital he passed the offer on to the composer Edward Williams, who was able to take it up. In 1984 Robin Wood moved to Cornwall and started production chiefly of vocoders.

In 1985 a new device, the DTV (distance to voltage) converter, was developed by another EMS designer, Richard Monkhouse, who in 1974 had been responsible for the innovative EMS 'Video Synthesiser', which applied sound-synthesis techniques to the generation of video graphics, and which had found favour chiefly in Europe. The DTV used an ultrasonic beam over a range of up to six metres to detect the distance of any object which entered the beam. In 1988 it was adapted to include a *MIDI interface and renamed the EMS 'Soundbeam'.

Enhancer

The general name for a processor that adds small controlled amounts of harmonic *distortion to a signal to add brightness and presence which may have been lost though previous processing (for an explanation of harmonics, see ACOUSTICS 1). The original enhancer was the Aphex 'Aural Exciter' (1975). This was initially available only for rental, the company maintaining, to begin with, an aura of mystery over the details of its operation, broadly described as 'psycho-acoustic enhancement'. The principle was reportedly discovered by accident when one of the founders of the company incorrectly wired up an amplifier circuit.

The input signal is split into two paths, one of which includes a variable high-pass *filter, which removes all frequencies below a few kHz. The output from the filter is passed to the 'harmonics generator' before being recombined with the unprocessed signal. Enhancers are now a common feature in recording studios and are available from a number of manufacturers. Modern refinements include dynamic control of the enhancement so that *noise present in the original signal is not itself enhanced when the signal level is low. An enhancer differs from almost all other signal processors in that it adds new components to the original, rather than boosting or cutting existing components.

Envelope

The term used in *acoustics and in sound *synthesis to describe the change in *amplitude of a sound over time. The simplest envelope consists of two elements or 'stages': the 'attack', during which the sound increases in intensity (and, usually, spectral richness) from silence to some maximum level, and the 'decay', during which the sound falls back to silence. This envelope would thus be described as a two-stage AD envelope, and is sufficient for the description of simple percussive sounds, such as that of a drum or of a piano string left to decay freely.

For more complex sounds, further stages are required. For example, many sounds remain at a steady amplitude for much or most of the time, and thus require the addition of a 'sustain' stage in the envelope description. Since, moreover, the sustain intensity is often less than the peak intensity (of the attack), a second decay stage is required between attack and sustain. The envelope is now described by four stages—ADSD—with which most of the familiar musical sounds can be described with reasonable accuracy, and upon which the envelope generator of a *synthesizer is modelled. Clearly the description of an instrumental envelope characterized by expressive nuances (such as the 'swell' or *messa di voce*) will require corresponding stages to be added to the basic ADSD pattern.

It is often necessary (e.g. for sound synthesis or when using *signal processors) to consider the amplitude envelope of individual frequency components (partials—see ACOUSTICS) of the sound, that is to say, the *timbral envelope (see, in particular, SYNTHESIS II I). For example, in the recording studio, it is often better to alter the level of an instrumental sound by cutting or boosting selected frequencies (see EQUALIZATION) rather than by simply changing the amplitude with a volume control.

The attack is normally the most tonally complex part of the envelope, and provides most of the auditory cues by which one instrument is distinguished from another. For example, in *musique concrète* and tape manipulation, a common technique is to cut off the attack portion of an instrumental sound. Although only a small fraction of a second of the sound will have been removed, this is often sufficient to render the resultant sound unrecognizable.

Envelope Follower

An electronic circuit which uses the dynamic *envelope of a sound to control an amplifier to which some different sound is connected. The amplified sound takes on the envelope characteristics of the controlling sound. The amplified sound is usually from a *synthesizer. See *also* GUITAR SYNTHESIZERS AND CONTROLLERS.

Envelope Generator (EG)

See ENVELOPE, SYNTHESIS II 2, SYNTHESIZER 1.

EPROM

Short for Erasable Programmable Read-Only Memory. The EPROM is a special memory chip (see COMPONENTS 6) used in *computers and some *synthesizers for storing data. Once programmed, the data is stored permanently, but can be erased by exposing the chip to ultra-violet light.

Equalization

The use of *filters to modify the *spectrum of a sound, either for creative effect or as a corrective. A graphic equalizer provides controls over a large number of filters (twenty or more) covering the audio range, allowing selected bands of frequencies to be cut or boosted. One application is to compensate for any undesired room resonances (determined through spectrum *analysis; see *also* ACOUSTICS 4) which might otherwise lead to inappropriate adjustments being made during the recording process, the equalizer being applied between the monitor output from the mixing desk and the main amplifiers. A 'parametric equalizer' is a tunable tone control, giving variable boost or cut of a selected frequency, usually also with a control to vary the *bandwidth.

Expander

The general name for a *synthesizer without a keyboard. It is externally controlled through *MIDI from a *sequencer or a MIDI controller. The latter is normally a keyboard, which may be either part of a complete synthesizer or a so-called 'mother keyboard' which contains no synthesis hardware but is designed specifically for controlling external instruments. Many expanders are 'multi-timbral'—each voice can be assigned to separate MIDI channels and thus to different sounds (patches). Such a facility can only properly be used in conjunction with a sequencer, which can be programmed to attach the required channel code to each item of note or patch change data, or with a MIDI controller such as a *guitar synthesizer.

Expansion

An electronic treatment applied to a sound to 'expand' its *dynamic range. Expansion is normally used to reverse the effects of *compression in the recording process (e.g. as part of a *noise reduction system), but it can also be used on its own to reduce the *noise content of a signal by progressively attenuating signals at a low level, at which noise is most apparent. The action of an expander is similar to that of a *noise gate, the two effects often being combined in a single unit. The combination of compression and expansion in a single unit is usually termed a 'compander'.

F

Fairlight CMI

A *digital *synthesizer developed in Australia by Peter Vogel and Kim Ryrie from a prototype instrument called the QASAR M8, and first manufactured in 1979. The CMI (short for Computer Musical Instrument) was the first commercial instrument to offer facilities for the real-time control of digitized sound (see SAMPLER), together with a wide range of *synthesis, *analysis, and composing facilities. A unique feature was the facility to draw a *waveform on the screen using a light pen. The hardware included a computer box containing two floppy-disk drives and memory cards for each of the eight voices, a six-octave keyboard (with the option of a second 'slave' keyboard), and a standard computer terminal consisting of a keyboard and visual display unit.

Later models feature multiple *MIDI ports, a hard disk, and the use of faster sixteen-*bit microprocessors (see COMPONENTS 6) instead of the original eight-bit devices, together with a considerable increase in memory. The original CMI had what was at the time a massive memory capacity of 208 Kbytes, rising to 14 Mbytes in the Series III system (1986).

Software (loaded from disk and thus easily updated) is arranged on a series of 'pages', each concerned with a particular function. For example, on the original instrument page 4 was concerned with the drawing of amplitude envelopes of harmonics for additive synthesis, and page 8 was concerned with sound sampling. Page D offered what became one of the most famous (and much imitated) of the facilities, a so-called '3D' display of consecutive wave cycles, which served to illustrate the change in waveshape over time. Later models have used the same format to present the results of digital *spectrum analysis (see acoustics 1).

While the earlier models found favour as much in academic institutions as in the commercial world, the modern Fairlight is designed uncompromisingly for the latter market as a self-sufficient sound production system, with the emphasis on comprehensive sampling, direct-to-disk digital recording, *sequencing, and *time code synchronization facilities.

Feedback

1. Acoustic Feedback

The penetrating whistle that occasionally occurs when a microphone is being used for live amplification (e.g. in a public address system) is caused by the microphone picking up the signal from the loudspeaker. The signal is thus 'fed back' into the amplifier, appearing at the loudspeaker at a higher level, to be picked up by the microphone in a continuous cycle. The effect is not dependent on the microphone pointing directly at the loudspeaker—smooth walls can act as acoustic mirrors, reflecting the sound from the loudspeaker towards the microphone.

The avoidance of feedback depends on careful placing of microphone and loudspeaker, the selection of directional microphones designed to resist feedback, and judicious trimming of the amount of amplification. Since the feedback is usually at a particular frequency, it is sometimes possible to use a notch *filter to remove that frequency from the signal path. In most cases, the simple principle that the microphone is behind the loudspeaker, pointing away from it, is a sufficient precaution.

2. Electronic

Feedback is an important technique in the design of amplifier circuits, being used to reduce *distortion and to smooth the frequency response (and in some cases to construct a particular response, as in a *filter, the elements of which are often incorporated into the feedback circuit). The feedback in this case is 'negative'—part of the output signal is subtracted from the input in such a way as to reduce the degree of amplification or 'gain' of the circuit. The opposite process, of adding part of the output to the input (therefore 'positive' feedback), gives the possibility of 'infinite gain', i.e. an output with no input, and is the basis of many *oscillator circuits.

Fender

See GUITAR.

Fender-Rhodes

See RHODES, *also* PIANO.

Filter

I. Analogue: Basic Types

A filter is an electronic circuit designed to attenuate a selected range of frequencies. It is defined by the range of frequencies it processes. A 'low-pass' filter allows low frequencies to pass unaffected, but attenuates high frequencies. Similarly, a 'high-pass' filter attenuates low frequencies. These two types form the basic building blocks for more complex filtering processes. Depending on the exact configuration, the combination of a high-pass and a low-pass filter results in either the attenuation of all but a selected range of frequencies ('band-pass') or in the attenuation of a particular mid-range of frequencies ('band-reject' or 'notch').

An 'active' filter is based on an amplifier circuit and therefore requires a power supply, whereas a passive filter (e.g. the tone controls fitted to most electric *guitars) gives no amplification and does not need a power supply.

As one might expect, the most important parameter of a filter is the frequency at which the filtering action begins to take effect. Referring to Fig. I, it can be seen that the removal of frequencies is a gradual process. Thus an arbitrary point on the curve of the filter has to be selected as the 'cut-off frequency'—this is the point at which the level of the signal has been reduced by 3 dB (see DECIBEL). In a band-pass filter there are two such points; the distance between them is termed the 'bandwidth' of the filter.

Fig. I also illustrates a second parameter of great importance, the rate at which the filtering takes place, generally referred to as the 'slope' of the filter. This is normally measured in terms of 'decibels per octave' (dB/oct.). For example, the relatively simple filters used in the tone control circuits of domestic audio amplifiers have a gentle slope of 6 dB/oct. Such a filter is termed a 'first-order filter'. This means that it employs a single circuit configuration, almost always involving a resistor and a capacitor (see COMPONENTS 2), in which case the configuration is an 'RC section'.

In order to increase the slope of the filter, one RC section must be added for each 6 dB/oct. increase in slope. Thus a 12 dB/oct. slope would require two RC sections, giving a 'second-order filter'. The filters usually used in analogue *synthesis are fourth order with a 24 dB/oct. slope.

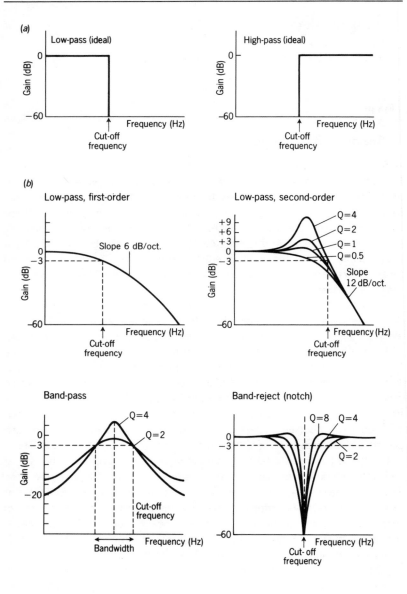

Fig. 1. FILTERS. (a) Ideal responses, low- and high-pass; (b) Practical filters.

A side-effect of the use of filters is that the *phase response also varies with frequency. The high frequencies lag behind the low frequencies, the more so the higher the order of the filter. Although the ear is largely insensitive to phase (see WAVEFORM 1), the phase lag can become a problem with filter orders of two and above, resulting in a ringing effect, and ultimately spontaneous oscillation.

In a second-order filter this effect is rarely audible, but in higher-order filters it can be exploited to good effect (see e.g. SYNTHESIS II 2(d)). Such filters can be designed to develop a resonant peak near the cut-off frequency. The height of this peak is determined by the 'Q' of the filter—the higher the Q, the higher the resonance peak. If the Q is made high enough, the circuit will oscillate at the cut-off frequency. ('Q' is most easily understood in relation to a band-pass filter, in which case it is equal to the ratio of the centre frequency to the bandwidth. The calculation for low- and high-pass filters is rather more complex.)

When band-pass and band-reject filters are designed with steep slopes, the results are respectively a 'tuned circuit' and a 'notch' filter. The former is familiar from its use in a radio receiver. The latter is used to remove frequency-specific interference, such as mains 'hum'. A single circuit can be designed to provide both band-pass (boost) or band-reject (cut) filtering according to the setting of a single control; this is the basis of the parametric and graphic equalizer (see section 3 below).

2. Digital Filters

The subject of *digital filtering is deeply complex and mathematical, and by no means confined to musical and audio applications. However, it is possible to describe the basic principles and explain the most important technical terms without recourse to complex mathematical analyses.

The starting-point for any study of digital filtering is the concept of the 'unit impulse'. While in analogue circuit design this is a somewhat theoretical idea, it has a very real meaning in a digital system as it signifies a single digital 'sample'. A digitized *waveform consists of a series of such impulses, the amplitudes of which arise from the shape of the waveform. A processor is described in terms of the relation between the input and output impulses. For example, a simple volume control can be implemented by calculating successive output impulses as the product of the corresponding input impulses and some constant value.

A digital filter requires that at least two input samples are used together to calculate a single output sample. For example, a rudimentary low-pass filter can be implemented by calculating the output sample as the average of two successive input samples. This can be represented by the simple formula:

$$y[n] = 0.5x[n] + 0.5x[n-1]$$

where n signifies the current sample, $n-1$ signifies the previous sample, y signifies output samples, and x input samples. An equally rudimentary high-pass filter results if the difference between the two input samples is calculated, rather than the sum.

There is some further terminology that can be conveniently introduced here. Since the output of the filter depends only on the values of input samples, the filter is said to be 'non-recursive'. This is equivalent to saying that there is no *feedback from the output to the input. The 'previous input' in the example above has, in effect, been delayed by one step (its value has to be temporarily stored within the filter in order to make the calculation). This is thus a 'first-order non-recursive filter'. Just as the order of an analogue filter depends on the number of RC sections, so the order of a digital filter depends on the distance in samples between the current sample and the most delayed sample—one in this case.

These expressions derive from the formula given above, which has the general form of a 'difference equation', since it is concerned with the differences between samples. An alternative and important way of describing the filter is in terms of its 'impulse response', i.e. the response to a single sample (or 'unit impulse') of maximum amplitude. In the above example, and assuming an input impulse of amplitude 1 (and all subsequent inputs 0), the output is two samples of amplitude 0.5. The impulse response is strictly finite, as in fact it always will be if the filter is non-recursive. Accordingly, this is a 'finite impulse response' (FIR) filter.

Most practical FIR filters calculate each output sample from several input samples. Each delayed input will have its own coefficient (the value by which it is multiplied). The impulse response consists of a number of output samples equal to the number of coefficients, and one more than the filter order. A ninth-order FIR filter, for example, will have an impulse response ten samples long. The process by which these output values is arrived at is known as 'convolution', a highly appropriate term as it turns out; each output sample is (in the above case) the result of ten multiplications and additions, a task which (yet modest by FIR filter standards) may already be beyond the ability of a processor to accomplish in real time (see DIGITAL SIGNAL PROCESSOR).

It remains to consider the structure and behaviour of a 'recursive' filter. As its name suggests, this calculates output samples using values of previous outputs—i.e. it involves feedback. Past inputs may be used as well, but, so long as one or more past outputs are involved, the filter is recursive. The great advantage of the recursive filter is its computational efficiency. A variety of useful filters can be designed using not more than two past outputs (i.e. two recursive coefficients) and the 'current input'. Even more powerful is the 'general second-order recursive filter' combining the current input with two recursive and two non-recursive terms.

A certain amount of care must be taken in designing a recursive filter, since it is possible for the output to continue indefinitely (resonate) after the input has finished—i.e. it is an infinite impulse response (IIR) filter. At worst, the output may grow without limit, resulting in numerical overflow and massive *distortion. Fortunately the conditions for a stable filter are well known (if mathematically complex); however, they do require that coefficients be determined by rigorous mathematical calculation rather than by trial and error.

The mathematical basis of filter design leads to a further way of describing a filter—in terms of its 'poles and zeros'. Poles are points of resonance, determined by the recursive coefficients, while zeros are points of frequency attenuation, determined by the non-recursive coefficients. A non-recursive filter is an 'all-zero' filter; similarly, a purely recursive filter is an 'all-pole' filter.

Direct comparisons between analogue and digital filters are less than straightforward. Although as a rough rule of thumb the number of poles of the digital filter can be taken to correspond with the order of an analogue filter, the characteristics of the slopes show marked differences. For a given order, the slope of a digital filter can vary considerably according to the way the coefficients are calculated.

3. Applications

The uses of filters fall into two general categories, which can be summarized as 'musical' and 'technical'. The former includes the electric guitar tone controls referred to above, the *vocoder and the filters used in sound synthesis. Filters have also been used as musical 'instruments' in live performance, most significantly in a number of works by Karlheinz Stockhausen, including *Mikrophonie I* (1964), *Prozession* (1967), and *Kurzwellen* (1968). The filters were used to transform the sounds of a large tam-tam picked up by microphones moved by performers over the surface. In the latter two works the filters were also applied to the sound from a contact microphone attached to a viola.

The purpose of 'technical' filtering is twofold: to remove undesirable *noise (e.g. rumble, mains hum, and hiss), and to boost or cut bands of frequencies that have been modified by the recording or reproduction process. This process is known as *equalization (often abbreviated to 'EQ'), and is the basis of several important pieces of equipment used both in the studio and on stage, most importantly the parametric equalizer and the graphic equalizer.

In practice, the difference between musical and technical filtering is not clear-cut, equalization in particular being used as much for musical effect as for technical reasons.

Flanger

See DELAY LINE 2(c).

Formant

See ACOUSTICS 3.

Fourier analysis, Fourier transform

See ANALYSIS.

Frequency Modulation

See MODULATION; *also* SYNTHESIS II 2(b), 3(c).

Fundamental

The lowest mode of vibration of an oscillating medium, such as a *guitar string, the column of air inside an organ-pipe, or more generally the lowest-frequency component of any periodic sound, for example from an *oscillator. See ACOUSTICS 1.

G

Gibson

See *GUITAR.

Guitar, Electric

1. Origins and Development

The electric guitar developed in America out of the steel-string acoustic guitar, which by the 1920s was well established in folk and Country and Western music, and was also eclipsing the banjo in popularity, especially in the new dance and jazz bands. Experiments were directed not only towards the basic problem of amplification, but also towards an increase in sustain. Associated with the former objective was the problem of acoustic *feedback, which was virtually eliminated with the development of the solid-bodied guitar, at the expense of the loss of the 'acoustic' quality of the sound (see ACOUSTICS 3).

The key figures in this early experimental period were Lloyd Loar, who worked for the Gibson company (a long-established manufacturer of steel-string guitars) between 1920 and 1924, and Adolphe Rickenbacker, who, after working for the Dopyera brothers ('Dobro') on their National 'resonator' metal-bodied acoustic guitars, went on to form the Electro String Company with two ex-National employees, George Beauchamp and Paul Barth, who had, like Lloyd Loar, been experimenting with magnetic pick-ups. The new company was the first to enter commercial production, in 1931, with an all-aluminium electric Hawaiian (lap) guitar which was soon dubbed the 'Frying Pan'. At about the same time the Rowe DeArmond company introduced clip-on magnetic pick-ups for steel-string guitars. Gibson followed in 1935 with the ES-150, an F-hole hollow-body acoustic fitted with a magnetic pick-up employing a large single fin-shaped pole-piece (see section 2(c) below). The jazz guitarist Charlie Christian took up the instrument with such success that the pick-up became named after him.

(a) Leo Fender (1909–1991)

The Gibson company showed little enthusiasm for the idea of a solid-bodied electric guitar and the initiative passed to Leo Fender, who had also been experimenting with pick-ups. In 1944 he set up the K & F company with an ex-employee of Rickenbacker, 'Doc' Kauffman, producing experimental steel guitars and amplifiers. Two years later Fender broke with Kauffman and formed the Fender Electric Instrument Company. In 1948 he introduced the 'Broadcaster' solid-body electric guitar, shortly afterwards renamed the 'Telecaster'. This was followed in 1954 by the 'Stratocaster', which has remained one of the most enduring, and most copied, classic designs, second only to the 'Gibson Les Paul' (see section (c) below). Earlier, in 1951, he had introduced the world's first solid-body bass guitar (see section 3(a) below), the 'Precision'.

Fender continued to experiment, producing several new models between 1956 and 1965; none of these, however, attained the degree of popularity enjoyed by the Stratocaster. In 1965 he sold the company to CBS, retaining a role as design consultant until 1970. In 1972 he formed Music Man with two former Fender employees, Forrest White and Tom Walker, continuing to concentrate on design, especially of bass guitars. He also began to use active electronics (pre-amplifiers) in both guitars and basses. In 1980 he formed G & L (the 'G' standing for a long-time associate George Fullerton) to develop and market a new range of instruments, combining the classic styling of the early Fender instruments with advanced pick-up, tremelo, and bridge design.

(b) Les Paul and Gibson

It is hardly possible to overestimate the contribution to the development of the modern electric guitar made by Les Paul. Many seemingly recent innovations, such as the headless guitar (see section 3(c) below), may be traced back to the experiments Paul made in the early 1930s, directed towards the two primary objectives noted above: the elimination of feedback and increased sustain. The principle of the solid body served both objectives: little acoustic energy was drawn from the strings, and there was no pick-up movement caused by body resonances. Paul himself has reported that early experiments used old railway sleepers.

In 1941 Epiphone, an established manufacturer of arch-top steel-string guitars, allowed Paul the use of their workshops. The resulting prototype, essentially an Epiphone acoustic guitar with a solid block of wood down the middle on which two pick-ups and a Gibson neck were mounted, became popularly known as the 'Log'. He offered his ideas to Gibson, then enjoying a high reputation for hollow-body electric guitars, but they were unimpressed and turned him down. It was only the success of Fender's first instrument (Fender himself was well acquainted with Paul and his work) that finally moved Gibson to offer Paul a contract. Even then, such was their caution that they suggested that the new instrument be known simply as the 'Les Paul' model, without the Gibson name. In the event, the instrument introduced in 1952 was called the 'Gibson Les Paul Standard'. It was heavier than the Fender instruments, being made of mahogany with a maple facing, rather than of solid maple, and the neck was also somewhat wider.

The next significant development came in 1956 when Gibson's Seth Lover and Ted McCarty invented the twin-coil 'humbucking' pick-up (see section 2(c) below), which, in addition to eliminating the electrical *noise and interference to which the single-coil was prone, had a characteristically warmer, more mellow tone. The Gibson Les Pauls produced between 1957 and 1960 and fitted with two humbucking pick-ups are now among the most sought after in the world.

At the time, however, the Les Paul guitars did not sell well, and in the 1960s the instruments were restyled. Les Paul's contract with Gibson ended in 1962; Gibson's subsequent instruments were designated the 'SG' series, though they clearly retained many 'Les Paul' characteristics. In an attempt to modernize their image Gibson also introduced a number of radical new designs, of which the most successful was the 'Flying V' (1958). They maintained their production of hollow-body electric guitars, and consolidated their position with the purchase in 1957 of Epiphone.

Shortly afterwards Gibson introduced a new hybrid instrument, the 'semi-solid' electric guitar, the first model (the ES-335) appearing in 1958. In essence this was a thin hollow-body twin-F-hole guitar with a central solid block of wood carrying the pick-ups and bridge, an arrangement not so far removed from that of Les Paul's original 'Log'. The design sought to combine the sustain characteristics of the solid-body with the warmer sound of the acoustic instrument. The idea proved very popular, especially among jazz and blues guitarists, and the semi-solid (also often referred to as the 'semi-acoustic') became rapidly accepted as a 'type' in its own right.

By the late 1960s, guitarists were paying large sums of money for 'vintage' Les Pauls, and in 1967 his association with Gibson was re-established, resulting in the reissue of the original 'classic' designs as well as the introduction of several new models. Gibson have also produced 'custom' instruments at regular intervals, reflecting the design ideas of individual players.

2. The 'Standard' Electric Guitar

(a) Body and Neck Construction

Although commonly referred to as a 'solid-body', the modern electric guitar cannot be assumed to be made of a single piece of wood. The simplest arrangement is, certainly, a carved block of wood for the body and a glued-in or bolted-on neck, and the classic Fender instruments featured just this type of construction. Many designers have chosen more elaborate methods whereby a number of separate pieces of wood are combined in a sandwich or laminated pattern. The Gibson arrangement noted above, of mahogany with a carved maple facing, is but the simplest of these methods. The choice of woods undoubtedly influences the tonal qualities of the finished instrument at least as much as the choice of construction methods. Walnut, alder, and ash are regularly used as well as mahogany and maple, the final mixture being determined by the slightly conflicting demands of high sustain, requiring a heavy wood such as mahogany, and lightness of weight, where maple would be preferred.

A third method of construction, regarded by many as superior, is that of the 'neck-through-body', in which the neck wood (which may itself be made of laminations) continues the length of the body, carrying the pick-ups and bridge, with either single pieces of wood or laminations glued to either side. The disadvantage of this method is that damage or deformation is usually irreparable. The bolt-on neck construction favoured by Fender not only avoids this problem but also enables subtle alterations to the tilt of the neck to be made by the player.

The neck (typically of maple) also contains a steel 'truss rod' which can be adjusted for tension to suit different string gauges. Access to the truss rod is usually immediately behind the nut on the headstock. On Gibson guitars the fingerboard facing is usually a dark hardwood such as ebony or rosewood, in contrast to the lighter-coloured rosewood or maple characteristic of Fender instruments. The frets (and sometimes also the nut) are usually of a nickel alloy, and the fingerboard is inlaid with decorative dot markers. Sometimes the wood between the frets is scalloped out to make string-bending easier.

(b) Body Styling

Released from the structural constraints of the acoustic guitar, designers of electric guitars, including Fender and Gibson, have produced some startling un-guitar-like body shapes, often for little reason other than visual impact. There are, however, two aspects of body shaping that serve entirely practical purposes. Firstly, the body can be contoured, both sectionally and in outline, to achieve as much comfort as possible for the player. Secondly, the body can be cut away at the point where the neck meets the body, allowing easier access to the higher frets; the resulting 'horns' can be proportioned not only for aesthetic reasons but also to fine-tune the balance of the instrument. (A few acoustic guitars have featured a single cutaway. The most well known is probably the Maccaferri, associated in particular with Django Reinhardt; other manufacturers to offer the feature include Gibson and Martin.)

(c) Pick-ups

The operation of a magnetic pick-up is very simple in principle. A bar magnet mounted across the body under the strings provides a magnetic field through which the steel strings pass. Disturbances to this field caused by the vibrating strings are detected by a coil wound round the magnet. The distance between the magnet and the strings is critical; other factors which affect tone quality and strength are the strength of the magnet itself, and the gauge and number of turns of wire in the coil. Most magnets are made of Alnico, an alloy of aluminium, nickel, and cobalt. More recently, ceramic magnets have been used by several manufacturers, and piezo-electric (contact) pick-ups incorporated directly into the bridge (and thus not dependent on the use of steel strings) are also used.

Early magnetic pick-ups, such as the 'Charlie Christian' type, used a single fin-shaped pole-piece, its upper surface curved to follow the curve of the fingerboard. Although this type is still used, the most usual modern type, following a pattern first employed by Fender, uses six individual magnetic pole-pieces, threaded so that each may be set to the optimum height with a screwdriver. Such a pick-up is known as a 'single-coil pick-up' to distinguish it from the 'humbucking' pick-up, which uses two single-coil pick-up assemblies side by side (each with six pole-pieces) and wired in series. The pick-up magnets have opposite magnetic polarities and the coils are wired out of *phase with each other, so that any mains-borne hum or other interference (induced equally in both coils) is cancelled out, while the desired signal from the string is duplicated. This arrangement has the additional effect of reducing the treble content of the signal by comparison with the single coil. Thus in general the twin-coil humbucking pick-up has a fatter, warmer sound than the single coil, which is correspondingly clear and biting. It is common for a modern guitar to be fitted with one of each. Traditionally, however, single-coil pick-ups are associated with Fender guitars, and humbucking pick-ups with Gibsons.

There are three recognized positions for pick-ups on a guitar, giving varying degrees of brightness according to their distance from the bridge: the 'neck' or 'rhythm' pick-up (furthest from the bridge), the middle pick-up, and the 'bridge' or 'lead' pick-up. Switches on the body enable the player to select pick-ups individually or in combination. The possibilities for variation can become quite complex. For example, the two coils of the humbucker can be used separately as single coils; pick-ups can be wired in series (one after the other) or in parallel (side by side), in or out of phase. Some pick-ups are made with a central 'coil tap' (emulating two series-connected single coils), the output of which (at half the *impedance of the full coil) is particularly 'clean' and bright.

As a rule, each pick-up will have associated controls for volume and tone (treble cut—i.e. a simple low-pass *filter). The Fender Stratocaster was noted for the provision of a single volume control close to the bridge pick-up, making it possible for the player to alter the volume with his little finger while playing. Such circuitry is 'passive'—no amplification of the signal is provided. Many modern instruments use 'active' (powered) electronics, boosting the signal within the guitar. This reduces the risk of signal degradation from interference or noise picked up by the signal cable, and makes it easier to connect elaborate tone controls and other effects. It also makes it easier to overdrive an amplifier into *distortion, as required by some forms of 'heavy' rock music.

(d) The Bridge

Depending on the design, the strings may terminate at the bridge itself, or at a separate tail-piece, or at the back of the body. Modern strings are fitted with ball ends, so that they have merely to be threaded through the appropriate fastening and then wound on to the tuning ('machine') heads.

The bridge on an electric guitar needs to be rather more sophisticated than that of an acoustic instrument, in order that the height and length of each string can be precisely adjusted. On the Broadcaster/Telecaster, Fender used three adjustable bridge 'saddles', but the most popular design was that used on the Stratocaster, which used a small saddle for each string. This was in effect a combined bridge and tail-piece design; Gibson in contrast have consistently favoured a separate tail-piece, in conjunction with their own 'Tune-O-Matic' bridge.

(e) Tremelo

This should perhaps more properly be called vibrato, since its purpose (at least as originally conceived) is to emulate the wide vibrato associated with slide guitar playing. In essence, it consists of a short arm connected to either the bridge or the tail-piece—pressing on the arm slackens the strings, thus lowering the pitch. It is normally used monophonically, since for a given movement the strings change pitch by different amounts.

Most modern tremelo designs are based on that developed by Fender for the Stratocaster. The bridge assembly is mounted on a block which passes through the body and is free to pivot longitudinally. The tension of the strings is balanced by a set of springs anchoring the base of the block to the body so that, when the tremelo arm is released, the 'floating' bridge automatically returns the strings to their original pitch. The pitch can also be raised slightly, depending on the usually limited amount of back travel available to the bridge assembly.

The bridge-based tremelo is, however, not without its problems. The movement of the bridge alters the height of the strings above the pick-ups, thus affecting the response. The most troublesome problems relate to errors of intonation caused by the failure of the strings to return exactly to their original pitch. This is caused by the strings sticking in the nut and/or the bridge. On modern instruments a locking nut is fitted which clamps the strings securely to prevent slippage. Similarly, tremelo systems from specialist manufacturers such as Kahler and Floyd Rose incorporate roller bearings on the saddles themselves together with string clamps. Many modern designs avoid the use of springs in favour of a cam or torsion bar mechanism, obviating the need for a cavity in the guitar body.

The alternative arrangement, of a fixed bridge and a flexing or pivoting tail-piece to which the tremelo arm is connected, is also popular for its relative simplicity (e.g. the 'Accent' tremelo designed by Rickenbacker in the early 1960s) and its ability to maintain the strings at a constant height above the pick-ups.

One of the most advanced tremelo systems is the 'Trans-Trem' by Steinberger. By means of some highly ingenious mechanics this maintains the relative tuning of all the strings as they are 'bent' up or down. An indexing system enables the tremelo to be locked (i.e. transposed) in almost any desired key within the available range—down a fourth and up a minor third.

The overall bend range of a tremelo system depends as much on the characteristics of the strings as on the mechanics of the tremelo itself. Clearly it is possible to lower the pitch to a point at which the strings slacken completely (an effect known as 'dive-bombing'); on the bass strings this may embrace an octave, while the treble strings drop a third or fourth. Modern systems (with selected strings) also allow the pitch to be raised by as much as a fifth; such a range should not, however, be taken for granted.

3. The Bass Guitar

(a) Fender

The bass guitar was developed by Leo Fender as a solution to the problem of amplifying the acoustic double bass. His first instrument, introduced in 1951, was the 'Precision', so-called because it was fretted like the standard guitar, enabling 'precise' pitching. (The 'fretless bass' has nevertheless developed alongside the fretted instrument, being particularly associated with the modern jazz group as an similar-sounding alternative to the double bass.) The tuning was that of the acoustic bass—E, A, D, G—sounding an octave below the corresponding strings of the standard guitar.

The Precision had the usual bolt-on neck, a single single-coil pick-up, and the double cutaway body shape later used on the Stratocaster. A later refinement, peculiar to the bass guitar, was the use of two pole-pieces for each string, to reduce the distortion that could arise when a single pole-piece failed to encompass the extremes of movement of a long heavily vibrating string. Rather than use a single 'in-line' pick-up, post-1957 Precisions used a 'split' pick-up—in effect two separate pick-ups each serving two strings. This has the added advantage that the 'treble' pick-up can be placed slightly nearer the bridge. Both types of pick-up are in general use on modern instruments.

(b) Other Designs

The idea of the bass guitar was rapidly taken up by other manufacturers. In 1953 Gibson introduced their EB-1 bass (styled to look like an acoustic bass and soon dubbed, somewhat misleadingly, the 'violin-bass'), following it in 1960 with the EB-0 and EB-3. These more conventionally styled instruments were given the same double cutaway shape (more symmetrical than Fender's) which Gibson introduced with their new SG range of guitars. In the same year Fender brought out the 'Jazz' bass—essentially a more luxurious version of the Precision with a slightly narrower neck and a second pick-up.

This period also saw the appearance of Rickenbacker's '4000' bass, the first of what proved to be a highly successful series of instruments. They were of 'neck-through-body' construction, the early models being of mahogany, later ones of walnut. Other features worthy of note include the provision of stereo outputs, and a sliding mute incorporated into the bridge. In the 1970s Alembic gained a high reputation for their expensive handmade basses, which were among the first production instruments to include active electronics.

(c) Steinberger and the Headless Bass

This radical design from the American Ned Steinberger was introduced in 1981. Les Paul had in fact included the idea in his early experiments, but without taking it into production. The objective in reducing the length of the neck was to eliminate certain acoustic dead spots that arose from neck *resonances. Steinberger took the idea very much further with a headless bass made of a specially developed blend of aramid fibre, carbon fibre, and glass, moulded in one piece under high heat and pressure. No truss rod was needed, whatever the gauge of the strings. The tuning heads were relocated at the back of the bridge, an arrangement that has become popular in its own right. The strings are made precisely to length with double ball ends.

The extreme rigidity of the body maintains accurate intonation over long periods, and a highly sustaining, clear, and balanced sound throughout the range. The futuristic black trapezoid styling has spawned many less expensive wood imitations. In 1983 Steinberger introduced an otherwise identical standard six-string guitar. More recently he has produced some highly sophisticated tremelo systems (see section 2(e) above).

(d) Extended Basses

Bass guitars have been produced with five and six strings. In the former case, the added string is usually a low B, reflecting the increased demand (fostered to a great extent by the use of *synthesizers) for extra-deep bass tones. Six-string basses either duplicate the tuning of the standard guitar (i.e. high B and E strings are added) or add a high C and a low B, thus preserving the fourths tuning of the four-string instrument.

4. Playing Techniques

In addition to the standard picking and strumming techniques associated with the acoustic guitar, there are several specialized and idiomatic techniques which take advantage of the sensitivity of the pick-ups and the extended sustain of the electric guitar.

(a) String Bending

By firmly displacing a string sideways (most easily in the middle of the neck) the pitch can be raised by up to a tone. Skilled players can bend several strings together or in sequence. For example, the first string is bent; as it is returned to its original pitch a second string is bent, creating a double-note bend in contrary motion. Vibrato can be performed either by string-bending or by means of a tremelo, if fitted.

(b) Pull-Off and Hammer-On

Because of the long sustain, legato fingering has a much greater impact on the electric guitar. Taking up a finger after the note has been picked (the note still sounding) is called a 'pull-off', and can be regarded in many cases as a form of left-hand pizzicato. The opposite action, fretting vigorously above an already fretted and picked note, is called a 'hammer-on'; given a sensitive pick-up this action can easily cause an initially silent string to sound clearly.

(c) String Tapping and Two-Handed Fretting

The logical extension of the hammer-on is the use of both hands on the neck, firmly tapping the strings, rather than picking in the conventional manner. With this technique, complex rapid melodic and rhythmic patterns can be performed.

(d) Thumb Slap

A technique particularly associated with (though not confined to) the bass guitar, this is similar to the string-tapping technique, except that it is performed nearer the bridge in the usual picking position. The thumb is used percussively in conjunction with fretting techniques such as those described above, the emphasis being on rhythmical energy and complexity rather than on melody. Used in this way the bass guitar can be seen very much as a percussion instrument, especially in combination with a rock drum kit.

(e) Amplification and Electronic Effects

In practice it is not possible to speak of the 'sound' of an electric guitar independently of the amplifier, which for many players can even take precedence over the guitar itself. A fully equipped amplifier may include a graphic *equalizer as well as conventional tone controls and a *reverb system. A player's sound and style depends similarly on his choice and use of external *signal processors (usually in the form of compact foot-controlled units). Many of these, such as the *wah-wah, originated from hobbyist workshops before being developed commercially. The most important effects include *distortion (which can be induced directly by overdriving the amplifier, as well as by means of an external 'fuzz box'), reverb, and a number of related treatments based on the use of a *delay line, such as phasing (see DELAY LINE 2), flanging, and chorus effects.

Guitar Synthesizers and Controllers

I. The Acoustic Controller

Often called simply a 'guitar synthesizer' this is a conventional electric *guitar which has been provided with extra electronics which enable the player to control a *synthesizer. The central circuit element is a pitch to voltage (P/V) converter which receives signals from a special 'hexaphonic' pick-up (i.e. with six separate pole-pieces—one for each string) mounted close to the bridge. Some systems use a special replacement bridge with contact pick-ups built into each string saddle.

To track the pitch of a plucked string accurately, the P/V converter has to 'see' usually at least two cycles of the *waveform, resulting in a sometimes noticeable 'tracking delay' (particularly on low notes) between the moment of picking and the output of the control signal. If the sensitivity of the pick-up is too high, signals from sympathetically vibrating strings, and signals caused by the squeaks and other incidental noises associated with guitar playing, may also unintentionally trigger the synthesizer. On the other hand, if it is too low, the decay of the string may be prematurely cut off and softly picked notes may not register at all. For this reason, a 'threshold' control is usually provided so that a player can adjust the sensitivity to suit his needs.

In addition to detecting pitch, it is possible to track the dynamic *envelope of the sound (see ENVELOPE FOLLOWER), generating a signal which can be used independently of the pitch to control other synthesizer parameters (e.g. the *filter cut-off frequency). Some early so-called guitar synthesizers did not in fact contain any synthesis circuitry, but applied *distortion, filtering, and other techniques (see SIGNAL PROCESSOR) to the signals from the hexaphonic pick-up.

For the control of an *analogue synthesizer, the output of the P/V converter can be used directly. Modern (post-1983) controllers are required to output *digital control signals conforming to the *MIDI standard (hence, 'pitch to MIDI converter'). For best results this requires the use of a 'multitimbral' MIDI synthesizer, which enables each voice (assigned to a different MIDI channel) to be controlled by a different string. Some synthesizer modules have been designed specially for this application, providing independent pitch-bend control for each voice, a facility not normally available on MIDI instruments, which assume control from a keyboard with a single 'global' pitch-bend controller.

One problem associated with the P/V system is that of the difficulty in using a tremelo arm (see GUITAR 2(e)). The software associated with the P/V converter has to make decisions (which may well be wrong) about the detected pitch in order to generate the correct note and pitch-bend data. Additionally, certain types of tremelo cause the critically important distance between the strings and the pick-up to change. The solution used on some instruments is to provide a 'soft' tremelo arm which serves solely to send MIDI pitch-bend and other control data.

2. History and Development

Pitch to voltage converters have been available since the early days of *analogue *synthesis (usually as part of a 'modular' system), but specialized guitar synthesizers appeared on the market only towards the end of the 1970s, with models from a number of manufacturers, including 360 Systems, *ARP (the 'Avatar'), and, most importantly, Roland, who have a unique record of development and manufacture, starting with the GR-500 (1978), followed by the GR-300 (1981) (both analogue controllers), and the GR-700 MIDI controller (1984). These models all consisted of an otherwise standard electric guitar, fitted with a hexaphonic pick-up and a number of extra controls, connected to a separate synthesis module.

The GR-700's guitar is fitted with a special bar connecting the headstock to the top of the body, designed to eliminate certain body resonances (see ACOUSTICS 3) which could confuse the pitch detection circuits. Unlike those of earlier models which were designed for manual setting of synthesis parameters, the synthesis module of the GR-700 (based on one of their early MIDI keyboard-based synthesizers) is controlled by a set of foot pedals, so that patch changes can be made while playing.

Roland have also introduced 'retrofit' MIDI adaptor units (1987 onwards) which can be simply fitted to any electric guitar without the need for structural alterations. Similar products (both complete guitars and retrofit systems) have been introduced by Shadow (a leading manufacturer of guitar pick-ups), Ibanez, Zeta, and K-Muse. The latter's 'Photon' controller (1986) is notable for using an optical (infra-red) pitch detection system which obviates the need for steel strings and which is claimed to resolve the pitch of a note in a single cycle.

The American company New England Digital (NED) has designed a guitar controller interface for their *Synclavier digital synthesizer, which could be used by any guitar fitted with a hexaphonic pick-up. The system is celebrated chiefly for its use by the guitarist and composer John McLaughlin playing a Roland G-303 guitar (originally designed for the GR-300 system) fitted with a NED remote-control panel.

The 'Mirror 6' Guitar and MIDI Controller (c.1987) from Zeta Music Systems combines pitch detection (necessary to follow pitch-bend and tremelo effects) with a patented fret-scanning system which enables a MIDI note to be triggered either by the picking of the string or simply at the moment when the string makes contact with the fret. The modified mechanical (Kahler) tremelo can also function as a 'soft' MIDI controller.

3. Alternatives to the P/V System

Although the great majority of guitar controllers use the P/V system, its inherent limitations coupled with the difficulty of extracting higher levels of synthesizer control have encouraged the development of a variety of alternative systems which act purely as MIDI controllers and cannot be used as conventional electric guitars.

The futuristic-looking 'SynthAxe' developed in 1984 in England by Bill Aitken uses separate neck and trigger strings to isolate the picking and damping action of the right hand from the fretting, string-bending, and other actions of the left hand. Pitch information is obtained from the electrical contact between the neck strings and special split (hexaphonic) frets. String bending is detected electromechanically by small coils mounted in the body. The trigger strings are conductive, and detect damping through the change in electrical characteristics caused by contact with the hand. A set of piano-like keys (*velocity- and pressure-sensitive) are also provided, enabling groups of strings, or indeed all six, to be triggered simultaneously.

In 1988 Yamaha introduced their G10 controller, which detects pitch with great speed and precision by sending ultrasonic signals along each string and analysing the echo. Further sensors detect velocity and string bending. The streamlined body also carries rotary volume and *modulation controllers, two patch select buttons, and a 'soft' tremelo arm. The instrument connects to a rack-mounted control unit which can in turn be connected to any MIDI synthesizer.

4. Self-Contained Guitar Synthesizers

In 1986 the British designer Steve Randall introduced the Stepp DG1 electronic guitar. Similar in many respects to the SynthAxe (using, for example, two sets of strings), it sought to avoid the problems of translating guitar gestures into MIDI data (which was conceived in terms of the piano keyboard) by incorporating a specially designed synthesizer (providing six digitally controlled analogue voices) with its own communication system. One noteworthy feature was the special 'ADSM' envelope generator (signifying attack–decay–sustain–mute), which recognized the technique peculiar to the guitar of picking a string while simultaneously muting it with the hand. Control of external MIDI instruments was also possible, though with some compromises which reflected the Stepp's unique methods of control. A controller-only version, the DGX, was introduced in 1987, but the company was by then in financial difficulties and ceased trading the following year.

Also in 1987, Casio introduced their DG10 and DG15 electronic guitars, which used plastic strings and offered 'easy-play' facilities similar to those available on many electronic *organs, including preset voices and automatic rhythm accompaniments (see drum machine). A more serious instrument was the PG-380 (1988), which combined a conventional P/V system (which enabled the instrument to be used as a standard guitar) with an internal 'interactive phase distortion' (IPD) digital synthesis module.

H

Hammond Organ

An influential and highly successful electric (later, electronic) *organ designed by the American inventor Laurens Hammond. Introduced in 1935, it used an earlier Hammond development, the synchronous motor. The speed of this motor was determined by the supply frequency (60 Hz in the USA) and could therefore be maintained with a high degree of stability. This motor drove ninety-five contoured 'tone wheels' approximately 30 mm in diameter. Close to the edge of each wheel was a small electromagnet; changes in magnetic flux caused by the changing distance of the edge of the wheel induced an alternating current in the coil of the electromagnet (see COMPONENTS 3). This current was then amplified and passed to a loudspeaker. Each disk was profiled so as to produce a sinusoidal *waveform, which could thus be used either as a fundamental tone or as a harmonic (see ACOUSTICS 1). A series of graduated draw-bars enabled the player to set the level of the fundamental, a sub-octave, and seven harmonics; each key of the keyboard thus had nine tone-wheels assigned to it.

Although Hammond insisted that the new instrument was not intended specifically as a replacement for a pipe organ, it provoked numerous protests from builders of pipe organs, who insisted that the instrument should not be called an 'organ' at all. A dispute with the Federal Trade Commission (at least in part caused by some grandiose advertising claims) led ultimately to a dramatic experiment at the University of Chicago, in which a pipe organ was tested 'blind' against the Hammond organ, the latter's claim to be an organ being finally vindicated. While a major proportion of sales were to those who saw it as a significantly cheaper alternative to a pipe organ, the instrument had a much wider appeal, being adopted by jazz and dance bands (for whom the portability of the instrument was a major attraction), and by some composers—George Gershwin was one of the first customers.

The most popular model was the B3 (1936), which had two 61-note manuals and a 25-note pedalboard. Ten preset settings were available on each manual, selected by means of an octave of reverse-coloured keys to the left hand of each manual. Two notes were reserved for voicings created by means of the draw-bars.

In 1939 Hammond introduced the first purely electronic organ, the 'Novachord', immediately followed by a monophonic synthesizer, the 'Solovox'. This was a piano attachment, to be played with the right hand, while the left hand accompanied on organ or piano. The tone-wheel organ, however, remained the mainstay of the business until the mid-1960s, when integrated circuit technology took over.

After World War II the company flourished, introducing several new instruments. There was a greater emphasis on instruments for domestic use. In 1949 a 'spinet' organ was introduced, called the 'Cinderella'. Two relatively short manuals were offset by an octave, with the lower-pitched manual in front, an arrangement which was rapidly accepted as a standard layout. A variety of new instruments and facilities were introduced for amateur players, notably the 'chord organ', a 'solo' keyboard (either monophonic or polyphonic) with extra keys or buttons, each of which produced a chord.

A device for long associated with the Hammond organ (especially the B3) is the *Leslie tremulant system. Organs with Leslie systems built in were introduced in 1967, and the company (Electro Music) was purchased by Hammond from CBS in 1980.

Competition in the electronic organ market increased markedly in the 1970s, with a corresponding decline in Hammond's fortunes. The introduction in 1979 of the B-3000, a revival of the classic 1936 Model B instrument, failed to avert a break in production in the early 1980s. In 1985 the company was bought by the Australian Noel Crabbe. Manufacture is now by Hammond Suzuki in Japan, with research and development in Australia. As a result a new generation of instruments has emerged which exploits modern *digital technology to the full, while preserving the traditional draw-bar system.

Harmonic, Harmonic Series

See ACOUSTICS 1; *also* WAVEFORM.

Harmoniser

See DELAY LINE 2(*d*).

Helmholtz

See ACOUSTICS 3.

Hertz

Abbreviation Hz. The name is the modern replacement for the quantity 'cycles per second', a measure of frequency. It is named after Heinrich Rudolf Hertz (1857–94), a German physicist celebrated for his pioneering work in electromagnetism.

Hexadecimal

Counting to base 16. Hexadecimal uses the letters A to F in addition to the denary digits. See COMPUTER 1. See *also* Appendix 1.

I

Impedance

The total resistance 'seen' by an electrical circuit feeding into another (input or 'load' impedance), and also the internal resistance experienced by a circuit applying a signal to another (output or 'source' impedance). This resistance can in many cases vary with the frequency of the signal, especially where the circuit contains capacitors or inductors (see COMPONENTS 1–3). For optimum signal transfer it is important that the input and output impedances are properly matched. A low impedance load (e.g. a loudspeaker) needs to be fed from a high-power (low output impedance) source. On the other hand, many signal sources, such as gramophone cartridges, generate very little power and need to be connected to a circuit which does not draw too much of this power away. Such a circuit would need to have a high input impedance.

Output impedance is the ratio of open-circuit voltage (i.e. with no load connected) to the current which flows when the output terminals are shorted together. Clearly, the measurement of open-circuit voltage presents just the problem outlined above. Many electronic test instruments are designed to have an extremely high input impedance so that they draw virtually no power from the circuit under test. If this were not the case, the measurement would not be a true representation of the circuit's performance.

In many cases it is necessary to calculate the output and input impedances by a mathematical model of the circuit. In the case of the gramophone cartridge, the output impedance is included in the manufacturer's speci-fications; amplifiers are designed to offer sufficiently high input impedance to suit the majority of cartridges. This is made easier by the fact that, so long as the input impedance is higher than the device's output impedance by a factor of 10 or thereabouts, few problems will arise.

In the case of a power amplifier feeding a loudspeaker, problems can arise due to the fact that the speaker's impedance, which may be specified as 8 ohms, does, being mostly inductive, in fact vary widely with input frequency. At certain frequencies at which the speaker coil is naturally resonant, impedance may drop significantly, possibly to little more than the residual resistive impedance of the wire, therefore drawing more power from the amplifier. Apart from the physical hazards of this possibly excessive power transfer, this phenomenon can be apparent in the sound as a lack of fidelity to the original signal.

Impulse Response

See FILTER 2, *also* REVERB 3.

Inductance, Inductor

See COMPONENTS 3.

Integrated Circuit

See COMPONENTS 6.

Interface

The term used to describe the electronic 'dialogue' between two pieces of *digital equipment. For example, in order for a computer to receive information from peripheral equipment such as a disk drive, special chips (integrated circuits: see COMPONENTS 6) are required (known as 'disk controllers'), which are responsible for sending the correct instructions to the disk drive, and similarly for passing messages and data from the drive to the computer for processing. It follows that the interface involves not only special hardware (the chips, plugs, and sockets, and so on) but also special software (built into the chip, which in turn is sent instructions by the system software) which sends the correct data at the correct time and which also understands the data from the external device. A complete interface specification covers everything from the speed of the data to the type of connector used and the precise electrical characteristics of the signal.

An interface transmits and receives data either serially (i.e. one *bit at a time down a single wire) or in parallel, using a separate wire for each bit.

A number of interfaces for common needs have been standardized. The most common standard for the serial transmission of data is known as 'RS232'. Thus, any computer fitted with an RS232 interface can communicate with any other piece of equipment similarly equipped. This might be another computer, a printer, or a modem, which is used to send digital data down a telephone line. A different serial interface is *MIDI, used for the exchange of data between electronic instruments such as the *synthesizer, *sequencer, and *drum machine.

L

Leslie

A keyboard amplifier with a built-in electromechanical tremulant system, developed by the American Don Leslie in Los Angeles between 1937 and 1940 and marketed from that date under the company name Electro Music. Although commonly said to use rotating speakers, in fact most often the drive units themselves are fixed; the sound from the treble drive unit is projected by a rotating treble horn, while that of the bass driver is reflected off an angled hardwood baffle enclosed in a revolving drum with a single aperture. However, Leslie experimented with a range of designs, and, in the case of the bass driver, has in some models mounted a revolving speaker inside the drum.

The rotation (exploiting the Doppler effect; see ACOUSTICS 1) causes the sound source alternately to advance and recede with respect to the listener, giving the effect of a subtle simultaneous *amplitude and pitch *modulation. Two speeds are available: a 'fast' vibrato speed of about 7 Hz and a 'chorale' speed of about 0.5 Hz. The Leslie is particularly associated with the *Hammond organ, although it has also found favour with many rock guitarists. In 1965 the business was sold to CBS, who in turn sold it to Hammond in 1980. Hammond and Electro Music were sold to the Australian Noel Crabbe in 1985; Hammond was acquired by Suzuki in 1988 and Crabbe licensed the Leslie name to Calo Corp. of Batavia, Illinois.

Limiter

A *signal processor (usually *analogue), used mainly in the recording studio, which prevents the level of a signal from exceeding a specified limit. Signals below the limit are unaffected. The action of a limiter is thus simpler than that of a *compressor, which reduces signal levels progressively. The two functions are often used in combination.

Loop

The term 'loop' is widely used in electronics and in electronic music for any process which repeats cyclically, and for any signal path wherein the output is returned to the input. Thus in an amplifier a *feedback loop is used to control gain (the amount of amplification) and frequency response.

In electronic music the term is most associated with tape manipulation techniques in which a sound is recorded on tape in the normal way; the tape is then cut so that the end of the sound can be spliced on to the beginning. The resultant tape loop may be designed to last for a few seconds or several minutes. In the latter case the loop may be passed between two or more machines, or bottles or jam jars are used to maintain tension in a long loop.

Instruments have been designed which exploit this technique, the most notable being the WEM Copicat, a small self-contained tape recorder with multiple heads and a single loop of tape, used for the creation of loop and *delay effects.

Looping is of great importance in many modern electronic (and especially *computer) music processes, particularly in *digital sound *sampling, where a short section of sound is looped under program control to create a continuous or repetitive sound. This may be done to save memory or to create unusual sound effects.

M

Mellotron

An electromechanical keyboard instrument for the playback of pre-recorded sounds, designed by Leslie, Norman, and Frank Bradley in Streetly, Birmingham between 1962 and 1963 and marketed by Mellotron Manufacturing from 1964. The principle of using a set of magnetic tapes linked to a conventional keyboard was first exploited in an instrument called the 'Chamberlin', for which Leslie Bradley's previous company, Bradmatic, had been asked to supply tape heads. The first instruments included features derived from the electronic *organ, especially in the division between left and right hands of accompaniment material (rhythms and chords) and melody. The Mark II instrument (1965) employed two manuals; however, the later, single-manual instruments proved the most successful—the Model 300 (1968) used a 52-note keyboard, and the Model 400 (1970) 35 notes.

Through a complex series of take-overs in the 1970s the designers lost the rights to the name 'Mellotron' (now an American company marketing sample playback systems), and in 1977 the instrument was reissued by the Bradleys' new company, Streetly Electronics, as the 'Novatron'.

Tapes were mounted in interchangeable racks, with three tracks per tape, which ran at $7\frac{1}{2}$ inches per second. The tape was broader than standard, at 9.5 mm; later, conversion units were made available to enable the use of standard recording tape.

The Mellotron/Novatron found particular favour with the 'electronic' bands which formed in the 1960s and 1970s, such as Tangerine Dream and Kraftwerk, and as a sound-effects source for broadcasting stations such as the BBC. It remained in production until the early 1980s, when it was at last eclipsed by *digital technology (see SAMPLER).

Microprocessor

A single *digital integrated circuit (see COMPONENTS 6) implementing the processing functions of a *computer, used in most modern electronic instruments such as the *synthesizer, *sampler, *sequencer, and *drum machine, as well as in many *signal processors. The *digital signal processor is a specialized form of microprocessor.

The power of a microprocessor is measured by a number of factors, including the internal 'word length' (e.g. sixteen *bits), the clock speed (which controls the overall processing speed), and the amount of external memory (measured in *bytes) which it can *address. See e.g. COMMODORE, APPLE, ATARI.

MIDI

The Musical Instrument Digital Interface developed from proposals from a number of Japanese and American manufacturers (chiefly Roland, Oberheim, and Sequential Circuits) for a 'universal' *digital *interface which would enable instruments such as the *synthesizer, *sampler, *sequencer, and *drum machine, from any manufacturer, to communicate with each other. A preliminary specification was developed by the end of 1982, and the first MIDI-equipped instruments, the 'Prophet 600' from Sequential and the 'Jupiter 6' from Roland, both *analogue polyphonic synthesizers, were introduced in the early months of 1983. A final version of the specification, known simply as 'version 1.0', was published by the MIDI Manufacturers' Association in August 1983.

1. Hardware Specification

MIDI data, representing not only the notes to be played but also information about program (patch) and control (such as volume and pitch-bend) changes, is sent serially (see INTERFACE) down a cable terminated at each end by a five-pin DIN plug. The rate of transmission is defined as 32.25 kbaud, i.e. 32,250 bits per second (see BAUD RATE).

A MIDI cable permits transmission in only one direction. The specification provides for three distinct sockets (usually referred to as 'MIDI ports') labelled OUT, IN, and, optionally, THRU. MIDI OUT outputs data generated by the instrument itself, whereas MIDI THRU outputs a copy of the data (i.e. without changing it in any way other than to 'buffer' or strengthen the signal) received at the MIDI IN port, which itself must include an opto-isolator (see COMPONENTS 4) to eliminate the risk of electrical interference between the MIDI signal and the instrument's internal electronics.

2. Software Specification

A synthesizer operates under a system of 'voice assignment'. As keys are pressed on the keyboard they are assigned in sequence to the internal voices up to the limit of the instrument. Clearly this process is entirely the responsibility of the synthesizer—MIDI itself imposes no limit on the number of voices an instrument may contain, nor does it, except in very specific circumstances (described below) instruct an instrument to assign a particular note to a particular voice.

(a) Channel Commands

MIDI data does not include distinct codes for different devices. Instead, it attaches to the majority of commands a channel number. This number determines, according to the MIDI mode of the receiving instrument (see below), whether a command (e.g. to play a note or select a patch) is to be obeyed or not. Sixteen channels are available over a single MIDI cable. This can only be increased by the addition of further MIDI OUT sockets, as found, for example, on some 'master' keyboards, *workstations, and high-performance sequencers.

In normal circumstances a synthesizer will transmit on one channel only. If an instrument includes a 'split-keyboard' facility it is possible for each section of the keyboard to transmit and receive on different channels.

The MIDI specification defines three modes of channel assignment for receiving instruments: OMNI, POLY, and MONO. When OMNI is set to ON (either at the instrument itself or remotely by a mode command), the instrument will respond to commands on all channels; when OFF it will respond only to commands associated with the channel(s) to which it has been set.

In POLY mode incoming note commands are assigned polyphonically up to the limit of the instrument in the usual way (indeed, the MIDI mode 'OMNI OFF—POLY' is now the standard mode for most instruments, to the degree that they will automatically enter that mode when switched on). In MONO mode, notes are assigned to one monophonic voice per channel. An eight-voice synthesizer would thus behave as if it were eight monophonic synthesizers. This mode encouraged the development of the 'multi-timbral' synthesizer, which can assign a different patch to each voice. Clearly such a facility can only be properly exploited with the aid of a sequencer, which can be programmed to attach the correct channel number to each note. Such an instrument is also well suited to receive input from a MIDI *guitar synthesizer or controller.

(b) Control Commands

MIDI distinguishes between two types of controller: the continuous controller and the switch. Up to thirty-two of each type are provided for. Continuous-controller messages cover functions such as volume, keyboard *after-touch and *velocity sensitivity, *modulation, and pitch-bend—the codes for these are prescribed by the MIDI specification. For instruments with unusual controls the player may have to spend some time sorting out which codes relate to which controls. MIDI allows the user to direct control data from one controller to another; for example, after-touch data (to which not all instruments can respond) can be redirected to the modulation wheel. The switch control commands deal with ON/OFF functions such as sustain and portamento.

(c) System Commands

MIDI includes a number of commands for use with sequencers and drum machines (e.g. to start and stop a particular sequence or pattern, and to synchronize instruments together) and some 'housekeeping' commands, such as one to turn all notes off when a sequence is stopped prematurely (a note once turned on cannot be simply turned off from the keyboard—it requires a 'NOTE OFF' command).

One of the most important command formats is that of 'System Exclusive', which as its name suggests permits the exchange of commands and data specific to a particular model and 'exclusive' to one manufacturer, each of whom is assigned a unique identification number through the MIDI Manufacturers' Association. Typical uses for System Exclusive include the transfer of patch data and the alteration of instrument-specific parameters.

(d) Implementation

The design of an instrument clearly will affect the range of available MIDI-controllable functions. For example, a keyboard may not be able to send velocity data, or respond to after-touch data. Manufacturers are required to include with their documentation for an instrument a 'MIDI implementation chart', which indicates precisely those messages which are or are not transmitted and recognized.

3. Extensions to the Specification

The success of MIDI in the years since its inception is reflected not only in a proliferation of equipment using the interface but also in an increased need for standardized synchronization, data storage, and transfer formats, as both sequencers and samplers have increased in sophistication and importance. In professional studios, stand-alone hardware sequencers have largely given way to software packages running on *computers such as the *Apple 'Macintosh' and the *Atari 'ST'.

To meet the demand for a standard file format for sequence data that could then be transferred not only between computers but also between different programs, a proposal for a MIDI File Standard was made by Dave Oppenheim of USA-based Opcode Systems in 1986 and taken up by a number of software companies; a final version was fixed in June 1988. The MFS provides three data formats, 0, 1, and 2. Format 0 is the simplest, recording all data, regardless of track assignment, sequentially with respect to time. Format 1 enables multiple tracks using the same MIDI channel to be preserved, and Format 2 allows multitrack files to be ordered sequentially.

An important extension to the basic specification is the MIDI Sample Dump Standard, also dating from 1986, the result of discussions between Sequential Circuits and E-mu. It introduced a new category of message, 'Universal System Exclusive', indicated by a particular data *byte sent after the standard System Exclusive code.

The specification allows a wide range of sample word lengths (from 8 to 28 *bits). It is the responsibility of each manufacturer to ensure the conversion of its own format, where necessary, to one compatible with the MSDS.

A unique feature of the MSDS is the use of what are termed 'handshaking flags'—commands which in effect ask the receiving instrument to confirm receipt of a block of data by sending an acknowledgement message. One criticism of the original MIDI specification has been that it made no provision for such two-way communication (which could thus only be implemented using System Exclusive). The MSDS handshake flags are themselves optional—data transfer can be accomplished without them if necessary.

One disadvantage of the MSDS is the slow transmission rate of MIDI itself—a full sample library could take in excess of twenty minutes to transfer, during which time the instrument cannot be used. On the other hand, the MSDS has made possible the development of 'generic' sample-editing and sound-synthesis programs which need not be tied to a particular instrument.

The need to synchronize MIDI data with studio equipment such as multitrack tape recorders and with film and video sound-tracks led to the development in 1987 of an additional standard within Universal System Exclusive, MIDI time code (MTC). The primary purpose of MTC is to add to MIDI a *time code format as close to that of the industry standard SMPTE code as possible. However, MTC has been provided with a powerful extra facility, a 'set-up' format, which sends a previously prepared 'cue list' of events, each tagged with MTC or SMPTE time codes, to all instruments, which perform the required actions when they receive the designated time codes. Any changes can be implemented simply by re-editing and sending the cue list.

4. MIDI Equipment

Since its introduction, MIDI has been applied to an increasingly diverse range of instruments and equipment. The development of the 'pitch to MIDI converter' not only as the basis for instruments such as the MIDI guitar controller but also in general-purpose devices such as the *Fairlight 'Voicetracker' means that in theory any monophonic instrument can be used as a MIDI controller. MIDI has also been applied to studio mixing desks, amplifiers, and stage lighting systems.

See also PIANO, ORGAN, SIGNAL PROCESSOR, STRINGED INSTRUMENTS, and WIND SYNTHESIZERS AND CONTROLLERS. Appendix 2 gives details of the principal MIDI command codes, including those of the MSDS. More detailed technical information on all aspects of MIDI may be obtained from the following organizations:

MIDI Manufacturers' Association, 2265 Westwood Blvd, Box 2223 Los Angeles, CA 90064, USA.
International MIDI Association, 5316 W. 57th St, Los Angeles, CA 90056, USA.
United Kingdom MIDI Association, 26 Brunswick Park Gardens, New Southgate, London N11 1EJ.
Japanese MIDI Standards Committee, Gakki Kaikan, 2-18-21 Sotokan, Chiyoda-Ku, Tokyo 101, Japan.

Modulation

The process by which one signal is used to modify another. The controlled signal is referred to as the 'carrier', and the controlling signal as the 'modulator'. It is of the greatest importance in both sound *synthesis and *signal processing.

The two parameters of a sound to which modulation is commonly applied are those of *amplitude (loudness) and frequency. Amplitude modulation of a signal causes changes in loudness in that signal. If the control signal is a slow regular *waveform (e.g. a sine wave) the result is a tremolo—similar to (and often confused with) vibrato, except that there is no pitch deviation. Once the frequency of the modulator is raised above 10 to 15 Hz the tremolo amalgamates into a complex sound with added frequency components (see ACOUSTICS 1) derived from the pitches of carrier and modulator. An irregular or transient control signal is generally associated with *envelope generation.

Frequency modulation causes the pitch of the carrier to rise and fall according to the shape of the modulating waveform. If this is, as above, a slow regular waveform, the result is vibrato if the depth of the modulation is low, otherwise becoming a wide siren-like effect. If the modulating waveform is a series of discrete steps, the result is a series of discrete pitches. Particularly complex sounds arise when the frequency of the modulator is close to or even higher than that of the carrier (see SYNTHESIS II 3(c)). See also DELAY LINE, RING MODULATOR.

Moog

A series of *analogue *synthesizers designed by the American engineer Robert Moog (b. 1934, Flushing, New York). His first commercial products were *Theremins, sold to finance his studies at Queens College, Columbia University, and later at Cornell University, Ithaca. One of Moog's customers was the composer Herbert Deutsch, who suggested to Moog the idea of a voltage-controlled *oscillator (VCO) and amplifier (see SYNTHESIS II 2). In 1964 Moog invited Deutsch to join him as a consultant. A prototype VCO was soon completed, and in the same year Moog published a paper on voltage control which was presented at a convention of the Audio Engineering Society.

The first Moog synthesizer, employing a modular design principle (see SYNTHESIZER 1(a)) originally proposed by Harald Bode, was produced in 1966. It was, however, only the publication in 1968 of the album *Switched-On Bach* by Walter Carlos that brought the potential of the synthesizer to public attention. The large modular systems marketed by Moog at this time were not intended for live use on stage, and in response to the interest from rock musicians Moog introduced the 'Minimoog' (1979), a self-contained and portable monophonic instrument that proved both highly successful (over 13,000 were sold) and influential. In particular, the location of pitch-bend and modulation wheels to the left of the keyboard was soon accepted as the standard arrangement (see SYNTHESIZER 1(b)). Also noteworthy was the provision of three oscillators, each with a wide selection of *waveforms and *modulation options. It is generally felt that the Minimoog's filters (the subject of a Moog patent) have never been surpassed (not even in later Moog instruments) for their 'musical' quality.

During the lifetime of the Minimoog a number of compact synthesizers were introduced to meet particular requirements of the rock market, including the 'Liberation' (designed to be worn round the neck like a guitar), the 'Prodigy' (a cheaper version of the Minimoog with two rather than three oscillators) and the 'Taurus', a foot-pedal-operated synthesizer. Other products included a *vocoder, a percussion controller (see DRUM PAD), and a ribbon controller based on that originally used on the *Ondes Martenot. The studio modular systems were available only to special order, in three sizes known as models 15, 35, and 55. The model 15 was portable, whereas the model 55 occupied three walnut cabinets.

In 1971 the original R. A. Moog Co. became Moog Music, and in 1973 this became a division of Norlin Industries. Production of the Minimoog continued until 1981, when it finally gave way to more up-to-date designs such as the 'Source' (monophonic, one of the first synthesizers to offer *digital parameter access) and later the polyphonic 'Memorymoog' (1983). None of Moog's instruments attained anything like the success of the Minimoog, and by 1985 production of synthesizers had ceased. Moog himself left Norlin in 1977 and in the following year set up Big Briar, specializing in control systems for synthesizers. He has worked with electric *guitar makers Gibson on guitar electronics, and more recently he has acted as a consultant to Kurzweil, manufacturers of advanced digital synthesizers and *samplers.

N

Noise

Noise has been defined as 'any unwanted sound'. However, for engineers it has a number of specific meanings, and in so far as noise constitutes a component of many natural and 'musical' sounds, it is of considerable importance to musicians concerned with electronic sound *synthesis.

In contrast to most 'musical' sounds, which have a definite pitch and a predominantly harmonic *spectrum (see ACOUSTICS 1), noise consists of a theoretically infinite and continuous range of frequencies. The *waveform consists not of regular periodic cycles but of random fluctuations of amplitude. In the present context, the *bandwidth of the noise may be considered limited to that of human hearing; as will be seen, it is possible to speak of noise limited to a variety of bandwidths.

It is usual to use analogies to visible light when discussing different types of noise. Thus, noise which has equal intensity at all frequencies is referred to as 'white noise'. Because the human ear is more sensitive to high than to low frequencies, white noise will be heard as a high hissing sound.

Many acoustic instruments produce sounds with a noise component—not only those of indeterminate pitch, such as some percussion instruments, but also, for example, the flute and some organ-pipes, in whose sound the 'chiff' and breath sound is an integral and characteristic component. Similarly, the bow noise is an important element in the sound of stringed instruments. As might be imagined, however, white noise by itself is insufficient for the realistic synthesis of these complex sounds.

By passing white noise through a *filter, different 'colours' can be obtained. 'Pink noise' results if white noise is passed through a mild low-pass filter. Whereas white noise has equal power at all frequencies, pink noise is defined as having equal power in each octave band (corresponding more closely to the response of the ear). Thus the power varies inversely with frequency—for this reason it is often referred to as '1/f noise'. Similarly, 'red noise' is referred to as '1/f² noise', the high frequencies being much more attenuated than in pink noise.

A common use for electronically generated pink noise is in the frequency response testing of equipment and in the testing of studio *acoustics (see *also* ANALYSIS). It is clearly important that a recording studio does not favour some frequencies over others, otherwise what is heard over the speakers will not correspond to the actual recorded sound.

By passing white noise through a band-pass filter it is possible to create band-limited noise of precisely defined characteristics. The narrower the bandwidth, the more prominent the peak in the spectrum, and the more apparent the frequency of that peak. The sound changes from a broad hiss to that of a whispered vowel, or more precisely to that made by someone attempting to whistle but not achieving a clean pitched tone. A sufficiently powerful band-pass filter can extract what is virtually a single frequency from the original white noise. The tone is not, however, identical to that which would be produced by an *oscillator because it still retains the random fluctuations in amplitude, which are unaffected by the filter. Thus it is possible in this special sense to speak of a pitched tone being 'noisy', despite the absence of any other sound component.

Because of the random nature of noise, it can be described using the language of probability and statistics. Thus band-limited noise (of which white noise is a special case) may also be referred to as 'Gaussian noise'. The Gaussian probability graph, which has a symmetrical bell-like shape, is here analogous to a spectrum plot. The amplitude measurement for a given frequency can be understood also as a measure of the probability of the presence of that frequency.

This mathematical view of noise is of great importance to composers of *computer music, since all sounds, including the different types of noise, have to be generated numerically in software, rather than by the use of hardware oscillators (see SYNTHESIS II 3). The principle has been extended by many composers, notably Xenakis, to the compositional process itself, notes and other musical 'events' being chosen and ordered using random and stochastic techniques.

Noise Gate

Many electronic instruments generate a certain amount of *noise which can be tiresome when the instrument is not actually being played. A noise gate detects when the signal level from the instrument falls below a preset threshold and cuts the signal completely—closing the gate, so to speak—using a preset decay *envelope. A similar threshold has to be exceeded by the signal before the gate is opened, using a similarly preset attack envelope.

In addition to this 'cleaning up' function the noise gate can be used for special effects, for example by imposing an exaggerated decay envelope on a signal by setting a high threshold. One classic example is gated *reverb, in which a normally long reverb 'tail' is abruptly terminated.

Noise Reduction

1. Single-Ended

A single-ended noise reduction system is used to reduce the *noise content of an already recorded signal (e.g. from a tape recorder). Since the most intrusive noise is high-frequency hiss accompanying a signal at a low dynamic level, a simple method of reducing noise is to use a dynamically controlled low-pass *filter; that is to say, the cut-off frequency of the filter depends on the level of the input signal. If this is high, the noise is largely masked by the signal so the filter is fully open, passing all frequencies; as the signal level falls so does the cut-off frequency, progressively cutting the high-frequency content of the signal.

2. Double-Ended

The most important application of noise reduction is in the process of recording on to magnetic tape. The best professional tape recorders can achieve a signal-to-noise (S/N) ratio around 75 dB (see DECIBEL). Nevertheless, the noise added by the recorder ('tape hiss') is still intrusive, especially at low signal levels. A double-ended noise reduction signal compresses the signal during recording and re-expands it on playback. Since the noise from the tape arises after the *compression stage, the *expansion has the effect of reducing the noise on playback, increasing the overall S/N ratio of the system. A tape recording made on such a system is said to be 'encoded', and requires the correct decoder to be installed in any machine on which the tape is played back.

The two noise reduction systems in common use are 'Dolby' and 'DBX'. The Dolby 'A' system for professional use splits the signal into four frequency bands which are compressed and expanded separately. The system responds dynamically to the signal level, only processing signals at low level. High-frequency noise is reduced by up to 15 dB. The lower-cost Dolby 'B' system (developed for use in cassette recorders) uses a single high-frequency channel of compression and expansion, reducing hiss by about 10 dB. More recently, Dolby 'C' and 'SR' have been developed. Dolby 'C' works like Dolby 'B', but reduces hiss by up to 20 dB; Dolby 'SR' ('Spectral Recording') has been developed for professional use, reducing noise throughout the audible range by up to 25 dB.

The DBX system is a relatively straightforward but powerful compression/expansion system, reducing the signal by half during recording (a 2:1 compression ratio), and also applying treble 'pre-emphasis'—the high frequencies are boosted by 12 dB per octave, to be cut (with any added noise) by corresponding 'de-emphasis' and expansion circuits on playback. DBX can improve the S/N ratio by up to 30 dB. On the other hand, the high degree of processing can sometimes be heard as a 'pumping' or 'breathing', especially on low-frequency transient material, such as bass drum sounds.

Novachord

See MOOG.

Novatron

See MELLOTRON.

Nyquist Frequency

See ANALOGUE TO DIGITAL CONVERSION.

Ondes Martenot

A monophonic electronic instrument designed and built by Maurice Martenot (1898–1980), and introduced in 1928 at a concert at the Paris Opéra. Like the *Theremin introduced four years earlier the Ondes Martenot generated a signal of continuously varying pitch, but with much greater control available to the performer. Pitch was controlled by means of a sliding ribbon (to which a finger ring was attached) connected to one plate of a variable capacitor (see COMPONENTS 2) which in turn controlled the frequency of a beat frequency *oscillator. This provided a potential range of seven octaves, though only some four-and-a-half octaves were available without transposition.

To facilitate accurate pitching a visual guide in the form of a conventional keyboard template was provided, over which the ribbon was mounted. Articulation was made possible by means of a touch-sensitive carbon strip functioning as a variable resistor, played by the left hand. In the absence of any pressure the instrument was silent, thus obviating the main limitation of the Theremin, which could only produce sliding pitches. The carbon strip was sensitive enough to allow the use of vibrato in addition to a wide range of dynamic expression. Also associated with the left hand were tone controls (see FILTER) and a tuning control. A second version of the instrument replaced the keyboard template with a real keyboard, the keys of which could be moved laterally to produce vibrato or microtonal inflexions.

The sound was projected not only through a conventional loudspeaker but also through two visually as well as tonally striking systems unique to the Ondes. The first of these was the 'Palme'. Twenty-four tunable strings are mounted on an elegantly curved sound-box. At the bottom the strings are mounted on a block in direct contact with a transducer (loudspeaker movement). With minimal damping imposed on the strings, they are able to resonate freely, adding considerable richness to the sound, which suggests that of a bass viol or of a harp, depending on the manner of performance.

The *diffuseur métallique* was added in 1947. This is in effect a hard cymbal-like plate attached at the centre to a transducer, imparting a lustrous, bronzed quality to the sound.

The Ondes Martenot was years ahead of its time, and the extraordinary expressive potential of the instrument attracted the attention of several composers, including Milhaud, Honegger, and Varèse, who revised *Equatorial* (1934) in 1961 in order to use the Ondes as a replacement for the Theremin. A concerto was written for the instrument in 1947 by André Jolivet. It has, however, become chiefly known through the music of Olivier Messiaen, who included obbligato parts for it in *Trois petites liturgies de la présence divine* (1944) and *Turangalîla* (1948). As early as 1937 he had written *Fêtes de belles eaux* for six Ondes.

In 1947 Martenot established a class for the instrument at the Paris Conservatoire. In 1950 Pierre Boulez, himself an accomplished 'Ondist', wrote a quartet for Ondes. The performer most associated with the Ondes is the pianist Jeanne Loriod, a pupil and later the wife of Messiaen. The Ondes, like the Theremin, has also been much exploited for its sound effects by composers of film music.

Organ, Electric and Electronic

The term 'electronic organ' has come to be applied to virtually any electronic keyboard instrument, regardless of size or styling, which falls outside the recognized categories of electronic *piano, *synthesizer, or *sampler. An electronic organ is essentially an instrument that provides a variety of preset voices (predominantly but not necessarily sustaining) which can be combined in the manner of conventional pipe organ registrations.

There are, however, certain more specific subcategories into which a given organ may fall, according to the method of tone generation used, the nature of those sounds, and the musical context for which the instrument is intended. Thus while the 'classical' organ will attempt to emulate both the sounds and console layout of the traditional acoustic instrument, the 'concert' or 'theatre' organ will include imitations of orchestral and other instruments, sound effects, rhythm generators, and automatic accompaniment facilities.

1. Electromechanical Organs

The development of keyboard-controlled electric instruments dates from the 1890s, and includes the use of vibrating reeds (*see also* PIANO) and opto-electrical systems. However, the most important class of instruments is that based on the use of rotating wheels. An early example is the *Telharmonium (c.1904); more significant in the present context were those instruments developed during the 1920s and 1930s. These were immediately seen by manufacturers of pipe organs as direct threats to their own business; the right of such instruments to be called 'organs' was vigorously challenged in the courts, on both sides of the Atlantic (see HAMMOND ORGAN).

The two most important instruments of this period, the Compton 'Electrone' and the Hammond organ, may be taken as representative of two parallel paths of development: the pursuit of an electronic alternative to the pipe organ, and that of an essentially new instrument with applications far removed from those associated with acoustic organs.

Nevertheless, the two instruments were markedly similar at the technical level. The Hammond organ used an electromagnetic system of tone generation based on small non-circular tone-wheels. The changing distance of the edge of the wheel from the pick-up created an alternating current which was then amplified. Variation of tone was achieved by means of a set of adjustable draw-bars which were used to control, in a manner suggestive as much of 'additive' *synthesis as of conventional organ-stops, the mixture of upper *partials being supplied by other tone-wheels. These partials were therefore tuned in equal temperament, rather than in the exact ratios of the harmonic series (see ACOUSTICS, TUNING AND TEMPERAMENT).

The Compton 'Electrone', so named to avoid the legal problems described above, was based on design work conducted by Leslie Bourn since the mid-1920s and marketed by the English organ-builders Compton from 1938 until 1970, when production was taken over by J. & J. Makin Organs. It used an electrostatic system by which twelve disks each engraved with sine *waveforms for seven octaves of a single pitch rotated against fixed 'stator' disks. As in the Hammond organ, alteration of *timbre depended on adding partial tones from other wheels to the fundamental. Early versions of the system were used in Compton's theatre and cinema organs. Later more advanced models designed particularly for use in churches used complex waveforms which more closely approached the tonal characteristics of pipes.

2. Early Electronic Organs

The basic electronic building block of the early electronic organ was the valve *oscillator (see also COMPONENTS 5). A single oscillator can generate a variety of harmonically rich waveforms; instruments using such oscillators can employ *filters to vary the timbre according to the principles of 'subtractive' synthesis.

There were two basic techniques of polyphonic tone generation: a separate oscillator could be used for each note (a costly but musically superior method, especially for the imitation of acoustic pipe organs), or a set of twelve 'master' oscillators could be used, each tuned to the highest octave of a single pitch, lower octaves being generated by a technique of frequency division. The latter method (which clearly has much in common with that used in the Electrone) had the advantages not only of reduced cost but also of a much reduced burden of tuning. On the other hand, the former method offered greater scope for timbral control and variation over the range of the keyboard.

Instruments of the former type include the Allen organ (1939), which was the first all-electronic organ to enter into general commercial production (converted to transistor-based circuitry in 1959), and a large (up to three manuals) church organ (1930) designed by the organ-builder Eduard Coupleux and the engineer Armand Givelet. The latter was also a pioneer of automatic control systems for electronic instruments, and collaborated with Coupleux in the design of an early *synthesizer-like instrument using four oscillators, controlled by punched paper tape.

The method of frequency division became of great importance in the expanding domestic and light-music markets. The sequence of technical development is well illustrated by the organs produced by Wurlitzer from 1946, when they acquired from the Everett Piano Company rights to the 'Orgatron', an instrument based on vibrating reeds, and which they developed into a compact electric organ. A fully electronic organ using twelve master oscillators was introduced around 1960; this system was in turn superseded in the early 1970s by one based on the use of a single high-frequency oscillator (1 MHz and above) from which a full range of equally tempered pitches could be obtained by frequency division.

3. The Modern Electronic Organ

(a) The Theatre Organ and its Derivatives

The electronic theatre or 'concert' organ is derived from the acoustic theatre and cinema organ, the latter being associated very much with the Wurlitzer company, whose instruments offered an extravagant mixture of organ and instrumental sounds and special effects. As films acquired sound-tracks the organists (many of whom had substantial personal followings) were in many cases retained by cinemas to entertain audiences with a mixture of classical and popular arrangements, and improvisations.

The new electronic organs reflected the emergence of this new musical genre not only by offering voicings modelled on orchestral instruments as well as recognizably organ-like voices, but also elaborate facilities for automatic percussive and chordal accompaniment. In 1939 Hammond produced their first fully electronic organ; however, their introduction in 1949 of the 'spinet' organ was of much greater significance, as it featured the now standard arrangement (emphasizing the different roles of the left and right hands) of two 44-note manuals offset by an octave. Hammond had also developed the idea of a 'chord organ', in which whole chords could be played from a single key.

In 1958 Yamaha introduced their 'Electone' range of organs, generally regarded as the single most successful organ ever developed. New features included portamento and a vibrato controlled by lateral movement of the key (a system previously used on the *Ondes Martenot).

The 1960s saw a rapid increase in the number of manufacturers (notably Baldwin, Conn, Hohner, Lowrey, Selmer, Thomas, and Wurlitzer) producing organs for a diverse market, ranging from large console concert and theatre organs (in both spinet and full-length keyboard configurations) to small single- and double-manual instruments for domestic use and provided with a wide range of automatic 'easy-play' facilities (see below) to meet the needs of the untrained player. Lowrey introduced their now generally accepted term 'automatic organ computer' (AOC) to describe their system, which enables a single finger of the right hand to play full chords according to the chord held on the lower manual. Competition between manufacturers is as much over the promotion of new performance facilities as over technical advances in tone generation.

Small single-manual organs, most notably those by Farfisa and Vox, were used by a number of pop and rock groups. The Vox in particular is celebrated for its use in the hit song 'House of the Rising Sun' by the Animals. Among jazz musicians the Hammond organ remained a favourite, especially on account of its touch response; it has also been used in a number of contemporary classical works, including pieces by Luciano Berio and Karlheinz Stockhausen.

The pace of technological development continued in the 1970s, as keyboards (both organs and synthesizers) played a role of increasing prominence in rock music. The instruments produced during this period featured an increased use of automatic rhythm generators (with rock as well as dance rhythms), bass-line ('walking bass') and chord generators, and, from about 1975 onwards (i.e. consequent to the development of the microprocessor 'computer on a chip'), programming facilities such as preset chord sequences, automatic replay, arpeggiators, and memories for the storage of registrations. Such instruments were not only used on stage; they were also popular in the home as instruments which could, to a degree, 'do everything' and were thus valued both as a versatile foundation for home music-making and as aids to composition.

Keyboards could be 'split' electronically so that an instrument with a single manual could mimic the functions of the two-manual organ. In many cases, and especially in Japan, manufacturers of organs were also active in the manufacture of synthesizers, and a number of instruments were introduced (e.g. Yamaha's 'SK' 'Symphonic Ensemble' series (1980)) which combined in one console the functions of electronic organ, synthesizer, and 'string ensemble'.

In 1980 Casio entered the market with a series of portable 'home keyboards', including, for the first time, several with miniature keyboards. Battery operated with built-in speakers, the instruments opened up a large new market amongst children, as well as among those adults who could not justify the expenditure on a full-size instrument but who were happy to have a sophisticated musical 'toy'. The 'VL-1' (1981) looked more like a calculator than a musical instrument (and was small enough to be carried around in a pocket), but carried a 29-note keyboard, ten preset rhythm patterns, and a 100-note *sequencer memory. Casio have continued to introduce several models (with full-size, 'midi-size', and miniature keyboards) each year, offering increasingly rich combinations of facilities; single-finger chords, arpeggiators, programmable and preset rhythm patterns, the ability to load complete songs from cartridge, 'ROM-Card' or bar-code reader, and synthesizer-like (but much simplified and relatively limited) tone programming.

Casio was soon joined by other manufacturers, including Yamaha, Seil, JVC, and Korg, all of whom were active in the concert organ market. Products from Casio and Yamaha account for the great majority of portable keyboards sold; both companies are also prominent in the manufacture of synthesizers and related equipment, and much of that technology, such as the use of *'PCM' *sampled sounds, touch-sensitive keyboards, and *MIDI interfaces, and the use of advanced *digital synthesis techniques, has been carried over to the concert organ and home keyboard.

In the context of the general history and development of the electronic organ, it is worth bearing in mind that it has from the earliest stage of its development been a focus of attention not only from the commercial sector but also from amateur electronics enthusiasts, supported by technically comprehensive literature both in books and in periodicals. Apart from the pure satisfaction derived from the construction, if not always the design, of an electronic organ, there is also a clear cost advantage in home construction. The tradition has been maintained, despite the steady demise of *analogue designs in favour of the new digital technology (less amenable to amateur development), in particular by the German companies Böhm and Wersi, who have maintained their reputations almost entirely on the strength of organs supplied in kit form.

(b) The Digital Theatre and Classical Organ

The Allen organ has already been cited as the first electronic classical organ. In 1971 Allen introduced the world's first digital organ, based on a compact digital tone generator developed by Philips in the late 1960s and further refined by Ralph Deutsch. The sounds were based on digitized (sampled) recordings of selected acoustic pipes. Some models used a card reader to load alternative timbres and registrations. In 1983 Allen introduced their 'ADC' range of two- and three-manual organs, followed at the beginning of 1990 by the MDS series, which includes a full *MIDI implementation.

In England, a research team at Bradford University led by Dr Peter Comerford, who in addition to being a senior lecturer in computing was also a church organist, developed between the mid-1970s and early 1980s what has proved to be a most important and influential digital synthesis system, now known as the 'Bradford Computing Organ'. The time-varying timbral characteristics of a wide range of different pipes were analysed (see ANALYSIS), and the resulting data (giving the time-varying amplitudes of each component partial, which may number up to 100 for low notes) used to re-create the sound following the principles of 'additive' synthesis (see also SYNTHESIS II 1). By loading alternative sets of data from magnetic disks it was possible to reconfigure the instrument completely, for example from a classical church organ to a theatre organ.

The principal licensees for the Bradford Computing Organ are the long-established organ-building company Wyvern, who worked closely with the Bradford team throughout the development period and assisted in the construction of the early prototypes, the Dutch company Cantor, and the German manufacturers Ahlborn, whose British division is also based at Bradford.

Other European manufacturers to introduce digital organs (based on digitized acoustic pipe sounds) include Copeman-Hart and Norwich in England, Eminent and Johannus in Holland, and Viscount and Gem in Italy.

While both in Europe and America there has been a general move away from analogue tone generation towards digital techniques, the new instruments have often been introduced alongside established analogue designs; Wyvern, for example, discontinued their production of analogue organs as recently as 1989.

The amplification of an electronic organ is of vital importance; a number of channels may be required not only to produce adequate power but also to create a sufficiently broad and diffuse sound field similar to that of a large pipe organ. A medium-size church organ may use three or four stereo channels of amplification together with electronically generated *reverb. In such a situation the voicing of individual stops is as critical as it is in the case of a pipe organ, so that installation procedures differ little from those associated with the traditional pipe organ.

Oscillator

An oscillator or function generator is an electronic circuit which can generate a range of geometric (periodic) *waveforms. It is the primary source of sounds for *analogue *synthesis. The first oscillator circuits were developed soon after the invention of the triode valve (see COMPONENTS 5; also SYNTHESIS I .I) for radio transmission and reception. Audio signals were generated by the 'heterodyne' effect in which two high-frequency signals are tuned sufficiently close to each other so that they 'beat' together (see ACOUSTICS 2(b)), generating difference tones in the audio range (hence 'beat frequency oscillator'). This was the basis of several early electronic instruments, notably the *Ondes Martenot and the *Theremin.

The main obstacles to the direct generation of audio frequencies were the requirement, especially for the lower tones, for large inductors, and a general tendency to instability of pitch. The latter problem persisted even with the transistorized circuitry of the 1970s, and was only resolved with the introduction of *digital control.

Audio signals may also be generated electromechanically, for example by means of rotating wheels; this was the basis for the first polyphonic keyboard instruments (see, especially, TELHARMONIUM, HAMMOND ORGAN; also ORGAN, PIANO).

By the end of the 1940s the oscillator was an established item of audio test equipment and the single most important item of electronic equipment for the increasing number of composers active in electronic music (see SYNTHESIS I 3). The oscillator was available as a source for sounds for tape music composition, and as the tone generator in self-contained musical instruments, but it was only with the development of voltage control (see SYNTHESIS II 2; *also* BUCHLA, MOOG) that the oscillator was cast into a form suitable for both synthesis and live performance. The first commercial polyphonic synthesizer, the 'Prophet 5' (1975) from Sequential Circuits, contained five voices each using two oscillators. Subsequent developments have led to digital control, and ultimately the replacement of the analogue oscillator with fully digital methods of tone generation (see e.g. SYNTHESIS II 3; *also* SAMPLER).

Overdrive

One of the most characteristic sounds of 'hard' rock *guitar playing is the effect of forcing a stage amplifier into *distortion by applying an input at an excessively high level. This should not be confused with effects devices such as the 'fuzz box' which distort the sound before it is fed to the amplifier. The most sought-after sound is that of the overdriven valve amplifier (see COMPONENTS 5). The modern transistor-based amplifier distorts the sound differently, adding harsh odd-numbered harmonics (see ACOUSTICS 1) rather than the even-numbered harmonics of the valve amplifier. However, a wide range of transistor-based distortion effects units is now available, some successfully reproducing the character of the valve amplifier.

Overtones

See ACOUSTICS, *also* WAVEFORM.

P

Partial

Any one sinusoidal frequency component of a complex tone. See ACOUSTICS 1, WAVEFORM.

PCM

See PULSE CODE MODULATION.

Pedal Steel Guitar

An electric 'lap' or Hawaiian *guitar, developed from the 1930s, to which a number of pedals and knee levers have been added which alter the tuning of each string so as to put the instrument into different keys. A pedal may simultaneously lower the pitch of one string while raising that of another. Up to four strings may be controlled by one pedal; the knee lever rarely affects more than two. Although players tend to adapt instruments to their own requirements, a common 'standard' configuration would consist of a single neck with ten strings, connected to five pedals and one knee lever.

Double-neck instruments are also common, each with up to twelve strings, enabling the two 'standard' tunings—a chromatic based on E and a diatonic 'C' tuning—to be used together. Attempts have also been made to provide both tunings on a single neck, by using up to fourteen strings, ten or eleven pedals, and a similar number of knee levers. The pick-ups (usually one or two for each neck) differ little from those used on the electric guitar. Manufacture is inevitably concentrated in the USA, due to the instrument's special association with Country and Western music, and is largely the province of a few specialist companies, although Fender and Rickenbacker have been producing pedal guitars since the 1950s, and lap guitars (without pedals, but with up to four necks) from the mid-1940s.

Percussion Controllers

Drum sounds can be created either by *synthesis or by *sampling acoustic instruments, so that they may be played directly (via *MIDI) from a keyboard. Most usually, a separate 'rhythm' or *drum machine is used which is responsible for the automatic generation of rhythm patterns. Alternatively, they may be played idiomatically by means of *drum pads, or by means of devices such as the Palmtree 'Airdrums' (1986), two hand-held wands which use accelerometers to detect quasi-percussive gestures (i.e. without the need to hit anything) and convert them into MIDI control signals.

Controllers have been developed with a keyboard-like layout suited to the needs of players of tuned percussion. The 'Silicon Mallet' (1987) from Simmons is a highly responsive instrument with its own synthesizer, and the American-designed 'KAT' introduced in the same year is a modular system which can be expanded an octave at a time (to a maximum of four octaves), and which is purely a MIDI controller, including many functions associated with a MIDI 'master keyboard'.

Phase

The term 'phase' is used to indicate points within a single period (cycle) of a periodic *waveform. It is measured in degrees (or for some advanced mathematical calculations in radians), 360 degrees corresponding to one period. The addition of two waveforms implies that the amplitudes are summed. If there is no phase difference between them, the waveforms (here assumed to be identical) reinforce each other conversely if they are opposite in phase (equivalent to a phase shift of 180 degrees) they will cancel each other completely. It is therefore important that, for example, the outputs from a stereo amplifier are connected 'in phase' to each loudspeaker. On the other hand, an 'out-of-phase' connection can be deliberately used to eliminate unwanted signal components such as *noise or interference (see e.g. GUITAR 2(c)).

In considering the phase of a complex tone it is, strictly speaking, necessary to consider the phase of each frequency component or overtone (see

ACOUSTICS 1; *also* ANALYSIS) separately, each measured in relation to the *fundamental period. Although the ear is not sensitive to phase, it will certainly be aware of the result if two tones with some components relatively opposite in phase are sounded together. Such a situation can arise in relation to microphone placements for recording, and loudspeaker placements in a living-room or studio. It is important to avoid cancellation effects arising from the phase difference between the direct sound and sound reflected off nearby surfaces.

The effects of phase shifting are exploited in many types of *signal processor, especially those based on the use of a *delay line. See *also* FILTER.

Piano, Electric and Electronic

1. Electro-Acoustic Instruments

Experiments in the combination of a piano-like action with electronics date from the closing decades of the last century, when the ability of an electromagnet to induce and sustain vibrations in piano strings (see *also* E-BOW) was the basis of a number of instruments known as 'sostenente' pianos. More important, however, is the development, dating from the mid-1930s, of instruments using electronic amplification, applied both to conventional piano strings and to alternative electromechanical vibrating systems.

(a) The Electric (String-Based) Piano

In 1930–1 the American Benjamin Miessner developed an 88-note instrument which though retaining the overall appearance of a grand piano dispensed with the soundboard and used electrostatic *pick-ups to detect the vibration of the strings. Other advantages gained through amplification included the use of thinner strings, obviation of the need to use two or three strings for each note, and a generally much lighter construction.

In Germany, Oskar Vierling and Walther Nernst followed in 1934 with the 'Neo-Bechstein-Flügel', which used electromagnetic pick-ups similar in operation to those developed for the electric *guitar. Pick-ups were generally located at the far (non-striking) end of the string, but variation in *timbre was possible by using pick-ups in different positions, again a principle also used in the electric guitar. Further alteration of timbre was achieved by incorporating tone controls (see FILTER) into the amplifier, and a swell pedal was used to control the overall volume, giving the possibility to defy the natural *decay of the string (which was already longer than that in a normal piano as the energy of the vibrating string was not drained by a soundboard) by swelling the note after the *attack.

While a number of manufacturers consequently turned their hands to the design of electric pianos, the majority concentrated on new methods of sound generation (see below), which avoided to an extent the technical difficulties associated with acoustic piano design, and were less concerned to preserve the characteristics of the acoustic piano. The most important piano-like instrument of this type was the Hohner *Clavinet, which though it used strings was modelled on the action not of the piano but of the baroque clavichord.

In the late 1970s Yamaha introduced their CP70 and CP80 electric pianos, with respectively 73- and 88-note keyboards. These were designed to sound as like an acoustic grand piano as possible, using piezo-electric pick-ups, while being robust enough for touring and stage use. Specially designed bass strings were used, and the instrument was designed in two sections—strings and frame, and action and support—for easy transportation. The action was almost identical to that of the acoustic piano. The instruments proved highly popular, especially among musicians in the jazz, rock, and pop fields. More recently they have been enhanced by the addition of *MIDI (models CP70M and CP80M, and the CP60M upright) enabling, for example, a *synthesizer or *drum machine to be controlled from the keyboard.

In 1983 Kawai introduced their EP308 and EP608 electric pianos. The former is a grand piano broadly similar to the original Yamaha instruments, though without the sectional construction. The 608 is an upright piano which can be folded up for transit. Both use piezo-electric pick-ups built into the bridge, and include three tone settings and tremolo. MIDI control facilities were added in 1987.

(b) Non-String-Based Electric Pianos

Dating again from the 1930s, two techniques proved successful: the plucked metal reed, and the struck tone rod or tine. The plucked reed (using small adhesive pads) was used by Lloyd Loar (also important as a pioneer in the design of pick-ups for the electric guitar) in his 'Clavier', in Selmer's 'Pianotron', and, more recently, in Hohner's 'Pianet' (1976). More significant have been the instruments using struck rods, notably the Wurlitzer EP200 (1955) and the now classic *Rhodes 'Stage' series of instruments, introduced in 1968.

2. The Electronic Piano

The electric piano shared with the acoustic piano the important characteristics of being not only fully polyphonic but also 'touch-sensitive'—the harder the key was struck, the louder and longer the tone. From the point of view of a fully electronic version, this requires that independent *envelope control be available for each note. The technical difficulties involved (compared to the relatively straightforward task of creating an *organ-like sustained sound) were such that it was not until the early 1970s that electric pianos began to be seriously challenged by all-electronic designs, mostly from Japan (Roland, Korg, and Yamaha) and Italy (Crumar, Elka, and Farfisa). While the latter have subsequently concentrated on electronic organs, the Japanese manufacturers have continued to develop the electronic piano for both the domestic and professional markets.

It has been as important to achieve a faithful imitation of the sound of the electric piano (the Rhodes generally being regarded as the model) as well as that of the acoustic grand piano. Most instruments in fact offer additional voices including 'upright' and 'honky-tonk' pianos, harpsichord, vibraphone, and possibly ensemble string and brass sounds.

Many early electronic pianos limited the polyphony (for the reasons outlined above) to as few as eight simultaneous notes. Although this can prove too restricting for musicians wishing to play the classical repertoire, it is less so for the musician playing in jazz, rock, and pop idioms, which require techniques less dependent on the sustain pedal, ranging from simple held chords to complex staccato rhythmical figurations.

At the top end of the market, the best electronic pianos offer a full-length keyboard with keys weighted to feel as like an acoustic piano as possible. The sound may be based on sophisticated *synthesis techniques, or on the digitally *sampled sounds of a real piano. For example, Yamaha's instruments (notably their 'Clavinova' series) exploit FM synthesis as well as sampled sounds, while those from Roland feature their proprietary 'structured adaptive synthesis'.

3. Computer-Controlled Pianos

(a) The MIDI Piano

In 1985 the California-based company LA Piano Services developed the 'Forte MIDImod' kit, which enabled any electric or acoustic piano to act as a MIDI controller, using touch-sensitive switches fitted under each key. The system was endorsed most notably by the jazz pianist Chick Corea. In 1987 Yamaha added MIDI control to two of their existing grand pianos, using optical sensors under each key together with a pressure-sensitive strip to provide *after-touch control. The comprehensive MIDI implementation was controlled from a long panel built into the body immediately above the keyboard. The German company Seiler offer a similar option on their grand pianos.

(b) The Player Piano

In 1986 Bösendorfer introduced their '290 SE Computer-Based Piano', which adds player piano facilities to an otherwise conventional Imperial Grand. The computer uses fibre optics (which does not affect the action in any way) to scan the keyboard during a performance so that all details of nuance and timing can be recorded, in the manner of a digital *sequencer. It does not use MIDI as the density of the data, in recording the fine details of touch, is some ten times greater than that which MIDI can sustain. To play back the performance the computer triggers electromagnetic actuators under each key. The instrument can thus reproduce very accurately the details of the original performance. These details can also be studied and edited using the computer terminal.

At about the same time Yamaha introduced their 'Disklavier' grand and upright player pianos. Like the Bösendorfer instrument they use fibre optics to scan the keyboard, but unlike that instrument also include a MIDI interface. Built into the cabinet is a small control panel containing a disk drive for $3\frac{1}{2}$-inch floppy disks. Among the programmable facilities are transposition, speed changes, and the ability to isolate left and right hands. Playback can be started remotely using a hand-held controller.

Pick-up

The informal name for an electromagnetic or piezo-electric (contact) transducer. See, in particular, GUITAR; also STRINGED INSTRUMENTS.

Pitch-bend

Expressive pitch inflexions, for example of a *guitar string, or of an *oscillator, the latter usually by means of a sprung wheel. See SYNTHESIS II 2(g), SYNTHESIZER I(b); also MIDI, MOOG.

Pitch Shifter

See DELAY LINE 2(d).

Poles and Zeros

See FILTER 2.

Port

See INTERFACE.

Potentiometer

The technical name for a variable resistor (see COMPONENTS 1); the short form 'pot' is in common use when referring to a rotary control.

Pulse Code Modulation (PCM)

The serial transmission (see COMPUTER 5) of *digital audio data, for example as a radio signal or down a telephone line; also the recording of such data on magnetic tape. The data is usually digitized from an *analogue source (see ANALOGUE TO DIGITAL CONVERSION), but may also be computer-generated (see e.g. COMPOSER'S DESKTOP PROJECT). PCM encoding is widely used to provide *sampled *acoustic sounds in instruments such as the *drum machine, *organ, *piano, and *synthesizer.

Pulse Wave

See WAVEFORM.

Pulse Width Modulation

See WAVEFORM, also MODULATION, SYNTHESIS II 2.

Putney

See EMS.

R

Release

The final stage of a keyboard-controlled *envelope generator. See, especially, SYNTHESIS II 2(e).

Resistor, Resistance

See COMPONENTS 1.

Resonance

Of an elastic vibrating medium, see ACOUSTICS 3; of an electronic circuit, see FILTER.

Reverb

The electronically or electromechanically generated reverberant effect, and the processor that generates it (as distinct from 'reverberation', which signifies the acoustic phenomenon: see ACOUSTICS 4).

I. The Need for Artificial Reverb

Electronic instruments such as the *synthesizer can produce very convincing imitations of acoustic instruments, but not the sense of an acoustic space around that instrument. Reverb is used not only to create this sense of space but also, by varying the relative strength of the direct and reverberated sound, to create a sense of distance. Reverb can also be used to suggest the effect of the resonant sound-box of acoustic instruments such as the *piano and harpsichord.

Modern pop and rock recording techniques, which seek to isolate instruments from each other both in the studio (designed to be relatively 'dry') and on the multitrack tape, rely heavily on artificial reverb to give character and ambience to the music—different instruments may be given different reverb treatments. Reverb is thus a creative effect in its own right, beyond the basic requirements of acoustic realism.

2. Acoustic and Electro-Acoustic Reverb

(a) Live Room
This is a specially designed room, built as part of a recording studio, with a very reverberant acoustic, using brick, tile, and wood surfaces. The effect can be tailored to a degree by the use of mobile acoustically absorbent screens.

(b) Spring Line
This is the simplest and cheapest of the reverb systems. The signal to be treated is applied to one end of a long metal coil spring by a transducer and detected at the other end by a second transducer. The sound is reflected by the ends of the spring and will travel back and forth several times before *decaying. The vibration of the spring is sufficiently complex for the result to be remarkably authentic. The decay time is determined by the length of the spring. Only the cheapest systems will use just one spring. The use of two or three springs of different lengths gives a choice of reverb times; also each spring may be 'tuned' to respond to a particular part of the audio spectrum.

There are two basic disadvantages to the spring line reverb. Being electromechanical, it is vulnerable to both physical and electrical disturbance—a major consideration for those built into stage *guitar and keyboard amplifiers. Secondly, highly transient sounds, for example from drums, can induce 'ringing' from the springs, unless the input level is severely limited.

(c) Plate Reverb
This is a large and bulky system which, until the development of *digital reverb made it virtually obsolete, was regarded as the best reverb system after the live room. A large steel plate several metres square is suspended in a tensioning frame. Activated by a transducer (which need be no more than

a loudspeaker), waves travel to the boundaries of the plate and are reflected back to be detected by strategically placed transducers. The character of the reverb can be altered by changing the tension applied to the plate. It is regarded as being particularly effective in the treatment of high-frequency and percussive sounds. The quality and distinctiveness of plate reverb may be judged by the fact that most digital reverb systems include at least one preset 'plate' setting.

3. Digital Reverb

(a) History and Development

The digital simulation of reverberation is immensely complex, the more so if it is desired to reproduce the characteristics of a real hall. There is in fact a method of doing this, which entails *sampling (digitally recording) the 'impulse response' of the hall (literally, the reverberant response to an extremely short sound) and mathematically combining this response with the music signal through a process known as 'convolution'. Unfortunately, an extremely large number of calculations is required—possibly 50,000 for each sound sample. Research has consequently been concentrated on the development of computationally efficient techniques which approximate to a musically acceptable degree a range of acoustic environments.

The first paper on the subject was published by Manfred Schroeder in 1962. This described the use of two special digital *filter algorithms—the comb filter and the all-pass filter—which both use the principle of the recirculating *delay line and can be implemented relatively efficiently. By setting the delay times for each filter to be relatively prime, a high echo density can be achieved without the risk of sudden convergences that would result in a 'grainy' reverb. The all-pass filter is unusual in that it has a uniform frequency response (i.e. it passes all frequencies) but a complex *phase response.

Schroeder described two reverb algorithms: a 'cascade all-pass' using six all-pass filters in series, and a 'comb all-pass', which used four comb filters in parallel followed by two all-pass filters in series. The latter, though it proved superior to the cascade all-pass algorithm, still exhibited a number of problems, relating mostly to the beginning and end of the reverberation. It was found, for example, that the early reflections characteristic of real halls were not well represented, and the end of the reverb decay tended to ring metallically at frequencies related to the delay times of the filters.

The comb all-pass algorithm was refined firstly by Schroeder (1970) and later by James Moorer (1979) to include an initial tapped delay line to generate the early reflections, accounting for the first 80 milliseconds or so of the sound, followed by the reverb algorithm proper. This used six modified comb filters, each with a single low-pass filter in the *feedback loop to simulate the damping of high frequencies, followed by a single all-pass filter. The delay times were derived from an analysis of the characteristics of the Symphony Hall, Boston.

The first commercial digital reverbs appeared shortly before the publication of Moorer's paper, notably the 'DRS 78' from the German company Dynacord, introduced in 1978. It offered a maximum delay time of 420 ms and an audio *bandwidth of a modest 8 kHz. It was, however, somewhat eclipsed in 1980 by the introduction of the '224' from the Canadian firm Lexicon, which, with a delay time of up to 70 seconds, a bandwidth of 15 kHz, full stereo operation (including the possibility to program different reverbs for each channel), and thirty variable parameters based on six reverb types, set the technical standard.

Other manufacturers such as EMT (already established as manufacturers of plate reverbs), Eventide (famed for their 'Harmoniser' *pitch shifter), and the British firm AMS brought out successful models, which though cheaper than the Lexicon were nevertheless beyond the budget of all but the largest studios. The climax of this early period of development was probably the 'Room Simulator' from Quantec (1983), which offered a decay time of up to 400 seconds and a 'freeze' or 'infinite reverb' facility.

The first genuinely low-cost reverb to be produced was the R1000 by Yamaha (1983), which offered four preset algorithms covering decay times between 1.55 and 2.4 seconds, together with a three-band parametric *equalizer, for under £500. 1983 was also the year in which the *MIDI data interface was introduced, and the new generation of MIDI-equipped reverbs did not reach the market (which the R1000 thus had in the meantime virtually to itself) until 1985.

(b) The Modern Digital Reverb

Modern reverbs fall roughly into two categories: those that allow detailed programming of a number of parameters, and those that while providing relatively limited programming facilities (or indeed none at all) offer a wide range of preset reverb 'patches', covering a range of room sizes from a small cupboard to the largest cathedral, together with effects such as 'plate reverb', reversed reverb, and 'gated' reverb, in which the reverb is abruptly cut off as if by a *noise gate.

In the case of programmable reverbs, variable parameters include pre-delay (setting the time between the direct sound and the first reflection), early reflections, high-frequency damping, diffusion, and reverb time. Some systems offer 'macro' parameters such as 'room size', which use preset settings which may or may not be able to be modified by the programmer. Many models also include delay-based effects, such as phasing, flanging, and chorus. This has been extended by the modern 'multi-effects' unit, which enables a number of such effects, including reverb, to be used together.

Rhodes

An electric *piano developed by the American pianist and teacher Harold Rhodes during the 1950s and marketed in association with Leo Fender (see GUITAR) from 1965. It is thus also referred to as the 'Fender-Rhodes', particularly in England. It was the culmination of research into electric pianos that had begun during the 1940s using scrap Air Force materials. The final design was inspired by a study of the chimes used in clocks. The Rhodes is now regarded as a classic of its type, its sound being the model for most of the synthesized electric piano sounds found in modern *synthesizers and *organs.

The tone is produced by striking a small tuned steel rod or tine similar to piano wire and linked to a larger 'tone bar' (originally made of iron, later steel) whose vibrations amplify and sustain the sound, the whole acting as a sort of tuning-fork. The sound is amplified by means of electromagnetic pick-ups. Being electromechanical, the instrument is fully polyphonic and 'touch-sensitive'. The *timbre, much favoured by jazz musicians, is warm and bell-like, though in early models sometimes lacking in penetration, especially in the low register.

The first instruments were known as the 'Rhodes Suitcase 88', the number signifying the number of notes—shorter models with 73 and 54 notes have also been made. They were followed in 1968 by the 'Stage' series of instruments, culminating in the Mark V model introduced in 1984. A version including *MIDI was introduced the following year; however, the electro-mechanical instrument has now been superseded (1989) by a fully electronic version marketed by Roland and designed in consultation with Rhodes, including a range of grand piano and vibraphone sounds as well as re-creations of several 'classic' Rhodes timbres.

Rhythm Box, Rhythm Machine

See DRUM MACHINE.

Rickenbacker

See GUITAR.

Ring Modulator

An electronic circuit which combines two input signals, each modulating the other. Its effect can best be described by an example. Given two sinusoidal inputs (e.g. two sine waves—see WAVEFORM) with frequencies of 400 Hz and 700 Hz, the output will consist of a complex tone made up of the sum and difference of the input frequencies, in this case 1,100 Hz and 300 Hz. In the general case, each frequency component or partial (see ACOUSTICS 1) of the first input signal will be modulated by each partial of the second, giving an output with a number of partials equal to twice the product of the number of partials in each input. For example, if each input contains three partials, the output will contain $2 \times 3 \times 3 = 18$ partials. The only exception to this is if two partials have the same frequency, giving a difference of zero.

The output from a ring modulator has two important characteristics. Firstly, except in the very simplest cases, the *timbre of the output will not be harmonic, nor will it be harmonically related to either of the inputs. More particularly, neither of the input signals is passed to the output. Secondly, if either of the inputs is at zero volume the output is also zero. This is accounted for by the fact that, internally, the process is as if the two input waveforms are multiplied together.

Thus a harmonic, recognizable sound modulated with a simple synthetic waveform is converted into a complex inharmonic timbre which may bear little or no perceptual relation to the input. The ring modulator enables inharmonic, bell-like timbres to be generated with great ease; similarly, instrumental and vocal sounds can be subjected to a variety of complex transformations, according to the nature of the modulating waveform. It is therefore of great value in *analogue subtractive *synthesis, which cannot directly produce inharmonic timbres. The ring modulator is also very valuable as a signal processor in live electronic music. In particular, the composer

Karlheinz Stockhausen has employed ring modulators in a number of works, notably *Mixtur* (1964, revised 1967), modulating orchestral sounds with sine waves, and *Microphonie 2* (1965), combining the sounds of a chorus and a *Hammond organ.

S

Sampler, Sampling

The process of converting a continuous *analogue signal (e.g. from a microphone) into a stream of *binary numbers which can be processed by a *digital *computer is known as 'digitizing' or, more usually, 'sampling'. It is the basis of a wide range of *signal processing and *synthesis techniques, and has led to the development of new recording techniques offering greatly superior audio quality (low *noise and *distortion) by comparison with conventional analogue recording on magnetic tape.

The signal to be digitized is fed to an *analogue to digital converter (ADC), which measures the amplitude of the signal at successive instants of time and represents each measurement as a binary number, which can be stored like any digital data—in memory, or on magnetic or optical disk. Similarly, the data can be recalled and converted back into sound by a digital to analogue converter. This is the basis of the now familiar compact disk.

Alternatively the sound can be digitized, processed, and reconverted in 'real time', i.e. without any perceptible delay between the sampling of the sound and its playback. This is the basis of modern digital *signal-processing techniques (see e.g. DELAY LINE I (c), REVERB 3).

To avoid any risk of confusion in the descriptions that follow, the digitized sound as a whole will be referred to as the 'soundfile', and each individual binary number making up the soundfile as a 'sample'. In popular usage, the latter term is freely used for both.

The sampler is a special application of digital recording developed for live performance. It enables the real-time playback of a soundfile by means of a keyboard (or in modern instruments any *MIDI controller). Most importantly, the keyboard is used to change the rate at which the soundfile is played back, resulting in the sound being heard, possibly polyphonically, at higher or lower pitches. The density of the polyphony (i.e. the maximum number of simultaneous notes) is determined by the speed of the internal processing (see DIGITAL SIGNAL PROCESSOR).

There is a trade-off between fidelity of sampling and memory usage. The higher the sample rate, the better the fidelity as more (ideally all) of the high-frequency components (see ACOUSTICS 1) are preserved. On the other hand, a high sample rate also requires more memory to be used for a given sampling time. For example, at the compact disk sampling rate of 44.1 kHz, a second of (monophonic) sound requires storage for 44,100 samples. Were half that rate to be used (which would in many cases still give an acceptable audio quality), the same amount of memory could store two seconds of sound.

The basic principle of variable-pitch playback is (while maintaining a fixed playback rate for the system itself), for a higher pitch, to skip over a given number of individual samples, or, for a lower pitch, to repeat samples. However, for high fidelity, accurate pitching, and low noise, it is necessary to calculate new sample values intermediate between those in the soundfile, a process known as 'interpolation'. A related term, used mainly in the context of the compact disk, is 'oversampling', which signifies, for a given sample rate, a doubling or quadrupling (which would be 'four times oversampling') of the system sample rate, and interpolating the extra sample values into the source soundfile to reduce to a minimum the residual distortion caused by digital to analogue conversion.

An inevitable side-effect of changing the pitch of a sample as described above is that the duration of the sound is thus also changed (just as it would be if a tape recording was played back at a lower or higher speed). For high pitches, the length is compressed, for lower pitches, it is lengthened. The principal technique used to overcome this and provide a sustain over the whole playing range is that of *'looping', which continuously repeats a selected portion of the sound, which should therefore be as constant in volume and *timbre as possible. Most importantly, the start and end of the loop should form a smooth join, otherwise a transient click known as a 'glitch' will occur at each pass around the loop. Even with a smooth dynamic join, any timbral differences within the loop will remain as a pulsing in the sound (this may of course be acceptable as a form of vibrato, though it will vary with pitch).

Techniques of considerable sophistication have been developed to minimize glitches, based on the principle of the 'cross-fade loop', in which sections at each end of the loop are faded into each other; many are included with the software of an instrument, but others depend on the graphic *waveform display and editing facilities provided by a separate computer system.

Problems can arise when a sound is transposed. In particular, the timbral formants which characterize many sounds, especially the human voice (see ACOUSTICS 3), are transposed, changing the character of the sound. A vowel sound, for example, loses its identity once the transposition exceeds a few semitones. To avoid such problems a number of separate soundfiles can be used, each covering a relatively small range of pitches—in extreme cases, a separate soundfile for each pitch will be used. Seen another way, this technique of 'multi-sampling' enables the sound of a full orchestral string section, for example, to be distributed along the keyboard by using appropriate soundfiles of violins, violas, cellos, and basses in each register. Similarly, each key could play a different percussion sound (see DRUM MACHINE).

The sampler can apply synthesizer-like processing to the soundfile (e.g. by *filters and *envelope generators), and can combine several soundfiles under the control of a single key; for example, the key *velocity can be used to control the relative balance between two soundfiles ('cross-fading'). Similarly, it can be played 'multi-timbrally' under external MIDI control.

Sampled sounds can also be combined with synthesized sounds. For example, one solution to the problem of looping is to use a (possibly multi-sampled) short soundfile for the very beginning of the sound (the *attack) but a synthesized waveform for the remainder. Many digital synthesizers use this technique to combine the realism of sampled sounds with the high level of timbral control provided by digital synthesis.

Instruments which offer both sampling and digital recording facilities include the *Fairlight and the *Synclavier. Important samplers have come from E-mu Systems (the 'Emulator' series and the 'Emax'), Ensoniq, whose 'Mirage' was one of the first 'affordable' samplers, Kurzweil and Roland, and Akai, whose 'S' series of keyboardless *expander units (and especially the S1000) have become widely regarded as studio 'standards'. However, almost all modern electronic instruments, including synthesizers, *pianos, and *organs, signal processors, *drum machines, and an increasing number of personal computers, now exploit sampling one way or another.

Sawtooth Wave

See WAVEFORM.

Semiconductor

See COMPONENTS 4.

Sequencer

A sequencer is an electronic system for the recording, editing, composing, and reproduction of musical 'events' in the form of control signals for a *synthesizer (hence an alternative title, 'event recorder'). It is defined by the nature of these signals—*analogue voltages in the case of a synthesizer based on voltage control (see MOOG, BUCHLA; *also* SYNTHESIS II 2), or *digital in the case of those instruments using either a proprietary digital *interface (see *below*) or, since the end of 1982, *MIDI, now in universal use. The description 'digital' has also been used (at the risk of some confusion—the term 'hybrid' would be more appropriate) to describe those analogue sequencers which used digital circuitry to process analogue data, using special circuits (see ANALOGUE TO DIGITAL CONVERSION) to convert between analogue inputs and outputs and the internal digital representation.

While the descriptions below relate explicitly to 'stand-alone' sequencers, it is important to note that it has long been common for a sequencer to be built into a keyboard instrument. At its simplest, it may amount to little more than an *arpeggiator or monophonic pattern generator; on the other hand a modern built-in MIDI sequencer is often provided with sufficient power to serve as the control centre for a whole MIDI system (hence the modern *workstation), not just for the keyboard into which it is built. A specialized form of sequencer is the 'rhythm box' or *drum machine (which may also be built into a keyboard instrument), in which performance of a number of percussion sounds is controlled automatically to generate preset or user-programmed rhythmic patterns.

The principle of sequencing (or 'automatic performance') has a long and fascinating history, embracing not only the subject of musical automata such as the musical clock, the music box, and the player piano, but also developments outside music such as the Jacquard loom. In the modern era of electronic music, sequencing of one form or another is central to the production of both commercial music and 'classical' computer music. The initiative for technical and musical developments has passed between both areas—while the development of the digital sequencer can be traced back to the first music 'computer', the RCA Mark I (see SYNTHESIS I 4), the development of MIDI arose from the need felt by commercial manufacturers for a common communications system.

The development of the sequencer is thus closely paralleled by those of the synthesizer and the *computer. The reader desiring to place it in as complete a historical and musical context as possible is encouraged to study these and other indicated entries in conjunction with the present article, which concentrates on the technical development 'towards MIDI'.

1. Analogue

The purely analogue sequencer must now be regarded as largely of historical interest, as its functions have been superseded not only by those of hybrid and MIDI sequencers but in many cases by the more elaborate control functions of the synthesizer itself. A small number of programmable stages (typically between eight and twenty-four), each of which stored a control voltage set by a potentiometer (variable resistor—see COMPONENTS 1), is sequenced by a simple electronic counter controlled by a variable-speed clock. In the context of an analogue 'modular' synthesis system, these control voltages could be applied to any suitable module. The most obvious application is to generate sequences of pitches by connection to an oscillator, but it is also usual to connect the sequencer to a voltage-controlled *filter or amplifier for the creation of complex *timbral and *amplitude *envelopes.

2. Hybrid (Digitally Controlled Analogue)

The introduction of digital circuitry to store and process synthesizer control signals offered not only the possibility of increased precision, speed, efficiency, and capacity (number of control steps), but also the ability to use the computer to supervise higher levels of compositional control. Thus on the one hand a relatively simple digital sequencer might have internal memory sufficient for some hundreds of steps (see e.g. EMS); at the other extreme, data relating to several parallel control streams might be stored on disk or tape and be subject to high-level compositional and editing procedures (see COMPUTER 3). Commercial sequencers have been generally of the former type, ranging from relatively inexpensive models with a single (monophonic) control voltage output and modest editing facilities to sophisticated polyphonic sequencers (notably models from Oberheim and Roland) offering up to sixteen analogue outputs. These were used not with polyphonic synthesizers, which did not offer independent external voltage control of each voice, but with separate monophonic instruments or modular systems.

(a) Programming and Editing Facilities

The basic editing facilities available in a typical commercial hybrid sequencer included copy, insert, delete, and transpose functions. These applied to single notes or to short segments of music which might be termed 'patterns' or 'chains' (the terminology was not, and to a degree still is not, standardized), or to the sequence ('song') as a whole—reflecting the assumed primary application of a sequencer, to facilitate the arrangement of frequently repeated material into song structures consisting of alternate verse/chorus sections.

(b) Recording and Playback

More sophisticated facilities included the choice of entering data either in 'real time' (i.e. recording a performance directly from a synthesizer keyboard) or in 'step time', in which pitch and duration data for each note was entered using the sequencer's control panel. In real-time recording, the sequence of notes has to be 'quantized' to fit the speed of the sequencer's timing clock, measured in fractions of a crotchet (= quarter-note, hence the clock speed is quoted as so many 'beats per quarter-note' or 'bpq'). On the one hand, if the clock resolution is too coarse, fine nuances of timing will not be preserved (e.g. separate notes might be recorded as chords, or missed altogether); on the other hand, an unrhythmical performance can be 'corrected' through the quantization process.

A new and important facility made possible by digital processing was that of 'overdubbing', whereby a second performance could be merged with a previously recorded sequence or, alternatively, recorded into a second channel while the first was being played back. If the sequencer was to be used in conjunction with a multitrack tape recorder, a special synchronization signal (see also TIME CODE) was first recorded on to one track of the tape. This was then used to synchronize all further recordings. Finally, cassette tape was used for permanent storage of sequence data.

3. The Digital Sequencer

(a) The First Computer-Based Systems

Computer-based synthesis 'workstations' such as the *Synclavier and the *Fairlight (both introduced in 1979) included powerful sequencing software which was able to take advantage of a large working memory and disk-based data storage to provide a high level of compositional and performance control over the internal (digital) voices. The Synclavier's sixteen-track sequencer was modelled on the functions of a multitrack tape recorder; the Fairlight included not only a real-time sequencer but also a proprietary Music Composition Language (MCL). Other similar instruments developed around this time include the *Buchla 'Touché' (including the 'FOIL' processing language), Con Brio 'ADS 200', the Crumar 'General Development System' manufactured by the New York-based company Digital Keyboards, the West German PPG 'Wave 2', and the 'Synergy', also from Digital Keyboards. Only the Synclavier and the Fairlight have established positions of dominance in the commercial market, and have in more recent models converted entirely to MIDI control.

(b) Digital Interfaces and MIDI

To achieve true polyphonic control of their synthesizers, as well as control of one instrument by another, proprietary (and thus incompatible) digital *interfaces were developed around 1980 by Oberheim, Sequential Circuits, and Roland, to enable each manufacturer to offer a complete 'system' comprising polyphonic synthesizer, drum machine, and sequencer. This made possible one valuable new facility (otherwise only available on the large digital systems described above), the remote changing of synthesizer patch and voice data from the sequencer. The same companies were responsible for the introduction, in late 1982, of the MIDI standard, which sets out precise details (both hardware and software) for the exchange of event and control data between instruments.

The facilities offered by the first MIDI sequencers, some of which, such as Roland's 'MSQ-700', were dual standard, with both MIDI ports and a connector for the manufacturer's own interface, departed little from what had gone before. As synthesizers themselves gained in sophistication, and control of individual MIDI channels (each of which could carry polyphonic note data) became of greater importance, so new sequencers were introduced which offered greater storage and extended editing facilities.

By 1984 the substantial market in personal computers was encouraging the development of MIDI sequencing software, together with the required hardware interfaces, which could take advantage of the computer's large text and graphics display facilities. Sequential Circuits produced a sequencer program, together with the necessary additional hardware, for the *Commodore 64, and Roland introduced their MPU401 interface with software for the *Apple II and the IBM PC. Yamaha introduced their 'CX5' computer, which included an FM sound module, built-in MIDI ports, and a suite of programs which included a voice editor for their 'DX7' synthesizer as well as a sequencer. It was discontinued after only a few years and in 1988 Yamaha introduced a much more powerful professional PC-compatible MIDI computer, the 'CI', which carries eight MIDI OUT ports and a built-in hard disk.

The introduction between 1984 and 1985 of firstly the Apple 'Macintosh' and then the *Atari 'ST' (the latter provided with built-in MIDI ports) established the superiority of the general-purpose computer, thanks mostly to the use of a high-resolution visual display unit (VDU), over the 'dedicated' hardware sequencer, which, though regarded as in principle more reliable (e.g. for stage use), is limited by a small display which makes the editing of sequences of any length and complexity a time-consuming and confusing process. However, in many cases it represents a considerably cheaper alternative to the combined cost of a personal computer and sequencing software.

The VDU gives the composer the ability to 'see' a large section of a sequence, in a variety of representations. Some programs offer an editable display in conventional staff notation, although the most usual is some form of grid or block display of note and related data, which can often be edited while the sequence is playing. During recording and playback, the display is usually designed to represent a multitrack tape recorder, offering appropriate forms of control over each track, together with auxiliary information such as elapsed time in a variety of formats. Sequencers which use MIDI *time code can synchronize the recording and playback of sequences to SMPTE-based equipment such as video, film, and audio tape recorders.

It would be impossible to list all the possible editing options available on a modern MIDI sequencer. In general, the emphasis can vary between real-time recording and playback of extended 'through-composed' sequences, or of 'pattern'-based sequences in which relatively short sections are frequently repeated. It is usually assumed that percussion tracks are generated by a separate drum machine controlled from the sequencer.

Note data can be edited to great precision. For example, the start and finish times of each note can be independently delayed or advanced by a single clock pulse, which in some sequencers is as rapid as 384 bpq. The 'mechanical' effect of strict quantization can be mitigated by 'humanize' functions, which, for example, delay alternate beats by a certain amount, or impose a specified 'swing' rhythm on the entire track. Whole tracks can be similarly delayed or advanced, not only for special effects, but also to accommodate the delays in response to which some instruments are prone.

At the other end of the compositional scale, global alterations can be made not only to speed and timing of tracks but also to pitch, volume, and dynamics (the latter, for example, by modifying the *velocity or *after-touch data). It is possible not only to create different arrangements of one set of material, but also to play a number of complete sequences (often referred to as 'songs') in a particular order. A common technique is to set aside a track for the recording of control (including 'System Exclusive') data, for example to change synthesizer patches and settings on MIDI-controlled *signal processors. Recently, programs have been developed which provide facilities for real-time interactive performance control, and for algorithmic composition, in which controlled random processes (see noise) are applied to short sequences of note data. Examples include 'MIDIGRID' from the *Composer's Desktop Project, and 'M', 'Jam Factory', and 'Realtime' from Intelligent Music, a software company founded by the American composer and performer Joel Chadabe.

Signal Processor

A signal processor is any electronic device which performs some controlled function on an input audio signal. This may come directly from an instrument or from another processor. The function may be remedial, such as the removal of unwanted *noise, or creative, such as the addition of artificial reverberation (see ACOUSTICS 4) or *reverb. These are treatments applied to a signal that is substantially complete; while a *filter is clearly a signal processor it is not usually described as such when it is part of a *synthesizer. Thus the term is widely used, for example to identify independent pieces of equipment that may be used in the recording studio, but it is less appropriate if applied to a function internal to a larger system.

The filter is the most familiar example of a family of processors which modify the *timbre of the sound. (See e.g. DISTORTION, EQUALIZATION, RING MODULATOR, VOCODER, WAH-WAH.) Filters also play an important role in *noise reduction systems.

A further important family of processors are those such as 'phasing', 'flanging', and 'chorus' which are based on the use of a *delay line. Although nominally a 'time-domain' process, the mixing of delayed and direct sound often affects the timbre, the difference lying largely in the time-varying nature of the process.

Most modern signal processors are *digital rather than *analogue, employing *analogue to digital conversion to transform the signal into a stream of *binary numbers for processing before being converted back to analogue. This leads to a distinction between processors which function in 'real time' (now the majority) and those which do not. The latter include in particular digital recording systems which enable spectrum *analysis, editing, and mixing functions to be performed on previously digitized sound. The advantage of non-real-time processing is that it enables the use of techniques which are too computationally demanding for a real-time *digital signal processor. See also FILTER 2, REVERB 3.

Signal-to-noise ratio

See DECIBEL, NOISE, NOISE REDUCTION.

Sine Wave

See WAVEFORM.

SMPTE Code

See TIME CODE.

Spectrum

A measure of the frequency content or *timbre of a complex tone. See ACOUSTICS 1, ANALYSIS, WAVEFORM.

Square Wave

See WAVEFORM.

Steinberger

See GUITAR 3(c).

Stringed Instruments, Electric

The solid-bodied electric bowed stringed instrument dates from the 1930s, and was developed mostly by those active in the design of other electric instruments, particularly the *guitar and the *piano, such as Benjamin Miessner, Oskar Vierling, Lloyd Loar, and the Electro String Instrument Co. under their Rickenbacker label. Although Miessner is acknowledged chiefly as one of the first (with Vierling) to develop an electric piano, he was a prolific inventor and designed not only electric violins, cellos, and basses but also a variety of electric guitars.

The body of a solid-bodied electric violin or bass is often of minimal size, serving merely as a mounting block for the tuning-pegs, fingerboard, bridge, and tail-piece. The electric violin has sometimes been styled with curved limbs giving it a skeletal but clearly violin-like appearance. Pick-ups are either piezo-electric, usually mounted directly on the bridge, or electromagnetic in the manner of pick-ups for the electric guitar and necessitating steel strings. Alternatively, simple electric violins are available that are structurally little different from the acoustic instrument, but are heavily lacquered to dampen body resonances and reduce *feedback.

In the early 1970s the American *computer music pioneer Max Mathews developed an electric violin so designed that the signal from each independently amplified string could be modified by powerful *filters. These enabled him not only to experiment with synthetic timbral formants (see ACOUSTICS 3) but also to synthesize brass and voice-like sounds. Similar principles have formed the basis of some *guitar synthesizers.

The upright electric bass has remained a specialist instrument, often made to special order, for players such as Joelle Léandre and Eberhard Weber. The electric violin is today associated mainly with the work of the jazz-rock artist Jean-Luc Ponty, though it is also occasionally used in pop and rock groups, as well as by larger ensembles such as the Electric Light Orchestra.

Modern manufacturers of electric violins and basses include, in addition to the guitar manufacturers such as Fender and Rickenbacker, smaller specialist companies such as Zeta Music Systems (known mainly for their range of *MIDI-based guitar controllers) of Berkeley, California, Barcus-Berry, who are well known as manufacturers of pick-ups for a wide range of acoustic and electric instruments, and Raad Instruments of Toronto, who have developed a series of instruments for specialists of contemporary classical music; in particular, they have been adopted by the Arditti String Quartet.

Synclavier

The Synclavier is a large-scale *digital *synthesizer and audio production system. It was the product of research into digital *synthesis conducted by Sydney Alonso, Jon Appleton, and Cameron Jones at Dartmouth College, New Hampshire, in the mid-1970s. In its prototype form it was known as the 'Dartmouth', and is referred to as such in some contemporary literature. The developers established a company, New England Digital (NED), to market the instrument commercially, production commencing in 1979. This initial model was succeeded the following year by the Synclavier II. Synthesis was based on additive and FM techniques, and the system included one of the first digital eight-track *sequencers.

Further substantial enhancements to both hardware and software were made in 1984, the instrument being known simply as the 'Synclavier'. The original five-octave keyboard was replaced by a 76-note *velocity- and pressure-sensitive keyboard originally developed by Sequential Circuits for their own 'Prophet T8' synthesizer. In addition to the retained synthesis facilities, the new instrument included substantial *sampling and resynthesis capabilities. Up to 32 voices could be used, each playing four wavetables (see SYNTHESIS II 3(b)), known as 'partial timbres', which could be combined under program and keyboard control—a method which has proved highly influential. One further feature retained from the original design was the distinctive control panel carrying a single large rotary control for parameter control, and some 160 buttons. Despite this being an increase of 32 on the original model, many buttons still had to serve several paged functions. Alternatively, the instrument could be controlled remotely from a *computer terminal.

The latest Synclavier is an 'open-architecture' system that can be configured and expanded in a variety of ways. There are two basic models, the 3200 and the 9600, the latter offering greater scope for expansion—a maximum of 96 voices rather than 32, and whereas the maximum RAM memory of the 3200 is 32 Mbytes, the 9600 starts at 32 Mbytes and can be expanded to 96 Mbytes. External storage capacities follow a similar proportion. An optical disk storage system is available as well as conventional hard disks.

Complementing the Synclavier console itself is a graphics *workstation based on an *Apple 'Macintosh' computer. In addition to a substantial *MIDI interface (two IN, eight OUT ports), both models can generate and read SMPTE *time code. NED also market a stand-alone 'direct-to-disk' digital recording system, which functions as a digital multitrack recorder with up to sixteen tracks.

The system is used not only for music production, but also for audio-visual work, where sound has to be synchronized to film and video. The Synclavier's processor has also been used for scientific research, in the field of data acquisition, most notably in a probe to visit Mars.

Synket

A small *analogue *synthesizer designed and built by Paolo Ketoff in Rome in 1964, and thus contemporary with Robert *Moog's presentation to the Audio Engineering Society of his paper on voltage control (see SYNTHESIS II 2). The voice configuration differed somewhat from that later established by Moog, *Buchla, and others for subtractive synthesis, providing three square-wave *oscillators (see also WAVEFORM) and a white-*noise generator as primary sound sources, together with a resonant band-pass *filter (which could also act as a sine wave oscillator), a filter bank (see EQUALIZATION), and facilities for *amplitude and frequency *modulation. Each of three such voices (relying mostly on internal connections, though external 'patch' cords could also be used) was controlled by a two-octave keyboard.

The instrument was not marketed commercially. Ketoff built seven to special order, the first for the American composer John Eaton, who made use of it in several works, exploring the use of micro-tones as well as the imitation of instrumental and vocal *timbres. The Synket is celebrated as pioneering the idea of a portable, self-contained instrument for live performance, at a time when composers interested in such combinations were largely confined to the use of pre-recorded tapes or of commercial electronic instruments (see e.g. SYNTHESIS I 6).

Synthesis I: Historical Overview

1. The First Electrically Based Instruments

Behind the sophistication and complexity of the modern *synthesizer lies a process of technical and musical development dating back at least to the industrial revolution of the nineteenth century, embracing not only theories of sound (see ACOUSTICS) but also work in mathematics, electricity, and electromagnetism, to say nothing of more general speculations on the nature and 'progress' of music itself.

The earliest electric instrument of importance was the *Telharmonium, patented in 1896 by the American inventor Thaddeus Cahill, although experiments into the generation of sound by electrical means had been conducted as early as 1874 by another American, Elisha Gray, best known for his pioneering work in telecommunications. Such experiments were inspired by the theoretical work of the German physician and mathematician Hermann Helmholtz (1821–94), who in 1860 published *On the Sensations of Tone*, the first book to present a rigorous physical and mathematical analysis of the behaviour of vibrating systems, especially those of string and wind instruments (see ACOUSTICS 3).

The Telharmonium used electromechanical means (rotating tone-wheels) to generate sound. The wheels were of formidable size, since they had to generate sufficient power to be connected directly to the telephone network. This approach was rendered obsolete in the 1920s by new techniques and applications made possible by the invention by Lee de Forest in 1906 of the triode valve (see COMPONENTS 5), developments in circuit design such as the Hartley *oscillator (1917), the Eccles-Jordan frequency divider (1919), and in particular the development of the free-cone moving-coil loudspeaker by Rice and Kellogg in 1925.

Of the many instruments developed during this period the most important were the *Theremin (c.1920), the *Ondes Martenot (1928), and the *Trautonium (1928–30). The techniques of amplification developed during this time made possible the design of compact electromechanical instruments (see PIANO, ORGAN, especially HAMMOND ORGAN, FENDER-RHODES). The new jazz and dance bands became increasingly dependent on amplification for instruments such as the guitar and the double bass (see STRINGED INSTRUMENTS), in conjunction with the continuing development of loud-speakers of higher fidelity and greater power. The mid-1940s saw the development of the electric *guitar, which depended entirely on electronic technology for its sound projection.

2. Developments in Sound Recording

The realization of the vision of electronic music would not have been achieved without the development of reliable high-fidelity audio recording equipment which offered the facility to store, mix, and edit sound material. The first magnetic recorder, using steel wire, was developed by Valdemar Poulsen of Copenhagen, as early as 1898. Developments were pursued chiefly in Germany and in America, encouraged to a great extent by the military. The race to develop reliable tape recording equipment was won by Germany, the AEG 'Magnetophone' being introduced in 1935. In the meantime, composers such as Edgard Varèse and John Cage who were interested in the use of recorded sounds developed compositions around the use of gramophone turntables. Cage's 'Imaginary Landscape No. 1' (1939) is generally regarded as the highlight of the work of this period.

By 1945 the AEG machines were capable of high-quality audio recording, and were dramatically superior to the American wire recorders. After the war the USA made the AEG patents available to any interested companies, and by 1948 high-quality magnetic tape recorders were available from several sources, including Ampex and Magnecord; other companies such as Minnesota Mining and Manufacturing (3M) concentrated on the development of the magnetic tape itself. The year 1948 itself proved to be a turning-point in the history of electronic music. In the USA Bell Laboratories developed the semiconductor transistor (see COMPONENTS 4), and in Paris Pierre Schaeffer promoted the principle of *musique concrète*, the recording and organization of 'natural' sounds on tape.

3. The Electronic Music Studio

The 1950s were years of intense activity for electronically minded composers. Formal electronic studios were established in 1951 in Paris and Cologne in association with radio stations, followed soon after by studios in Milan (1953, founded by Luciano Berio), Tokyo (1955), and Warsaw (1957). In England, the BBC Radiophonic Workshop was established in 1958, largely through the efforts of the composer Daphne Oram. The BBC has been widely criticized for not allowing access to the facilities to outside composers (Roberto Gerhard being a notable exception). Nevertheless, the Workshop introduced electronic music to a wide public, and to this day is known chiefly for its theme music (composed by Ron Grainer) for the cult science fiction TV series *Dr Who*.

The equipment available to composers during this period consisted of 'separates'—audio *oscillators, *filters, *ring modulators, mixers, and recording apparatus, as well as available electronic instruments. The Cologne studio was the first to make use of four-track tape recorders. Many fundamental synthesis and compositional techniques were established during this period, especially the principles of amplitude and frequency *modulation, the use of filters for timbral modification (especially in subtractive synthesis), and tape manipulation.

Of the composers active at this time the most significant were Messiaen (*Timbres durées* for tape, 1952), Karlheinz Stockhausen (*Electronic Study I,* 1953, *II,* 1954; *Gesang der Jünglinge,* 1956), and Varèse (*Poème électronique,* 1958). Other composers working in the medium included Pierre Boulez, John Cage, Herbert Eimert, Ernst Křenek, György Ligeti, Bruno Maderna, and Darius Milhaud.

4. The First Synthesizer

Important developments were also taking place in America. In 1955 RCA unveiled the Mark I Electronic Music Synthesiser. Designed by Harry Olsen and Herbert Belar, this was the first sound synthesizer in the modern sense. A larger Mark II version was completed soon after—it required over 1,700 valves and measured over 20 feet in length. It provided precise programmable control of oscillators, filters, and mixers on two channels (i.e. two notes at once). The original instrument used a multitrack disk sound recorder; this was replaced in 1959 by a system based on magnetic tape. The programmer had to define the parameters of each note to a high degree of precision, and enter the required data by creating a punched paper roll. The holes in the paper passed under a metal brush, which made contact with a metal drum, thereby activating relays which in turn controlled the corresponding analogue circuits. In the same year the Mark II instrument was installed in the Columbia-Princeton Electronic Music Center.

The designers saw mainly commercial applications of the instrument in creating electronic popular music on record, but the instrument is remembered today chiefly through its association with the composer Milton Babbitt, whose complex serial techniques were well suited to the degree of precision demanded by the system. The studio itself was host to a number of composers, including Mario Davidovsky and Charles Wuorinen, and, later, Luciano Berio, Edgard Varèse, Ilhan Mimaroglu, Walter (later Wendy) Carlos, and Jacob Druckman.

5. Digital Sound Generation

In 1957 Max Mathews, working at Bell Laboratories in New Jersey, demonstrated the technique of using a *digital *computer to create sound using a digital to *analogue converter. This led to the development of an important series of sound-synthesis programs (see COMPUTER 3; *also* SYNTHESIS II 3). Although developed on large mainframe computer systems, versions of some programs have been successfully adapted for use on personal computers (see e.g. COMPOSER'S DESKTOP PROJECT). Similarly, the techniques of synthesis, *analysis, *sampling, and *signal processing developed through this research later formed the basis for the development of commercial digital synthesizers and processors.

6. Into the Modern Era

With the advent of the 1960s it becomes less easy to present developments in a single historical sequence. Instead it is possible to identify several parallel strands of development, reflecting the proliferation of electronic studios for the serious experimental composer, the increasing commercial demand for electronic instruments and new sounds, and the accelerating search for new forms of musical expression.

Through the continuing work of Mathews and his colleagues Newman Guttman, David Lewin, John Pierce, and James Tenney, Bell Labs became established as the pre-eminent centre for research into computer music techniques, especially the analysis of acoustic instrument sounds. Mathews was joined in 1965 by Jean-Claude Risset, and towards the end of the decade by F. R. Moore. This collaboration resulted in the development of the digital sound creation program MUSIC V, and the program GROOVE for the control of analogue equipment.

The development of voltage control by Don *Buchla and Robert *Moog (see, especially, SYNTHESIS II 2) led to the design of a large number of relatively simple analogue synthesizers for both studio and concert use (see also EMS, ARP). Transistor-based circuitry made possible the design of compact *signal processing units for use on stage (as 'personal effects', exploited in particular by players of the electric guitar) as well as in the studio. Until the development in the late 1960s of synthesizers suitable for stage use, rock and pop groups were limited to the available keyboard instruments, such as the *Hammond organ and the smaller organs by companies such as Vox and Farfisa. Instruments such as the Theremin and the tape-based *Mellotron offered a dramatic alternative to the relatively predictable sounds of those instruments. The former is remembered in particular for its use by the Beach Boys in 'Good Vibrations' and the Mellotron for the flute sounds in 'Strawberry Fields Forever' by the Beatles.

In the classical field, the 1960s saw the expansion of studio-based tape music composition, and the development of electro-acoustic music, which combined electronic sounds with those of live instruments, and which also used signal processors (especially the ring modulator and the filter) to transform acoustic sounds. Stockhausen was active in both areas; his studio output included *Telemusik* (1966) and *Hymnen* (1967), and electro-acoustic works include *Mikrophonie I* and *II* (1964, 1965), *Mixtur* (1964), *Solo* (1966), *Prozession* (1967), and *Mantra* (1970). The alternative approach, of combining live performers with a pre-recorded tape, was epitomized by Roberto Gerhard's third symphony *Collages* (1960), and *Laborintus II* (1965) by Luciano Berio.

By the mid-1960s there was sufficient interest in the new medium to encourage the formation of specialist electro-acoustic music groups, most with a strong emphasis on free improvisation. In Europe Stockhausen's own performance group was joined by two groups in Italy, the Gruppo di Improvvisazione Nuova Consonanza and (made up mostly of American composers) Musica Elettronica Viva.

Musicians in Great Britain were especially active. AMM was formed in 1965 by Eddie Prévost, Cornelius Cardew, and others, concentrating on avant-garde performance techniques, which included the use of contact microphones, and Intermodulation was formed in 1969 by Tim Souster and Roger Smalley. A number of similar experimental groups were formed, often to reflect the interests of a particular individual, for example the experimental electromechanical instruments devised by Hugh Davies.

In America John Cage assembled a highly influential group of composers and performers, including his long-standing colleague David Tudor, Alvin Lucier, Pauline Oliveros, and others. Many were also members of the New York-based Sonic Arts Union, which included Robert Ashley and the experimental electronic and computer music composer David Behrman.

7. Aesthetics: New Sounds, New Thinking

The emergence of electronic music gave further impetus to the philosophical and psycho-acoustical speculations that had accompanied the twentieth-century musical revolution. The new technology led many composers to seek new forms of musical expression, with the concomitant need to propose new ways of perceiving as well as listening to music. One reason for this search for new aesthetic criteria was a desire shared by a number of composers and performers to create an alternative to the post-Webernian complexities of the mainstream avant-garde. Another was the increasing interest in the music and philosophy of the East (which were also important ingredients of the emerging 'hippie' culture)—John Cage's pursuit of musical 'indeterminacy', for example, was inspired at least in part by the tenets of Zen Buddhism.

The attraction of Eastern music, chiefly of India and Indonesia (gamelan), lay, among other things, in a combination of modality and pulsed rhythmic elaboration, and in the notion of music (at least as it was interpreted in the West) as a continuum of sometimes imperceptible 'processes' (rather than as a formal analytical structure of clearly differentiated elements), imbued with a magical, almost numinous quality. Meditation was in the air. Electronics was seen by some as enabling the perceptual separation of the sound 'object' from the psyche and personality of a performer. The new musical philosophy was later to be explored in the now classic book *Through Music to the Self* (1976) by the German composer Peter Michael Hamel.

One of the most striking expressions of these new directions (and viewed with some concern by many members of the mainstream classical avant-garde) was variously called 'process', 'systems', or 'minimalist' music. Composers associated with this music include, from California, Pauline Oliveros, Terry Riley (whose most well-known work *In C* (1961) began life as a tape piece before being adapted for instruments) and La Monte Young, who made use of drones created by sine wave oscillators; and in New York Steve Reich and Philip Glass (who took for their inspiration respectively the music of Africa and India) both made use of electronic organs and, later, synthesizers and samplers, in their subtly different types of process music. Reich's 'phasing' technique derived from a method of tape manipulation in which one track was slowly displaced in time from another (see e.g. DELAY LINE 1).

In the world of pop and rock music, the 'psychedelic' 1960s inspired many of the more experimental performers to explore the uses of electronics. Until the advent of the synthesizer towards the end of the decade this was confined to tape manipulation and simple signal processing (e.g. the use of 'fuzz' *distortion circuits). Nevertheless, some extraordinary results were achieved. The Beatles were among the most adventurous of the groups in incorporating *musique concrète* techniques such as random tape splicing, tape reversal, and the use of environmental sounds. The album *Sgt. Pepper's Lonely Hearts Club Band* (1967) was one of the first albums to feature such techniques extensively, and it proved highly influential not only to other musicians but also to commercial studios, the creative potential of which it revealed with great impact. This in turn helped fuel a demand for specialized electronic equipment for both stage and studio use.

With the rise of progressive and experimental rock in the 1970s, synthesizer design in particular became predominantly oriented towards commercial requirements, and correspondingly remote from the requirements of classical electronic music composers, who in general disparaged the technical and musical dependence on a conventional keyboard, preferring either the tape manipulation techniques of the analogue studio or the even more rarefied world of the mainframe computer, which nevertheless was to be responsible for the technical developments which were the foundation of the new commercial digital instruments.

8. New Directions in Recorded Music

As part of a conventional rock or pop group, the synthesizer (which was, to begin with, only monophonic) had limited, if important, roles to play—it would be used as a substitute for a bass or lead guitar, or for sound effects. However, the use of a sequencer broadened the possibilities considerably. A short repetitive melodic pattern ('riff') could be programmed into the sequencer, which would then control the synthesizer, leaving the live performers to concentrate on other things.

The German group Tangerine Dream, formed in 1967 by Edgar Froese and Christoph Franke, began as a rock band specializing in improvisation, issuing its first album *Electronic Meditation* in 1970. Soon afterwards it was joined by Peter Baumann and became a predominantly keyboard-based group, making considerable use of sequencers to create its own brand of atmospheric ostinato-based minimalism, while retaining the drums and guitar of its rock origins. Later albums such as *Phaedra* (1974) and *Rubycon* (1975) dispensed with even these, and used a mixture of string ensemble synthesizers, monophonic synthesizers, organs, and Mellotron to create slowly unfolding cloudscapes of sound merged with hypnotic sequencer-based repetitive melodic patterns, the latter predominantly in the bass to middle registers.

Thus was established a genuinely new musical genre, the electronic 'concept' album, and it was eagerly adopted by both groups and individual artists. The language of this essentially instrumental music (when not imitating familiar rock idioms) was that of meditation, dreams, magic, and fantasy, allied especially in modern 'New Age' electronic music to the idea of healing, the music serving as a therapeutic antidote to the stresses of modern life.

In England, the previously little-known guitarist Mike Oldfield caused a sensation with his 1973 album *Tubular Bells*, composed by overdubbing all the instruments (mostly played by Oldfield himself) using a multitrack tape recorder. The album sold some 10 million copies and established Virgin Records as a powerful force in the recording industry.

A highly influential artist active from this time was Brian Eno. Originally with the experimental rock group Roxy Music (1971), he left in 1973 to develop his own ideas. One of these was the creation of the Obscure record label for experimental composers; artists to record for Obscure included Gavin Bryars, John Adams, John Cage, Michael Nyman, and Harold Budd. Eno used the term 'ambient' to describe his particular type of pulseless, almost static but aurally hypnotic music, created with great subtlety and attention to detail. In his search for perfect harmony he makes use of 'natural' scales tuned in just intonation rather than equal-temperament (see TUNING AND TEMPERAMENT).

9. Experimental Rock Music

Eno was one of a small group of artists who strove to incorporate elements of the avant-garde into rock music. The attempt was not always commercially successful—the audience for progressive rock was only 'progressive' within its own terms. The group Pink Floyd produced in their second album, *Saucerful of Secrets* (1968), a title track in the style of a 'classic' tape music composition; by the time of their most celebrated album *Dark Side of the Moon* (1973) they had returned to a solidly rock idiom, while continuing to make imaginative use of electronics. A later group, Talking Heads, managed to be both experimental and commercially successful, attracting the interest of Brian Eno, who acted as producer for their second album, *More Songs about Buildings and Food* (1978). The sound of the group was distinguished by its clever use of studio effects to enhance and transform a largely orthodox rock instrumentation.

10. The New Technology

The major technological advances in musical electronics at the end of the decade, heralded by instruments such as the *Fairlight, the *Synclavier, and the digital 'Linndrum' *drum machine, with their powerful sequencing and sampling abilities, established the fact that electronic instruments were by this time not merely a potent addition to the conventional rock and pop instrumentation but were indeed alternatives to it, as was already clear from the number of solo artists and groups creating albums in the studio with entirely electronic means.

These instruments also demonstrated a blurring of the distinctions between the hitherto clearly separate functions of the synthesizer, sequencer, drum machine, and mastering recorder that was to become even more marked in the 1980s, with the introduction of *MIDI, digital synthesis and sampling, multi-timbral voicing, and digital recording. The technical sophistication of modern instruments has also encouraged hitherto cautious classical composers and performers to develop their own compositional and performing applications.

Synthesis II: Principles and Techniques

The electronic synthesis of sound falls into two broad areas of application: the accurate re-creation of natural acoustic sounds (e.g. of orchestral instruments—see ACOUSTICS), and the creation of 'new' sounds which may occasionally, but by no means necessarily, have an 'acoustic' quality to them. Common to both is the need to be familiar with the physical properties of sound itself, as well as with the electronic apparatus ('hardware') most suitable for the many synthesis techniques which have been developed.

The synthesis task therefore falls into three interdependent stages: the formulation of a theoretical or empirical model of the target sound, the development (or selection) of a suitable synthesis technique, and its practical implementation.

The hardware used for sound synthesis may be *analogue, comprising a variety of circuits made up of mostly standard electronic *components, each circuit serving a particular function (see below) and generating and processing continuous signals, or *digital, in which *computer techniques are used to generate and transform sounds represented by streams of numbers, or a combination of the two (a 'hybrid' system), for example the digital control of analogue circuits. Analogue oscillators generally produce simple geometric periodic waveforms; a digital oscillator can in principle generate any waveform.

A further important distinction in digital synthesis is made between synthesis using systems that can respond immediately to the control of a performer (i.e. in 'real time'), and synthesis that entails the 'non-real-time' construction of a sound for later playback. Non-real-time synthesis is generally confined to research and to tape music composition; however, many techniques developed on non-real-time computer systems have been subsequently incorporated into real-time digital synthesizers for use in live performance—see, in particular, section 3(c) below.

1. Timbral and Dynamic Models

The *timbre (frequency spectrum) of an acoustic instrument (see ACOUSTICS 1(b)) can be represented as the sum of a number of pure sine waves, which for a conventionally 'musical' pitched sound are normally harmonic. Spectrum *analysis reveals that the spectrum is rarely static: the relative intensity of the component *partials varies in time, depending, for example, on variations in performance. Synthesis techniques need to be able not only to create the 'overall' or characteristic spectrum of a sound, but also where necessary to control the change in spectrum with time.

Accurate imitations of acoustic instruments cannot be achieved, however authentic the timbre, without attention to the *envelope. The complexity of this task depends on the degree of variability in the target sound. The envelope of a note on a xylophone is relatively fixed, whereas melodic sustaining instruments such as bowed strings or softly articulated brass sounds exhibit a wide range of dynamic envelopes. Furthermore, the apparent dynamic change in a sound may be predominantly a change of timbre; typically, the high-frequency energy of a sound (to which the ear is relatively sensitive) will be significant only at relatively high dynamic levels.

(a) Additive Synthesis

The process of creating a sound by the precise addition of sine waves is called 'additive' synthesis (sometimes, though not always strictly correctly, 'Fourier synthesis'). It is a (usually prohibitively) cumbersome and costly technique with analogue equipment, unless major limitations on the number of oscillators are accepted, but it is relatively easy to implement using digital computers, which allow in theory any number of 'logical' oscillators to be used. Additive synthesis also lies behind the principles of registration used on pipe and some electronic *organs.

(b) Resynthesis

It follows from the above that any sound, once analysed to determine the relative strength of its component partials, may in theory be 'resynthesized' by the controlled mixing of correspondingly tuned sine wave oscillators. This in turn gives the possibility of creating interesting variations of the original sound. The Fourier technique is not, however, universally applicable. It has some difficulties, for example, in representing sounds with a significant *noise content, and the sheer amount of data generated by Fourier analysis can prove unmanageable. A variety of analysis and resynthesis techniques have been developed by audio engineers and specialists in computer music for particular purposes, for example in speech synthesis.

(c) Subtractive Synthesis

Waveforms such as the triangle, sawtooth, and square wave are easy to generate electronically and are rich in harmonics, which can be selectively removed by a *filter to arrive at the desired sound. Hence this technique is known as 'subtractive synthesis'. The technique is very economical in terms of hardware, and is more naturally accessible to musicians than additive synthesis. For this reason it is used by the great majority of commercially produced analogue synthesizers, despite the fact that it is not as flexible or as comprehensive as additive techniques. It is difficult, for example, to create sounds with non-harmonic partials using subtractive synthesis. A wide range of *modulation and *signal-processing techniques has been developed to overcome these limitations.

2. Voltage Control

An analogue subtractive synthesis system involves, therefore, three elements: signal generators, signal processors, and parameter controls. The extent to which these elements interact depends on the design of the hardware, and in particular upon the recognition that an audio signal might also be used as a control signal for another circuit. This leads to the design strategy of a system of circuit modules, each containing a signal input, one or more control inputs, and an output. The two pioneers of synthesizer design, Donald *Buchla and Robert *Moog, both designed (independently of each other) synthesis systems based on this principle. While Buchla preferred to keep signal and control paths separate, Moog designed circuits that were fully compatible electrically, so that the output from any module could be used to control any other without restriction.

Central to this approach is the technique, associated particularly with the work of Moog, of voltage control. This enables important parameters, such as the frequency of an oscillator or the cut-off frequency of a filter, to be controlled (modulated) not only by a manual control but also by a voltage applied to a control input. Thus the pitch of an oscillator can be controlled by a keyboard which outputs a voltage determined by the key played—a low key produces a low voltage and a high key a high voltage. Modulation techniques made possible by voltage control enable rich and complex sounds to be generated easily from simple sources.

Described below are the basic building blocks of subtractive synthesis using voltage control. These can be organized in a wide variety of ways, from a set of physically separate modules to a fixed arrangement designed by a manufacturer—see SYNTHESIZER.

(a) Voltage-Controlled Oscillator (VCO)

A single oscillator circuit can generate simultaneously a number of waveforms, including those listed above, over the audio range. In keeping with the principles of subtractive synthesis, a sine wave output is not normally included. Control inputs enable the pitch of the oscillator to be modulated by external signals. If a pulse (square) wave output is provided, a second control input can be used to modulate the width of the pulse (hence 'PWM'—pulse-width modulation); this creates a subtle sense of 'movement' within the sound by modifying the spectrum of the signal.

The primary control source for the VCO is usually a keyboard. While this may cover as little as $2\frac{1}{2}$ octaves, selectable octave ranges, typically from 16 ft to 2 ft (by analogy with organ registrations), give the VCO a potential range of some eight octaves. Clearly a waveform rich in harmonics is well able to reach the upper as well as the lower limits of the audible range.

The pitch may be further modulated by other control signals, for example from other VCOs (hence the general name for this technique, 'frequency modulation'; see also section 3(c) below). Other techniques include simple detuning, whereby two or more oscillators are tuned apart by a few *Hertz—this creates beats (see ACOUSTICS 2(b)), and a valued thickening of the sound—and *phase-locking, usually referred to as 'sync'. This forces the waveform of a second oscillator to synchronize with that of the first. While the frequency ratio is unity, the two oscillators sound as one. Any deviation of the frequency of the first oscillator forces the waveform of the second to make a discontinuous 'jump' so that the start of each wave cycle still coincides, resulting in the sudden and often penetrating addition of harmonics. The technique depends on a special hardware connection between the oscillators. Another valuable technique is *ring modulation, which is used not only with electronically generated signals (to generate bell-like inharmonic timbres) but also, for example, with the voice and other acoustic sources for 'robotic' effects.

(b) Low-Frequency Oscillator (LFO)

This is a specialized oscillator designed for the generation of slowly changing voltage signals specifically intended as control signals. A single cycle of an LFO may last in excess of ten seconds. Unlike the VCO, an LFO may generate a sine wave as well as other waveforms. The LFO can also have control inputs affecting the amplitude and frequency of the signal—in modern synthesizers the control signal can be taken from a *velocity- and pressure-sensitive keyboard. A press-and-release button can be used to trigger the LFO manually for delayed vibrato effects.

The most common application of an LFO is the creation of pitch vibrato (frequency modulation) by applying the output to the control input of a VCO, but its usefulness extends to virtually every department of a synthesizer. Applied to the cut-off-frequency control input of a VCF (see section (d) below) it can produce 'filter sweep' effects; applied to a VCO it can produce pitch sweeps as well as vibrato; and applied to a voltage-controlled amplifier (VCA—see below) it can produce tremolo. Limitations arise if a single LFO is responsible for too many functions. It is preferable to have at least two LFOs, so that the VCO and the VCF can be modulated independently.

(c) Noise Generator

White *noise is used for special effects (e.g. wind and sea sounds) and as a starting-point for the synthesis of drum and other sounds of indeterminate pitch. It is purely a signal generator—the output is normally sent to a filter (see below). However, since noise consists of a randomly changing voltage, it is possible by sampling the signal at regular intervals (by a 'sample-and-hold' circuit) to extract from it a slowly changing succession of random voltages that can then be sent to control the pitch of an oscillator. Random control signals of this kind can also be generated digitally.

(d) Voltage-Controlled Filter (VCF)

The filter is the single most complex and characterful circuit in a synthesizer. It is also the most expensive, and, where cost is a constraint, it is common for a single VCF to be fitted to an otherwise polyphonic instrument. The filter is, furthermore, the most difficult function to implement digitally (see below), especially in real time, as considerable arithmetic processing is required.

The standard VCF for subtractive synthesis is necessarily of the low-pass type (see FILTER for a description of the basic configurations), though in all but the most cost-reduced systems a high-pass filter (HPF) is also included. The VCF is powerful enough to reduce the most harmonically rich signal to its fundamental tone and, in tandem with the HPF, to pass individual harmonics. The standard control sources are the LFO, the keyboard, and the envelope generator. The effects obtainable from each of these sources can be summarized as follows:

LFO modulation. Assuming a low-frequency setting on the LFO, the VCF at its most resonant setting will 'scan' the harmonics of the signal. If this is a simple waveform such as a sawtooth, the resultant sound is closely similar to that of the violinist's glissando of harmonics. A milder resonance setting produces the characteristic 'ee-oo' sweeping effect. A faster LFO setting (at low *amplitude) will create a timbral vibrato. The more extreme effects are better imagined than described.

Keyboard modulation. The normal application of keyboard modulation (often termed 'key follow') is to maintain the timbral characteristic of a sound over the range of the keyboard by adjusting the cut-off frequency of the filter according to register. If the filter is pushed into self-oscillation (at maximum resonance) its pitch can be played by the keyboard like a VCO. At maximum modulation, the result will be the normal tempered chromatic scale. At lower modulation settings, microtonal scales can be created. With noise as the source signal, a wide range of percussive, wind, sea, and whistling effects can be created.

Envelope modulation (see below). Following from the above, a filtered noise source can be enveloped to generate a range of pitched or semi-pitched percussion effects. This is but one example of the wide range of available timbral enveloping effects. The *attack (see also below) of many acoustic instruments is harmonically rich, while the sustained portion of the sound is much less so—an envelope-modulated filter is needed to imitate this characteristic.

(e) Envelope Generator (EG)

The general concept of a sound's *envelope is described in a separate entry. The purpose of this section is to describe the operation of a practical EG within the context of subtractive synthesis. Since most synthesizers use a keyboard as the primary performance controller, the final *decay section of an envelope is (like the initial attack) triggered from the keyboard, giving a basic four-stage configuration of attack (time), decay (time), sustain (level), and release (time) (ADSR). The EG is used to control both the voltage-controlled amplifier (VCA) and the VCF.

It is important to remember that the sustain level is not necessarily the same as the attack level. The former establishes the 'steady state' of the sound, and in this limited sense may be thought of as a volume control. However, not only are many instrumental sounds characterized by a 'bite' at the beginning of the sound, some, such as the piano, actually have no steady state at all.

The attack parameter determines the time taken by the sound to reach its initial peak, the level of which corresponds to the overall output level of the system. Even in a percussive instrument such as a piano, the tone takes a certain amount of time to develop. On the other hand, the attack of a loud drum sound such as a tom-tom is somewhat more rapid, and the decay time very much more so. In such cases, the sustain level is set to minimum—the decay function reduces the level to that set by the sustain control. If a trumpet or similar brass tone is being synthesized, the sustain level will be set as high as possible, allowing just the necessary headroom for the extra intensity of the attack. The attack and decay parameters can also be used to mimic performance nuances.

The release stage of the EG may occur at any time—the dynamic level at the moment of release is reduced to nil over the time set by the release parameter. The rapid release of the key can mean that the EG never enters the decay stage; thus the unusual situation can arise in which a key pressed and held down results in a short sound (i.e. completed fast attack and decay stages), whereas a key struck and rapidly released results in a note with a lengthy decay (i.e. a long release time). Clearly a wide range of variation is possible through a considered combination of particular ADSR settings and playing technique.

The EG can be used to great effect to control the VCO and the VCF, as noted above. The former enables the creation of a variety of pitch sweep and other pitch-based sound effects, and the latter enables reasonably authentic timbre changes over time to be synthesized—the brass 'bite' referred to above is a timbral as well as a dynamic phenomenon. While in many cases the same EG settings will serve for control of both VCF and VCA, it is nevertheless desirable to have separate EGs for each function.

A valued facility especially on instruments with only one EG is the option to invert the output of the EG, for application to the VCF. Thus a sharp dynamic attack can be associated with either a closing or an opening of the filter; a reducing dynamic level can therefore be combined with an increasing timbral richness.

(f) Extended Enveloping Techniques

A small analogue *sequencer, with eight or sixteen stages, can be used to construct more complex envelopes than can be achieved with the basic

ADSR envelope. In many modern digitally controlled instruments the ADSR structure has been replaced by a more flexible arrangement in which a number of 'breakpoints' corresponding to dynamic levels can be programmed, with the time taken to move from one to another also programmable (hence a 'time-value breakpoint envelope'). This enables, for example, multiple-attack envelopes to be designed.

A further range of control is made possible by the modern velocity- and pressure-sensitive keyboard. The programmed envelope can be modified by the speed with which the key is struck, by pressure applied to the key as it is held down (see AFTER-TOUCH), and the speed with which the key is released. The internal envelope generator can be replaced by an *envelope follower, which tracks the envelope of an external source, or by a 'breath controller', a transducer which produces an electrical signal from the player's breath pressure and articulation.

(g) Performance Controls

This term embraces a range of mechanical dynamic, timbral, and pitch controls, acting on all the sections of the synthesizer. Basic controls are required for pitch inflexions (referred to as 'pitch-bend'), volume, and LFO modulation control for the application of vibrato. The practical implementation of performance controls is described in detail in the companion entry, see SYNTHESIZER 1.

The techniques of real-time synthesis embrace not only the creation of a particular sound, but also the provision of ways in which that sound can be modified, conventionally or otherwise, by the performer. Often the synthesist has to pay close attention to the way in which instruments are played, if a synthesis project is to be successful. In this respect it is important to note that the keyboard is by no means the only synthesizer performance controller—*guitar, *percussion, and *wind controllers have also been developed. The development of *MIDI has encouraged the design of a continually widening range of synthesizer controllers.

3. Digital Synthesis

(a) Hardware versus Software

Just as it is possible to represent a sound graphically, by drawing a waveform, so it is possible to represent that waveform numerically, using whole numbers (integers) or floating-point numbers within some given range. The representation of sound waveforms in a numerical format can be achieved by a software program, or directly by the process of 'digitizing' or *sampling (see ANALOGUE TO DIGITAL CONVERSION). The resulting data can be processed in a variety of ways before being converted back to sound by a complementary digital to analogue converter (DAC).

For high-quality sound a high processing speed is required. That is to say, the hardware (i.e. the processor and memory) must be able to perform calculations and data manipulation at high speed, and the software (the controlling program) must itself function as efficiently and as quickly as possible. A general-purpose *computer is unlikely to be fast enough to be used for synthesis in real-time. Instead, the data from a synthesis program must be stored on tape or disk in stages, and the completed digital soundfile then passed to a DAC for output. In contrast, a specialized *digital signal processor (DSP) can perform millions of arithmetical operations per second, so that sound can be sampled, processed, and output in real time. A number of manufacturers have developed their own proprietary DSP chips, usually optimized for a particular synthesis method.

There is therefore a distinction to be made between the use of general-purpose computers to calculate a sound using specialized programs (software synthesis), and the use of specialized digital hardware which can perform specific tasks automatically, in real time, but which cannot match the flexibility of the software approach. Practical digital synthesizers employ both approaches in a variety of ways—these are described in more detail in the companion entry, see SYNTHESIZER. For further information of a general technical and historical nature see also COMPUTER 3.

(b) The Theoretical Background

The pioneering research of computer music composers such as Max Mathews, Barry Vercoe, and Jean-Claude Risset was directed towards the most accurate and complete analyses of natural instrument timbres, with a view to their synthesis using additive and other techniques. Risset made a series of studies of instrument tones, of which the most important were the *Computer Study of Trumpet Tones* (1966) and *An Introductory Catalogue of Computer Synthesised Sounds* (1968). The 'MUSIC' series of programs developed by Mathews and Vercoe established the use of a set of 'unit generators'—a collection of small programs (subroutines) which imple-mented the functions of oscillators, filters, and envelope generators together with fundamental arithmetic operations. These could be combined as the composer wished, to create a 'logical instrument'. An 'Orchestra File' of such instrument specifications could be 'performed' by a separate 'Score File' to create an entire piece.

(i) The Wavetable As indicated above, a waveform is stored inside a computer as a sequence of numbers. This sequence is called a 'wavetable'. Its length (i.e. the number of memory locations, or data 'words', in which numbers may be stored) is a compromise between precision and economy of memory (and to some extent the sample rate), but is normally a 'power of 2' value. For example, if a single *byte (eight *bits) is used to store the table length, the wavetable will be (at most) 256 words long. Longer tables (giving lower *distortion and *noise) of 512 or 1,024 words are common in professional systems. The size of the data word itself also affects the audio quality of the sound. While many excellent systems, including, for example, the original *Fairlight synthesizers, have used eight-bit words, for the best results twelve- to sixteen-bit words are necessary. The latter is the size used by a compact disk.

The data entered into the wavetable represents one complete cycle of the waveform. The data is then scanned by an 'indexing counter'. This counts from 0 (the first number in the table) to the end, say 511 (for a 512-word table), and then 'wraps around' to 0 again. Mathematically, the counter represents the 'instantaneous phase' of the waveform. Similarly, the numbers representing the waveform may be called the 'instantaneous amplitude' of that waveform. A phase offset is achieved by adding a constant value to the indexing counter. In the example above, an index starting at 128 would create a cosine wave, given a wavetable loaded with a sine wave.

(ii) Frequency Control To create a continuous tone the data derived from the repeated scanning of the wavetable needs eventually to be passed to a DAC; the speed at which this is done is the 'sampling rate' of the system. Given that the wavetable contains a sine wave (though it could of course contain any arbitrary waveform), the system is thus outputting a single sine tone at a pitch determined by the wavetable length and the sampling rate. In order to obtain a continuous range of pitches the techniques of either truncating or interpolating 'table look-up' are used.

In calculating the table increment (index) for a given pitch, the result in most cases is a fractional number representing a position intermediate between two consecutive values in the table. In a truncating look-up the fractional number is truncated to give a whole-number index; in an interpolating look-up the values of those adjacent samples are used to calculate a new, much more accurate, intermediate value. The interpolating technique gives superior musical results but demands a larger amount of computation. The truncating look-up can, however, give acceptable results if a sufficiently large table of, for example, 8,192 words is used.

(iii) The Logical Oscillator   To create a timbre (e.g. by additive synthesis), an area of memory is set aside as a 'logical oscillator' (it could also be called an 'output buffer'), in which data from the wavetable look-ups is combined. In theory there is no limit to the number of partials which may be used, other than that imposed by the sample rate (which must be at least twice the highest frequency to be generated). Additive synthesis lends itself to an empirical graphics-based mode of data input—the composer draws amplitude envelopes (e.g. time-value breakpoints) for each partial, leaving the computer to calculate the numerical values.

The precise implementation of these principles depends on whether the system has to work in real time. In a non-real-time system the data from table look-ups is accumulated first in a *buffer in memory, then transferred to permanent storage. In real-time synthesis, the 'logical instrument' program (also termed an 'algorithm') is run continuously, generating output samples at the system sample rate in response to user input.

(c) Frequency Modulation (FM)

This very important synthesis technique was developed at Stanford University by the American composer John Chowning, who described it first in a paper published in 1973 in the *Journal of the Audio Engineering Society*. It was later licensed to Yamaha, who developed the highly influential 'DX' series of synthesizers based exclusively on the technique. The most popular model, and also one of the first to be introduced (though FM had been used in the earlier 'GS' keyboards in a non-programmable form) was the DX7 (1983 onwards), one of the first programmable digital synthesizers available to the general public.

FM differs from conventional analogue frequency modulation techniques as described above in two respects; firstly, that the modulating frequency (the 'modulator') not only lies in the audio range but may well be higher in frequency than that of the oscillator being modulated (the 'carrier'), and, secondly, that more than two oscillators may be employed—one modulator may itself be modulated by others. In the DX7 six sine wave oscillators (termed by Yamaha 'operators') were available for each note; these could be used in thirty-two preset arrangements termed 'algorithms'.

Referring to Fig. 1: the effect of modulating the frequency of one audio oscillator by another is that a series of 'sidebands' (frequency components) are generated symmetrically above and below the nominal frequency of the carrier. The number of sidebands increases (with complex variations of intensity) as the level of modulation (the 'modulation index') increases, and thus considerable timbral change is achieved through the alteration of a single parameter, the amplitude of the modulator. In the DX7, independent amplitude envelopes were programmable for each operator, allowing a very wide range of possibly complex dynamic timbral evolutions. No filters were provided.

A second important parameter is the ratio of the frequencies of the carrier and the modulator—the 'c/m ratio'. This determines the degree of harmonicity of the sidebands, which are harmonic for simple c/m ratios such as 1 : 1 or 2 : 1, but increasingly inharmonic as the c/m ratio itself becomes more inharmonic. It is therefore very easy, by using, for example, a non-integer c/m ratio, to generate complex inharmonic metallic and bell-like timbres, which are, as explained above, so difficult to achieve with conventional subtractive synthesis. Further timbral complexities can be obtained by using modulating waveforms other than sine waves.

FM has proved amenable to the synthesis of both conventional instrumental timbres, especially brass and metallic percussive sounds, and highly abstract sounds remote from any acoustic model, with (in the case of real-time instruments such as the DX7) a high degree of responsiveness to performance nuances; on the other hand it is hard to program by the empirical alteration of parameters as the results are difficult to predict.

(d) Waveshaping

Waveshaping is known by several alternative names, including 'non-linear distortion' and 'non-linear processing'. Jean-Claude Risset is credited with the first use of the technique, in 1969, though the principal technical papers on the technique were published independently ten years later, by Daniel Arfib, James Beauchamp, and Marc LeBrun.

Recalling the structure of the basic wavetable, and assuming that it contains a sine wave, the regular increment of the instantaneous phase can be represented by a straight line (see Fig. 2). This line is the 'transfer function' applied to the wavetable. This is best understood by analogy with the performance of an audio amplifier. An ideal amplifier will have a 'linear' response—the relationship between the input and output signals is a straight line. Thus a signal presented at the input will be represented by a perfect copy at the output. If the response is non-linear, the output will be a distorted copy of the original.

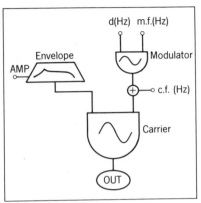

(a)

Key

d = amplitude of modulator=maximun
    frequency deviation imposed on carrier

m.f.= frequency of modulator=rate of
    frequency deviation

c.f. = carrier frequency

I = modulation index=d/m, determines
    spectral bandwidth

HARMONIC

c/m ratio=1 : 2

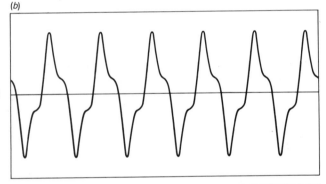

(b)

INHARMONIC

c/m ratio=1 : 1.3

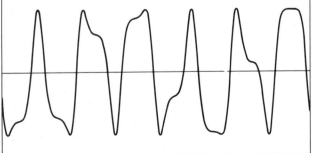

(c)

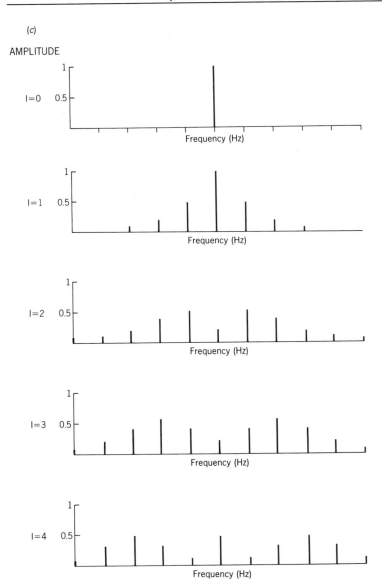

Fig. 1. FREQUENCY MODULATION. (a) Block diagram of basic FM configuration: both oscillators use sine waves; (b) Typical FM waveforms; (c) Effect on spectrum of Mod. Index (sidebands are spaced m.f. Hz above and below c.f.).

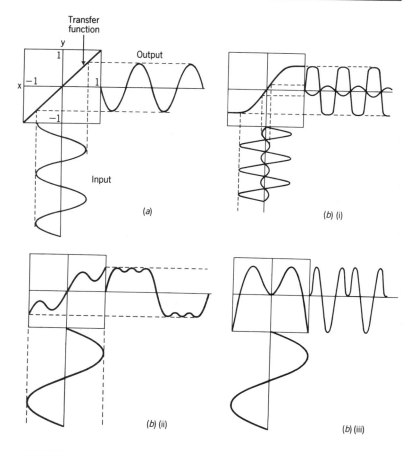

Fig. 2. WAVESHAPING. (a) Basic (non-distorting) transfer function; (b) Non-linear Transfer Functions. Functions b(i) and b(ii): at low input amplitudes signal is unmodified. At high amplitudes, waveform is distorted, adding harmonics. Functions b(i) and b(ii) are 'odd', adding only odd harmonics; function b(iii) is 'even', adding even harmonics, with a net doubling of frequency.

In waveshaping, a non-linear transfer function is created by the programmer and stored in a 'function table', which is then used to control the wavetable phase increment, which will now proceed at different rates, and possibly directions, at different stages through the wavetable. Fig. 2 gives some examples of simple non-linear transfer functions and their effect on the output from the wavetable. The effect of the transfer function can be made sensitive to the amplitude of the stored sine wave—at low amplitudes the function is linear, but as the amplitude increases so does the non-linearity. The technique generates periodic (harmonic) waveforms; however, inharmonic spectra similar to those created by FM can be achieved by simple extensions to the basic process, for example by amplitude or ring modulating the output of the non-linear processor.

Waveshaping thus offers similar facilities to those offered by FM, to which it is quite closely related. Complex timbral modification can be created by simple means, and this modification can be made amplitude-sensitive and thus reflect the behaviour of acoustic instrumental sounds. The transfer function can be drawn empirically, or it can be calculated by mathematical formulae such as Chebyshev polynomials, which give precise control of the harmonics arising from the waveshaping process. The degree of 'predictability' of the results is then considerably higher than is the case with FM synthesis. For this reason an adaptation of the technique was adopted by Casio for their 'CZ' range of synthesizers, under the name 'Phase Distortion'.

(e) Other Wavetable Techniques

Clearly the contents of a wavetable need not be confined to simple waveforms. The non-linear processing described above could equally well be applied to a digital sample of an acoustic sound. The use of samples as synthesis building blocks is a classic application of computer techniques, and since the mid-1980s has become increasingly important in the commercial world as the falling cost of computer chips has combined with higher processing speeds and greater sophistication in software.

As explained above, the attack of an acoustic instrument is usually the most timbrally complex part of the sound, and the most difficult to synthesize. It is also, in many cases, very short in relation to the sound as a whole. Sounds in this category include the 'chiff' at the start of flute tones, the scrape of a violin bow on the string, and the 'lip' noise at the start of a brass sound. On the other hand, the sampling of an entire note demands a great deal of memory, with little scope for modification in performance by comparison with the synthesized equivalent.

An effective and elegant solution to this problem is to use synthesis techniques to create the steady-state part of the sound, but to use a sample for the attack portion—the two components of the sound can be simply spliced sequentially, or the sample can be mixed with the beginning of the synthesized sound. These two basic techniques, splicing and mixing, applied to the combination of sampled and synthesized sounds, have formed the basis for a number of proprietary sample/synthesis methods developed by commercial manufacturers. The ESQ1 (1986) by Ensoniq was one of the first such instruments to be developed; other manufacturers to produce similar products include Roland (the D50, 1987, in which the technique was termed 'linear arithmetic synthesis'), Korg (the M1 workstation, 1988), and Kawai (the K1, 1988).

(f) Other Processing Techniques

Some techniques well established among computer music researchers and composers have remained, so far, unexploited in commercial instruments. 'Linear predictive coding' (LPC) is one of a family of analysis/resynthesis techniques developed in the search for techniques for speech encoding, transmission, and reception (see VOCODER) and is still the most widely used technique for computer-generated speech. LPC attempts to estimate the spectrum of a sound in terms of the filter coefficients (see FILTER 2) which would be needed to synthesize that sound when applied to an 'excitation source', which may be either noise (for unvoiced sounds), or a band-limited pulse wave in which all the harmonics are of equal amplitude. In a synthesis application, both the excitation waveform and the filter coefficients can be modified (in both the frequency and time domains) to create related variants of the original sound.

The 'phase vocoder' was first documented in 1966 but has only been popular since the mid-1970s; a complex signal-processing technique which includes elements of LPC, it uses continuous and overlapping Fourier transforms of a sound for several related objectives, ranging from resynthesis, and timbral interpolation from one sound to another, to 'time-stretching' (altering the speed of a sampled sound without affecting the pitch) and 'pitch shifting' (transposition of a sound without altering the speed). The phase vocoder is so called to distinguish it from the more familiar 'channel' vocoder.

A potentially significant technique is 'granular synthesis', first proposed as early as 1946 by the physicist Dennis Gabor, in the context of an inquiry into the theory of hearing. Taking his cue from quantum physics, Gabor proposed that sound was made up of 'grains' or musical quanta—these were the shortest sounds that could be discriminated by the ear. The duration of a grain is felt to lie mostly within a range of 10 to 50 milliseconds. In his book *Formalised Music* (1971) the composer and mathematician Iannis Xenakis took up the theory and developed a compositional approach drawing on computer techniques.

Granular synthesis draws on the principle of additive synthesis (since a sound demands the addition of perhaps thousands of grains) and also offers possibilities for sound transformation. In addition to the direct synthesis of grains, acoustic sounds can be 'granulated', and the parameters of pitch and time then separated as in phase vocoding. One of the first composers to use the technique was the American Curtis Roads, who in the course of a series of experiments starting in 1975 composed several pieces using the technique either in part or, in the case of 'Prototype' (1975), throughout. More recent research (1988) by Barry Truax has concentrated on methods of controlling granular synthesis in real time.

The sound world of granular synthesis is perhaps best understood by analogy with computer graphics, in which 'particle synthesis' is used to create images of smoke, clouds, fire, and water. It is thus, like the other specialized techniques described above, likely to be used as an adjunct to other techniques, rather than as a technique for general synthesis purposes.

More recent research at IRCAM (see COMPUTER 3(c)) by Xavier Rodet and others has resulted in the development of 'formant wave function' synthesis, or 'FOF' synthesis, to use the French title (*forme d'onde formantique*). It was developed as part of IRCAM's 'CHANT' project, which was devoted to the development of techniques for the realistic synthesis of the singing voice. It models the human voice as the sound from an impulse generator (equivalent to the vocal cords) passing through a set of band-pass filters (representing the characteristics of the vocal tract), each filter corresponding to a vocal formant (see ACOUSTICS 3).

Since the output from the impulse generator can be considered as a sequence of 'grains', the technique can be seen to be closely related to granular synthesis, the difference being that in FOF the grains are regular and synchronous, generating a coherent periodic waveform. FOF is a powerful but computationally expensive technique, capable of creating a wide range of instrumental and abstract timbres as well as convincing vocal imitations.

Synthesizer

A synthesizer is a system of electronic circuits, either *analogue or *digital, or a combination of both, for the creation of sounds, using one or more methods of sound synthesis (see SYNTHESIS II). Implicit in this definition is the assumption that a synthesizer is in the conventional sense a musical 'instrument' which can be played. This in turn implies that the various parameters which determine the sound can be varied in a controlled and predictable way by the player in 'real time'—there is no noticeable delay between the actions of the player and the output of the synthesizer.

The analogue synthesizer, by its nature, responds in real time, but will be limited, for example, by the general difficulty of providing performance controls for a possibly large number of parameters, especially where the objective is the authentic re-creation of an *acoustic instrument. It will also be limited to the use of the simple geometric *waveforms that can be easily generated by analogue circuits.

The digital synthesizer can, in theory, transcend all such problems, having access to a much wider range of techniques, but is limited in response by the speed of processing—the number of calculations that it can perform in real time.

1. The Analogue Synthesizer

(a) Modular Systems

The only technique that is really practicable using analogue circuits is that of subtractive synthesis, in which harmonically rich source sounds generated by *oscillators are modified by *filters and *envelope generators. Inharmonic sounds have to be generated by techniques such as *amplitude and *ring modulation. Filters need to be sufficiently powerful to isolate individual harmonics of a complex *timbre, and a single pitch out of white *noise.

Each of these functions can be implemented by a self-contained analogue circuit, which can thus be regarded as a 'module'. The development of voltage control (see SYNTHESIS II 2) made it possible for any module to control, and be controlled by, any other module, without fear of any signal mismatch. Signals can be summed or split by appropriate modules to enable, for example, a number of modules to receive the same control signal. Modules would ideally be housed in a mainframe or 'rack' which can supply power to each.

The early, fully modular systems gave the synthesist complete control over the choice of modules and the connections between them, made by 'patch cords'. Each particular configuration was thus known as a 'patch', a term that is still widely used even in the context of fully digital instruments, in which voice configurations are stored in memory.

While such freedom was necessary in the context of an experimental electronic music studio, the complexity and physical inconvenience of the patch cord system was a major hindrance to the fluent use of the system. This could only be overcome if the selection of modules was fixed at the time of manufacture. This approach was favoured by *ARP and the British company *EMS, who developed a series of modular but self-contained instruments which linked each module to a matrix board or 'patch panel'. Each socket in the panel corresponded to a particular signal path, which was activated by the simple process of inserting a 'patch pin'. Not only did this method completely eliminate the need for patch cords, it also made the documentation of module connections much easier.

(b) Portable and Self-Contained Instruments

The large-scale modular systems described above were designed to meet the demands of 'classical' electronic music composition. The selection and interconnection of modules was an important aspect of the composition process. The keyboard was itself a module, a source of control signals, that might or might not be needed for a given patch. For many applications, such as the imitation of acoustic instruments, a single basic configuration controlled from a keyboard was sufficient, and could be manufactured at relatively low cost in a lightweight console.

Fig. I illustrates the basic subtractive synthesis configuration for a single 'voice'. The physical layout of the synthesizer usually reflected the sequence of modules, from the VCOs on the left to the VCAs on the right. Early instruments used rotary controls (potentiometers or 'pots'), but later it became fashionable to use linear sliders, which gave a clear visual indication of settings for any patch.

The 'pitch-bend' and 'modulation' control wheels were features of *Moog synthesizers that rapidly became established as necessary standard fittings. The pitch-bend wheel was sprung with a central detent so that on its release it would return rapidly to the centre position. Its control range could be altered so that full deflexion would bend between a semitone and an octave. The modulation wheel controlled the LFO and was free-moving—it could be either left in a set position or adjusted for dynamic vibrato effects. The LFO trigger button was normally a separate control, but sometimes was incorporated into the pitch-bend wheel—an arrangement associated particularly with Roland instruments. Early Moog instruments included a 'ribbon' controller above the keyboard for portamento effects.

The performance controls were placed at the left hand of the keyboard, the latter usually having a range of three octaves (thirty-seven notes), which was sufficient for a monophonic instrument. The oscillators themselves had a much wider compass, typically from 16 ft to 2 ft in switched ranges. The

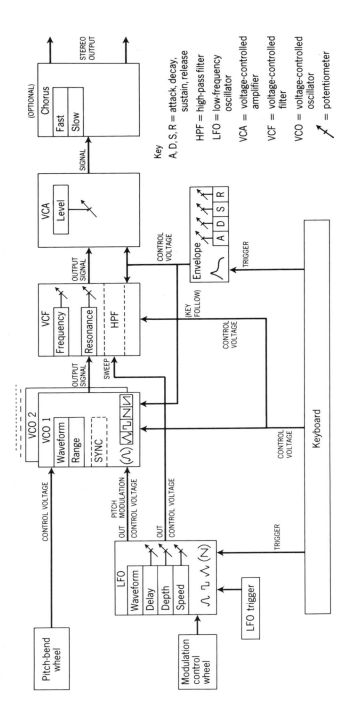

Fig. I. SUBTRACTIVE SYNTHESIS. Basic Voice Configuration.

keyboard was played by the right hand, the left hand being devoted to the performance controls and to parameter changes 'on the fly'.

In the context of a rock group, the synthesizer was used mainly for 'lead' (melodic) lines, often modelled on the gestures of rock guitarists (hence the importance of the pitch-bend wheel), and bass sounds, as a contrast to the bass guitar. Percussive effects were also popular, stimulating the parallel development of dedicated *percussion synthesizers and controllers (see DRUM MACHINE, DRUM PAD).

2. Digital Control

The latter half of the 1970s was a period of rapid progress in electronic *component design. The development of the single-chip computer ('microprocessor') initiated a dramatic increase in the production of memory and other support chips, an increase which was accompanied by falling prices. Parallel to this development was that of the general miniaturization of analogue circuits. Analogue synthesizers benefited considerably from all these developments.

(a) Polyphony

The single most important development arising out of the new technology was that of keyboard-controlled polyphonic voicing. Instead of a direct connection between the keyboard and the synthesis electronics, the keyboard is 'scanned' at high speed, and the identities of all active keys are translated into digital codes which are assigned to each voice in turn, up to the limit of the instrument. As each key is released, the voice it controlled is free to respond to a new key-press. Once all the voices have been assigned, further key-presses can have no effect, unless a voice is reassigned from an existing key to the new key. There are a number of ways of 'note stealing'—the lowest voice may be sacrificed, or the least recent note may be reassigned. The process as a whole is known as 'dynamic voice allocation' and will vary somewhat from model to model. It is also possible to assign more than one voice (possibly all of them) to a single key, for the creation of more powerful sounds.

The 'Prophet V' from Sequential Circuits, introduced in 1978, is regarded as the first modern-style polyphonic instrument, though Oberheim had introduced a comparatively primitive four-voice instrument two years earlier. The Prophet V offered five voices, each with two oscillators, played from a five-octave keyboard (sixty-one notes). This is still regarded as the standard length for a polyphonic synthesizer. The controls were arranged as for a monophonic instrument, but this time affected all the voices uniformly.

(b) Memory

The second valuable facility made possible by digital electronics was that of patch memory. Whereas in the case of the keyboard it was sufficient to know if a key was up or down, in order to record a patch the precise value of each variable parameter has to be converted into a digital code (see ANALOGUE TO DIGITAL CONVERSION) which can then be stored in memory for later immediate recall. Reserve ('back-up') power from a battery can be used to preserve the data in memory when the instrument is switched off.

Memory that can be programmed by the user is known as 'RAM'—random-access memory (see COMPUTER 4(b)). Read-only memory (ROM) can also be used by the manufacturer for permanent storage of patches, which are thus known as 'presets'. These serve not only to give the synthesist an immediate repertoire of good sounds, but also to advertise the power of the instrument to prospective purchasers. As synthesizers have become more and more complex, it has become common practice to create a new patch not from first principles but by adapting an existing preset.

(c) Electronic Control

Analogue circuits can be subject to instability. This is most noticeable in oscillators, which can drift in pitch to an unacceptable degree. Instruments often had to be left for some time after they were switched on so that component temperatures could stabilize. Digital circuits can be used to prevent this drift by monitoring, and where necessary correcting, the oscillator frequency. An oscillator so controlled is thus described not as a 'VCO' but as a 'DCO'—'digitally controlled oscillator'. Such an instrument has clearly left the original voltage control standard far behind, as digital electronics take over the task of controlling and connecting the analogue circuits. Benefits gained from this degree of digital control include increased possibilities for modulation and the ability to control many, perhaps all, of a voice's parameters remotely from a digital *sequencer.

3. The Digital Synthesizer

It is important to distinguish between those features of a synthesizer that are common to all modern designs and those that are particularly characteristic of digital synthesis. The latter may be summarized as follows:

Increased polyphony. In an analogue synthesizer each additional voice requires additional circuitry; in digital synthesis a voice can be implemented entirely in software, so that in theory there is no limit to the possible polyphony, though in practice real-time instruments are limited by processing speed. Nevertheless, digital synthesizers have generally offered many more than the six or eight voices common on analogue instruments. The Yamaha DX7 (1983), one of the first mass-market instruments, offered sixteen voices, a figure itself exceeded by more recent designs.

Wide range of synthesis techniques. Techniques (see SYNTHESIS II 3) which have been exploited commercially include FM (Yamaha), waveshaping (Casio), and additive (*Fairlight, *Synclavier, and others), as well as a variety of techniques (from manufacturers too numerous to mention) based on stored (sampled) wavetables.

Versatility in creating inharmonic timbres. Subtractive synthesis takes as its starting-point either noise or a harmonic waveform. There is no direct means of creating inharmonic sounds. Digitally implemented techniques such as those listed above can create inharmonic timbres directly. FM in particular is celebrated for the ease with which it can create 'metallic' and similar inharmonic sounds.

Increased frequency range. Analogue circuits tend to suffer from both low- and high-frequency 'roll-off'—a drop in signal level. With digital techniques both extreme low (sub-audio) and high frequencies can be generated at full amplitude; the high-frequency limit is set by the sampling rate (see ANALOGUE TO DIGITAL CONVERSION), and of course by the final analogue output stage. Digital instruments are generally considered to produce typically 'bright' sounds, compared with the 'warm' sounds characteristic of analogue circuits. One potentially hazardous consequence of this wide range is that loudspeakers may be damaged by high-level signals in the extreme frequency ranges.

Wide dynamic range. Subtractive synthesis uses filters to shape the spectrum; these filters can markedly reduce the energy in a sound, which has to be restored by amplification, which in turn will amplify any *noise present in the signal. The 'signal to noise' (S/N) ratio is thus reduced. A well-designed digital instrument can 'rescale' a low-amplitude signal without adding any noise. The S/N ratio is determined by the number of *bits used to represent amplitude—a sixteen-bit synthesizer can thus achieve a ratio comparable to that of compact disk. (See, however, NOISE, for a description of the 'quantization noise' which can be generated by digital synthesizers and signal processors.)

4. The Modern Synthesizer

The term 'modern' is here understood to apply to synthesizers which incorporate the *MIDI communications *interface. The first instrument to include MIDI was the 'Prophet 600' by Sequential Circuits, introduced in 1982, a year which can thus be regarded as a watershed in synthesizer design. In view of the rapid pace of development which would make any definition of a synthesizer instantly obsolete, the following descriptions should be understood as trends; only the hardware aspects of the modern synthesizer can realistically be said to be at all established or standard features.

(a) The Keyboard

As noted above, the standard length of keyboard for a polyphonic synthesizer is five octaves, though both four- and six-octave instruments have been produced. The most important refinement to the basic keyboard is the provision of velocity sensitivity. The time taken for a key to be pressed is measured, and the derived value is used to affect, for example, the volume of the sound. Additionally, a keyboard may be pressure-sensitive; as the name suggests, the finger pressure is measured and the derived signal can be used to modulate any suitable parameter, such as volume, LFO speed, and so on. In most instruments the keys are made of plastic, with a simple sprung action. An alternative is the 'weighted' keyboard, possibly with wooden keys, which seeks to emulate the feel of an acoustic piano.

(b) Performance Controls

The pitch-bend and modulation wheels, as described above, remain standard fittings, which can, however, be programmed to affect almost any parameter. Some instruments have included in addition a joystick, which can be used either to control two parameters simultaneously or to vary the relative levels of up to four wavetables in a complex sound (e.g. the Sequential Circuits 'Prophet VS'). The use of digital parameter access (see below) makes 'on-the-fly' alteration of voice parameters all but impossible, even assuming that the keyboard is still played with only one hand. Some instruments allow the use of a foot pedal as an alternative to the manual data entry control. Roland have provided optional remote programmers (carrying sliders for all the principal parameters) for many of their instruments.

In addition to a standard sustain pedal, most instruments provide for a pedal to be used to change patch, following either the internal incremental sequence or a user-programmed sequence of patch changes.

(c) Data Storage and Recall

Early instruments used audio cassettes (as also used by some early personal computers) for storage of patch and sequence data. This was superseded by the removable memory cartridge, available in both ROM (preset sounds) and RAM (for user programming) versions. It is provided with battery back-up to prevent data loss. Cartridges can be inserted and removed in a matter of seconds, and the synthesizer includes a software switch so that either the cartridge or the internal voices can be used. A more modern version of the cartridge is the memory card, which by virtue of its thinness is especially suited to use in rack-mounted synthesizer modules.

For a greater storage capacity the floppy disk (originally $5\frac{1}{4}$ inches, now replaced by the $3\frac{1}{2}$-inch 'micro-floppy disk') is in very general use. Even the synthesizer's operating system can be loaded from disk; this enables the instrument to be updated simply by issuing a new operating-system disk.

Any personal computer fitted with a MIDI interface can be used to store and edit patch data. The most popular computers for this purpose are the *Apple 'Macintosh' and the *Atari 'ST' series; the latter has its own built-in MIDI interface.

(d) Input and Output

The performance control inputs are described above. The MIDI interface must include IN and OUT ports; the THRU port is useful for channelling data through one instrument to the next, but is not essential. Worthy of special mention is the breath controller interface which Yamaha have included on all their instruments, and for which special modulation parameters are provided (see, especially, WIND SYNTHESIZERS AND CONTROLLERS).

Most early instruments provided a simple monophonic line output socket for direct connection to a mixer or to a stage amplifier ('combo'). In modern instruments a stereo output is expected; in the case of multi-timbral instruments (see below) the ideal is for a separate audio output to be provided for each individual voice. A general stereo output should still be provided, not least because such instruments can usually provide for multi-timbral voices to be panned within the stereo field. The headphone output may be provided separately, or will be incorporated into the line output in some way.

(e) Programming

A major proportion of the cost of a synthesizer is devoted to the mechanical parts—the keyboard, performance controls, knobs, and switches. To save costs manufacturers have cut down on the use of mechanical parameter controls in favour of 'digital parameter access' (sometimes called 'single-parameter access'), which uses a single rotary or linear controller in conjunction with a relatively small number of buttons which are used to select the desired parameter. The effect of parameter changes is reported on a central display (see COMPONENTS 7(b)), which may give a sizeable graphic display or as little as a single line of information.

Although undoubtedly less immediate than the traditional mechanical controls, digital parameter access has the advantage that many more parameters are made available to the programmer than would otherwise be practicable. Yamaha's original DX7, for example, provided the user with 64 voices (32 internal and 32 external in one bank of a cartridge), 145 voice parameters, and 23 performance parameters, all accessed by a total of 42 membrane switches, 1 incremental control, and 3 performance controls.

5. Performance and Composition Facilities

(a) Multi-Timbral Voicing

Early polyphonic synthesizers were mono-timbral—the same patch settings were used by all the voices. The simplest refinement was that of the 'split' keyboard, in which different patches could be assigned, for example, to the two halves of the keyboard's range. From the point of view of MIDI, each patch would be assigned its own channel. Thus on the one hand the two halves of the keyboard could control different external instruments; on the other a sequencer could address each patch independently. The modern 'multi-split' keyboard divides the keyboard into a series of ranges, perhaps eight, each of which plays a specified patch. A *sampler may take this principle much further, to the extent that each key may be assigned a different sound.

Full multi-timbral operation allows each voice to use a different patch over the whole range. Thus a sixteen-voice digital synthesizer can play sixteen different monophonic patches simultaneously. Clearly this is impossible from the keyboard; the facility can be exploited only by use of a polyphonic MIDI sequencer which can address each voice using a different MIDI channel. A multi-timbral instrument can also be played very effectively from a MIDI *guitar controller, each string transmitting over a different channel.

(b) Auto-Play Facilities

Many early analogue polyphonic synthesizers were provided with *arpeggiators similar to those commonly found in electronic *organs and home keyboards. In addition to its conventional application, the arpeggiator could also be used in conjunction with unusual patch settings for the creation of complex and dynamic sound effects.

A more valuable addition to the polyphonic synthesizer is a built-in sequencer. Early examples were limited to a few hundred notes programmed in 'step time', and were thus used mainly for the generation of ostinato figures. The modern keyboard-based sequencer has many of the features of stand-alone sequencers, including both real-time and step-time recording, multi-timbral operation, and comprehensive editing facilities, though without computer-based editing facilities it is much more awkward to use.

(c) Internal Signal Processors

The only signal processor normally built into analogue synthesizers was 'chorus' (see DELAY LINE 3), which gave a sense of movement and depth to otherwise rather thin, static sounds. All other effects had to be added by external equipment. It is now common for digital synthesizers to include functions such as delay, *reverb, and *equalization (in addition to any digital filters included as part of the voice architecture), with a flexibility of use and signal quality comparable to those of specialized 'multi-effects' units.

T

Telharmonium

Invented by the American Thaddeus Cahill (1867–1934) and patented in 1896, the Telharmonium (also known as the 'Dynamophone') was a remarkably imaginative and advanced concept that due to considerable technical and financial problems was never fully realized in terms of the original patent. It was the first instrument to apply the principle of 'additive' *synthesis. The sound was generated by means of massive metal wheels or 'rheotomes'; cogs on the rotating wheels passed over fixed brushes to create an electrical oscillation. The enormous size was required to develop sufficient signal power (in the absence at that time of any means of amplification) for direct connection to the telephone network. Twelve 'pitch shafts' were used (one for each note of the chromatic scale), and each shaft carried a number of tone-wheels catering both for different octaves of the same pitch and for up to five harmonics (see ACOUSTICS 1) of the same note.

The instrument was able to achieve convincing imitations of a number of orchestral instruments. In all, Cahill specified 408 rheotomes for an instrument with a seven-octave range. The keyboard itself was 'touch-sensitive'—the harder a key was struck, the louder the sound. The original patent also included a proposal for an electromagnetic speaker; so far as is known this was never developed, and instead the sound was transmitted over ordinary telephone wires to receivers fitted with large paper horns for amplification.

The first telephone music transmissions from a small prototype instrument took place in 1900 in Washington DC. In 1902 Cahill moved to larger premises in Holyoke, Massachusetts, where he completed a second, larger prototype, demonstrated in 1906. Later that year Cahill moved to New York, where he completed the final version—this used 144 rheotomes and weighed over 200 tons. Many formidable technical problems remained, both with the instrument itself and with the use of the telephone network, and Cahill's company ceased in 1911. In the same year the composer Ferruccio

Busoni published *Sketch of a New Aesthetic in Music*, in which he drew attention to the potential for the accurate creation of microtonal scales, which the instrument made possible.

The Telharmonium was conceptually many years ahead of its time, but based on technology that was already almost obsolete—the triode valve (see COMPONENTS 5), central to the development of truly electronic instruments, was invented in 1906. The touch-sensitive keyboard is a vital element in the modern *synthesizer (see *also* VELOCITY SENSITIVITY), and the tone-wheel method of sound creation was itself used with great success in the *Hammond organ (see *also* ORGAN 1).

Theremin

One of the first electronic instruments (originally called the 'Aetherphon' or 'Thereminvox'), developed by the Russian physicist Lev Sergeyevich Termen in 1919 (he later Westernized his name to Leon Theremin). In common with many other experimental instruments of the period it used the principle of heterodyning, in which two radio-frequency *oscillators are combined to produce difference tones (see ACOUSTICS 2(b)) in the audible range, over a range of some five octaves. While one oscillator had a fixed frequency, that of the other could be altered by movements of the performer's hand towards or away from an antenna. A second antenna could be 'played' by the other hand to control volume. No actual physical contact with the instrument was involved.

The instrument was promoted largely through the recitals given by Clara Rockmore (who like Theremin had arrived in America from Russia in the late 1920s) and was licensed to RCA in 1929 for commercial production, though it did not prove commercially successful. Musically the Theremin had significant limitations, due to the fact that it was difficult to establish precise pitches, portamento and other sliding effects being unavoidable if distinctive characteristics of the sound. In the 1930s various attempts were made to circumvent this problem. Varèse commissioned two keyboard-controlled Theremins for his *Equatorial* (1934); there is, however, some doubt as to whether these instruments were ever completed, and in the published score the Theremins are replaced by two *Ondes Martenot, which were used in the first performance in 1961. Theremin returned to Russia in 1938, leaving the instrument to be developed at the whim of performers, composers, and engineers (see e.g. MOOG). In 1964 he was appointed a professor of *acoustics at Moscow University.

Although gradually eclipsed as a solo and orchestral instrument it became very popular as a source of unearthly sound effects in horror, suspense, and science fiction films. The sound of the Theremin can be created easily with modern transistorized circuitry, and the instrument in this form has been in use since the 1960s, not only in film scores but also occasionally in pop songs, of which the most well-known example is the Beach Boys' 1966 hit 'Good Vibrations'.

Timbre

The term usually used to describe the tonal quality of a musical sound. Technically, the subjective timbre of a sound is closely related to its frequency spectrum, as determined by *analysis. Early attempts to define a single characteristic spectrum as representative of an instrument's timbre are now recognized as inadequate. The *attack of the sound (much relied upon by the ear to identify the instrument) is usually spectrally complex compared to the steady-state portion, and the identity of an instrument derives in most cases from the characteristic spectral evolutions during the course of a note.

While for a given instrument the details of the spectrum may change considerably at different dynamic levels and pitches, the ear nevertheless recognizes these variations as belonging to a single instrument. Modern research now classifies these differences as belonging to a particular timbral 'family', characterized by the presence and relative intensity of a number of spectral peaks or formants (see ACOUSTICS 3). It also recognizes the importance of context in the recognition of timbre, and, therefore, the potential for aural confusion if that context is modified in some way. Timbre is now treated by composers of *computer music as a potentially primary determinant of musical form, much as harmony is in more traditional forms of music. See also SYNTHESIS II.

Time Code

A *digital code recorded on to audio or video tape to synchronize recording machines and related equipment to each other. There are two principal applications: the synchronization of a sound-track recorded on audio tape with the video track on videotape, and the synchronization of two multitrack audio recorders so that they can be used as one extra-large recorder.

The time code used in professional studios is 'SMPTE code', a format standardized by the Society of Motion Picture and Television Engineers. It uses an eighty-*bit *binary 'word' to identify uniquely each video or film 'frame' (which may run at rates between 25 and 30 per second, depending on the format used) over a twenty-four-hour clock, and can be thought of as an extremely accurate 'intelligent' tape counter. The time is recorded in hours, minutes, seconds, and frames. SMPTE code can also include 'user information' such as the track number.

There are four standard frame rates: 30 frames per second (fps) are used for monochrome TV and audio-only recording; 29.97 fps (also known as 'drop-frame') for colour TV to the NTSC video standard used in America and Japan; 25 fps for colour TV to the EBU (European Broadcast Union) standard; and 24 fps for film.

The operating procedure is fairly straightforward. The code is recorded ('striped') on to each recording machine, as a modulated audio square wave (see WAVEFORM) at 1200 Hz. A time code synchronizer reads both time codes and treats one of the machines as the 'master', adjusting the speed of the 'slave' machine to maintain synchronization. As times are differentiated so precisely, a master recorder can be started at any point on the tape, and the slave machine will be instructed by the synchronizer to find the correct place on its own tape. One special feature of the encoding technique used (called 'bi-phase modulation') is that the code can be read not only forwards but also backwards, and at almost any speed. Thus a slave recorder can fast wind in either direction to a specified frame in response to commands from the synchronizer. If 'varispeed' is used to change the running speed of the master machine, the slave can follow the changes precisely.

If a *sequencer (e.g. controlling *MIDI instruments) can itself respond to SMPTE code, audio 'events' (whether music tracks or sound effects) can be synchronized directly to a given film or video frame. MIDI is well able to control the timing between instruments (for example, using 'song position pointers'), but lacks the intelligence of SMPTE code—times are measured relatively (i.e. from the previous mark) rather than absolutely. Nor does MIDI make any provision for the recording of synchronization tracks on to tape; this has to be handled by each sequencer in its own way, for example by recording an audio 'click track' on tape.

In 1987 an extension to the basic 'MIDI 1.0' specification was approved (by the MIDI Manufacturers' Association) which implements the principles of SMPTE code within the MIDI format. It is slightly slower than SMPTE, taking two frames to define the time completely. MIDI time code (MTC) also incorporates 'Set-Up' messages which are used to send a 'cue list' of instructions (e.g. to change patch, reverb setting, and so on) ahead of time to the receiving instrument. A SMPTE–MTC *interface unit is needed to convert between the two formats.

Trautonium

An early monophonic electronic instrument invented by Friedrich Trautwein in Germany between 1928 and 1930. It is noteworthy chiefly for its early application of the principle of subtractive *synthesis, in which different timbres are achieved by the removal of harmonics (see ACOUSTICS) from a harmonically rich source tone. Pitch was controlled by means of an electrically resistive fingerboard, similar in some respects to that used on the *Ondes Martenot developed at the same time.

An early champion of the instrument was Hindemith, who composed a concertino for it in 1931. The following year, Telefunken took up production of the instrument, which subsequently established a significant role in schools throughout Germany. Richard Strauss used the instrument in *Japanese Festival Music*, composed in 1940. In the 1950s Oskar Sala, a pupil of Hindemith and a virtuoso on the original instrument, collaborated with Trautwein on a new version, which was introduced in 1952 as the Mixtur-Trautonium. In the event only the one model was completed, used mostly by Sala as a studio-based source instrument for tape music compositions.

Triangle Wave

See WAVEFORM.

Tuning and Temperament

1. Intervals

The problem of tuning is one that has vexed both musicians and theorists since the time of Pythagoras, if not before, and remains a subject for discussion and experiment today. Since modern keyboard instruments offer considerable degrees of control over pitch, to the extent that many offer not only a selection of pre-set temperaments but the possibility to create one's own, it is necessary to understand something of the principles underlying the construction of scales.

The fundamental unit for any study of tuning is the octave, corresponding to a frequency ratio of 2:1. This octave can be divided into a 'natural' scale of seven notes, each of which may be flattened or sharpened by a semitone, giving a basic notational scale of twenty-one pitches—twenty-two if one includes the final octave itself.

The mathematical theory of consonance states that the simpler the frequency ratio between two notes, the less the dissonance. Thus, after the octave, the least dissonant interval is the perfect fifth, represented by a ratio of 3:2. By adding fifths (mathematically, by multiplying their ratios) it is possible to derive the seven tones of the natural scale. More interestingly, it is possible by adding twelve fifths to arrive at a pitch seven octaves above the starting tone. The problem of tuning arises from the fact that these two pitches are not in fact the same (as the calculation of the ratios would reveal): the pitch reached by twelve fifths is significantly sharper than that reached by seven octaves, by approximately a quarter of a semitone. This difference is known as the 'ditonic' or 'Pythagorean' comma and is given by the cumbersome ratio 531,441:524,288 (or $(\frac{3}{2})^{12}:2^{7}$). Ideally it should be equal to 1.

2. Scales and Temperament

The important consequence of this inequality is that it is not possible to construct a twelve-tone chromatic scale in which all the fifths are pure. The problem becomes even more acute if it is also desired to tune the thirds pure. The pure (or 'just') major third has the ratio 5:4 (equivalent to the interval between the fifth and fourth harmonics of the harmonic series—see ACOUSTICS); the difference between this tone and that derived from five ascending fifths is the 'syntonic' comma, ratio 81:80.

These conflicts are of relatively little consequence to singers, and players of instruments with fine pitch control, since they can continually make small adjustments to control intonation. The notes of the scale have a built-in degree of variability—the same note may be played sharper or flatter according to context. However, a practical keyboard must necessarily compromise between these conflicting criteria. The history of temperament is the history of efforts to find the most acceptable compromise, between the desire for pure thirds and fifths on the one hand, and the desire to play in all keys on the other. (This last requirement is of course peculiar to

Western music; oriental scales, for example, often include intervals remote from those derived from the natural scale. One of the most advanced tuning systems outside the West, and possibly of greater antiquity, is that of Indian classical music. The octave is divided into twenty-two intervals or 'srutis', to each of which is attributed a distinctive emotional character or 'expression', and from which a selection is made according to the râg. There is some evidence to suggest that the srutis combine both Pythagorean and just chromatic scales.)

A 'tempered' scale is one in which selected intervals are stretched or shrunk by precise amounts. The more thirds and fifths that are kept pure, the more other intervals become discordant and ultimately unusable. While the need to play in a wide range of keys is moderate, satisfactory 'mean-tone' tunings can be constructed in a variety of ways. Whereas pure intervals can be tuned by listening for and eliminating beats (see ACOUSTICS 2(b)), tempered intervals have to be found by tuning to precise beat rates, a skilled and time-consuming process.

In equal temperament, each fifth is reduced by the precise amount required to fit twelve within the octave, i.e. by one-twelfth of the Pythagorean comma. The octave is indeed the only pure interval, and the thirds are noticeably sharp. On the piano, if a low note is struck with a note two octaves and a major third higher (corresponding to the fifth harmonic), beats can clearly be heard.

In practice, things are a little more complicated, since the high stiffness of piano strings has the effect of sharpening the harmonics slightly. Piano tuners often tune by 'stretching' the octaves to eliminate octave beats. This has the added advantage of reducing the burden on the fifths somewhat. This phenomenon has been exploited in a recent proposal (1974) by the French tuner and mathematician Serge Cordier that the tuning be based on a division of the perfect fifth into seven equally tempered semitones. Advantages claimed include a reduced tuning time (seven semitones to be tempered rather than twelve), a better intonation when accompanying string players, and a systematic stretching of all octaves.

3. Interval Calculations: The Cent

To circumvent the awkward dependence on numerical ratios in describing intervals, the logarithmic unit of the cent, introduced by A. J. Ellis in the nineteenth century, is in very general use. The octave is divided into 1,200 parts, the cent being defined as the twelve-hundredth root of 2, approximately 1.00057779. The equally tempered semitone thus equals 100 cents. For simple calculations of frequencies in equal temperament the semitone ratio 1.059463 : 1 (the twelfth root of 2) can be used. To convert a ratio into cents, the logarithm of the ratio must be multiplied by a constant 3986.3137; the errors arising if the more convenient number 4,000 is used will be inconsequential for most purposes. The Pythagorean comma, for example, will be found to be approximately 24 cents. Appendix 3 gives comparative tables of tempered, Pythagorean, and just scales.

V

Velocity Sensitivity

Also 'touch sensitivity'. In an electronic keyboard, the detection of the speed (hence the force) with which a key is struck, to give a measure of the intended volume of the sound. The ability to respond dynamically to touch is natural to mechanical and electromechanical instruments such as the *piano (see also RHODES, CLAVINET). In a fully electronic instrument such as a *synthesizer or *sampler, control of intensity (which might also entail a control of the *timbre of the sound) must be performed electronically, in response to a suitable signal from the keyboard. The simplest method is to design each key to locate between two electrical contacts at the extreme up and down positions of the key. When the key is depressed, the time between the breaking of the first contact and the making of the second gives a direct measurement of velocity. A more sophisticated opto-electrical technique, which avoids most of the electrical and mechanical disadvantages of the contact method, uses beams of light (electrically and mechanically isolated from the main control system) instead of direct electrical contacts.

One interesting by-product of velocity sensing is that the same hardware can also give a measurement of the *release velocity, which can, for example, be used to affect the release time of a synthesizer's *envelope generator. Both attack and release velocity measurements are catered for in the specification for *MIDI. See also AFTER-TOUCH.

Vocoder

A *signal processor which enables the *timbre of one signal to be modified by that of another. The original vocoder (the word is derived from 'voice coder') was developed in 1936 at Bell Laboratories by Homer Dudley as a method for encoding, and thus reducing the bandwidth of speech signals. (The term 'bandwidth' here signifies the amount of information either in a signal or which can be carried by a communications channel.) The classic musical application of the vocoder is to impose the formant characteristics of the voice (see ACOUSTICS 3(b)) on some other signal, perhaps from a *synthesizer.

The basic working unit of the vocoder is an *analysis 'channel' comprising a pair of band-pass *filters. The first, acting on the modulating or control signal, measures the signal strength at a particular band of frequencies; this measurement is then used to control the resonance of the second filter, acting on the carrier signal. If the centre frequency of the channel corresponds to a spectral peak or formant in the modulating signal, the carrier signal will have that part of its spectrum correspondingly emphasized. A practical vocoder may have between eight and twenty channels, ensuring that, for example, the formant characteristics of the voice are well captured.

Beyond this basic structure, manufacturers have developed their own specialized and distinctive features. The most powerful vocoder was probably the 'Syntovox 221' from the Dutch company Synton, with twenty channels over a five-octave range, each with a maximum 54 dB/oct. slope (see DECIBEL), connected to a 20 × 20 patch panel. External *computer control was also possible. The *Buchla 'Programmable Spectral Processor' could be used under computer control as a vocoder, a graphic *equalizer, or as two eight-channel filter banks. The Roland 'VP-330 Vocoder Plus' combined the functions of a vocoder and synthesizer, with a four-octave keyboard which could play chords using the 'Strings' or 'Human Choir' presets as raw material for the vocoder section. More recently, the Korg 'DVP-1 Digital Voice Processor' (1985) offered, in addition to conventional vocoding effects, formant shifting and polyphonic pitch shifting or 'harmonising' (see DELAY LINE 3(d)), all under *MIDI control. Other manufacturers to develop vocoders include *EMS, *Moog, and Sennheiser. For a description of related digital processing techniques, see SYNTHESIS II 3(f).

Voltage Control

See ARP, BUCHLA, EMS, MOOG, SYNTHESIS II, SYNTHESIZER.

Voltage-Controlled Filter (VCF)

See FILTER, SYNTHESIS II 2, SYNTHESIZER I.

Voltage-Controlled Oscillator (VCO)

See OSCILLATOR, SYNTHESIS II 2, SYNTHESIZER I.

W

Wah-Wah

An early electronic *signal processor used widely by players of the electric *guitar. It is basically a tunable resonating low-pass *filter, whose cut-off frequency is under the control of a foot pedal, allowing sweeping tonal changes while playing. The name derives from the characteristic 'ooh-wah' effect caused by the rapid removal and restoration of high frequencies. It has now fallen somewhat out of fashion, having been superseded by processors using *analogue and *digital signal *delay techniques such as 'phasing' and 'flanging'.

Waveform

A waveform is a graphic representation of the variations of some continuous signal with respect to time. The waveform of a sound (see ACOUSTICS) represents the changes in air pressure (*amplitude) that are caused by excitation of the air by, for example, a musical instrument. That disturbance can be detected by a transducer such as a microphone and converted into an electrical signal, the waveform of which can then be displayed by an oscilloscope (see COMPONENTS 7(b)). Alternatively, these electrical signals may be generated directly by electronic circuits—see OSCILLATOR, also SYNTHESIS I, II.

Audio and electronic engineers need to define waveforms very precisely, in mathematical terms, so that they can predict and control the effect on a waveform of a circuit through which it passes, or so that a circuit can be designed (or a program written for a *computer) which creates that waveform.

It should be understood that this is not the only way in which a sound may be defined. A waveform represents the signal as it changes with time—it is a 'time-domain' representation. The sound can also be represented in the

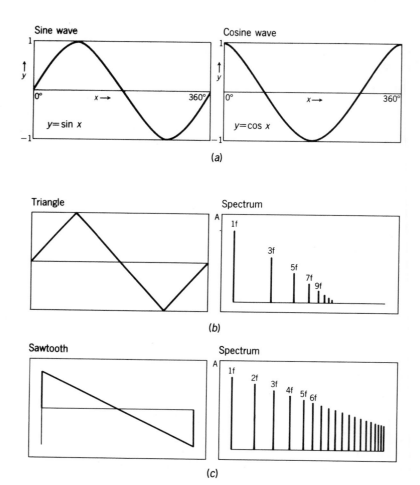

Fig. 1. WAVEFORM. (a) The spectra of these waveforms show only the absolute magnitude of each harmonic, and do not take account of any relative phase differences. (b) Triangle: Harmonics decrease by 12dB/Oct, i.e. inversely as square of harmonic number. Thus with a fundamental of amplitude A, harmonic 3 = A/9, harmonic 5 = A/25 and so on. (c) Sawtooth: Harmonics decrease by 6dB/Oct, i.e. in inverse relation to harmonic No: A,A/2,A/3 etc. (d) The square wave contains odd harmonics only, decreasing by 6dB/Oct.

Square wave (50% ($\frac{1}{2}$) duty cycle)

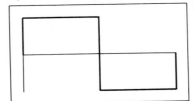

Spectrum

A

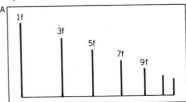

Pulse width (25% ($\frac{1}{4}$) duty cycle)

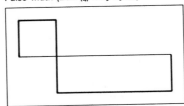

Spectrum

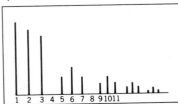

Pulse width (16.6% ($\frac{1}{6}$) duty cycle)

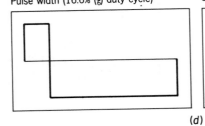

Spectrum

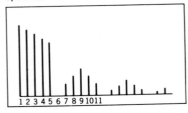

(d)

'frequency domain'; this is known as the 'spectrum' of the sound, giving a picture of the *timbre of the sound. A number of sophisticated *analysis techniques have been developed, many requiring the use of a computer, which can convert ('transform') the representation of a signal from the time domain to the frequency domain, and vice versa (the 'inverse transform'). Musicians interested in sound synthesis need to understand both representations, as they need to know the details of the spectrum of the waveforms that are being used in the synthesis process.

1. Periodic Waveforms

The simplest possible sound consists of a signal whose spectrum contains one frequency component only, such as the sine wave (see Fig. 1), represented mathematically by the formula $y = \sin x$. Since the values of the sine function vary for all values of x between the limits of ± 1, this formula defines a sine wave (theoretically of infinite length) with an *amplitude of 1. Each point on the waveform represents the 'instantaneous amplitude' of the waveform at that point. Also shown is the cosine wave. Though rarely mentioned in informal discussions of musical waveforms, it is of considerable theoretical importance. It is equivalent to a sine wave (i.e. it is 'sinusoidal' in form) shifted to the left by a quarter of a cycle, corresponding to a *phase difference of 90 degrees. Such phase shifts are not perceived directly by the ear, but 'cancellation effects' can occur when waveforms are combined. Two otherwise identical waveforms opposite in phase will cancel each other completely. A complete analysis of a complex sound must therefore include a measurement of phase as well as amplitude for each partial, which can be done by exploiting the many trigonometric and other algebraic relationships between the sine and cosine functions.

Different amplitudes can be created by multiplying $\sin x$ by different values. If those values also change with time, the waveform ceases to be a 'pure' sine wave. The result is that the now *distorted sine wave carries additional overtones or 'partials'—new sinusoidal frequency components have been added to the spectrum. If the sine wave is distorted in such a way that the periods of all the added partials fit into the same fundamental period, it is (as is the sound itself) deemed to be 'harmonic'. Mathematically, this means that each partial has a frequency which is an integer multiple of the fundamental.

Fig. 1(b) illustrates the waveforms, and associated spectra, most easily generated by electronic circuits, and thus most often used in an analogue *synthesizer. An inharmonic waveform is rather difficult to illustrate, since by definition the waveform does not repeat—for example the waveform of *noise, which contains, in theory, all frequencies, at random amplitudes and phases. See also SYNTHESIS II, Fig. 1(b).

The 'geometric' waveforms such as the triangle, sawtooth, and square waves have sharp changes of direction. This implies the presence of infinitely high harmonics. In practice, such waveforms are 'band-limited' by the finite high-frequency response or *bandwidth of the circuit. The effect in each case is to add a slight rounding to the peak of the waveform and ripples to the previously straight lines. As the bandwidth is reduced, for example by means of a low-pass *filter, the rounding and rippling becomes more and more pronounced, until only a sine wave remains. Alternatively, it is possible to approximate such waveforms by the addition of successive (sinusoidal) harmonics with the appropriate amplitudes and phases.

The square wave is one of a family of 'pulse' waves, in this case one with a 50 per cent 'duty cycle' (see Fig. 1(c)). As that proportion is changed, the spectrum also changes. This is the basis of the 'pulse width modulation' (PWM) which many synthesizers provide with a square-wave oscillator. The square wave should not be confused with the waveform in digital circuits. The square wave alternates between equal positive and negative peaks, whereas a digital pulse wave varies between zero (DC) and either positive or negative.

For information on the digital representation of analogue waveforms, see ANALOGUE TO DIGITAL CONVERSION; also SAMPLER. See also SYNTHESIS II 3.

Wind Synthesizers and Controllers

The 'Lyricon' was the first instrument which enabled wind players to control a *synthesizer. It was invented and developed by Bill Bernardi and Roger Noble from 1972 and marketed between 1974 and 1981 by Computone, which Bernardi had started in 1970 in Hanover, Massachusetts. The instrument makes no sound of its own; instead a transducer modelled on a clarinet mouthpiece converts breath and lip pressure into electrical signals which are used to control a separate *analogue *synthesis module built into the instrument's carrying case. The cylindrical solid metal body carries conventionally styled keys (but which function as electrical contact switches) arranged in a simplified Boehm clarinet layout. The basic three-octave range can be extended by transposition to over six octaves. The instrument found favour chiefly among session musicians, and was regularly used on film sound-tracks.

In 1975 the California-based trumpeter Nyle Steiner completed the first prototype of his 'electronic valve instrument' (EVI) or 'electronic trumpet'. Like the Lyricon, it used a specially designed analogue synthesis module to generate sounds. A later model was marketed by Crumar (1979), and won an award at the 1980 'Ars Electronica' festival at Linz. In 1986 the EVI and a complementary EWI (electronic wind instrument) were taken up by Akai and marketed from 1987 as the EVI/EWI-1000. Both instruments use touch-sensitive metal plates rather than moving keys, mounted on a square section metal tube, and arranged respectively to suit either trumpet (EVI) or clarinet and saxophone (EWI) players. Both use the EWV-2000 sound module, which functions as both synthesizer and control unit and also includes a *MIDI *interface for communication with other synthesizers.

Also in 1987 Yamaha introduced their WX7 wind controller, developed in consultation with Sal Gallina, a New York-based session musician and an experienced player of the Lyricon. Unlike the Steiner/Akai instruments, it is exclusively a MIDI controller, though like the EWI it uses saxophone fingering, with additional controls for pitch-bend, octave selection, and MIDI program changes. Response to both breath and lip control is adjustable by means of rotary controls and microswitches built into the upper section of the instrument. A 'key hold' feature enables the player to create and control drones and chords. Yamaha have incorporated breath control, using a simple transducer held in the mouth, in most of their synthesizers since 1983; recent compact synthesis modules such as their TX81Z are natural companions to the WX7.

In 1988 Casio introduced their 'digital horn', a relatively inexpensive instrument looking like a small 'toy' saxophone, but using recorder fingering, and intended for the educational market. It is self-contained, playing preset sounds through a small loudspeaker built into the 'horn' at the base of the instrument. It has a basic two-octave range which can be extended to four with transposition. It can also control external synthesizers through a MIDI interface.

Workstation

This is a generic term applied to an electronic music system which combines the functions of a *synthesizer, *sequencer, *sampler, *drum machine, possibly with *signal-processing and *computer-based editing facilities, in one package. The term is most appropriate to powerful systems such as the

*Fairlight and the *Synclavier, but has also been applied to smaller-scale keyboard instruments which offer all the essentials for composition and performance in one instrument.

Appendix I. Binary and Hexadecimal Conversion Table

Binary (1 byte)	Hexadecimal	Decimal	Binary (1 byte)	Hexadecimal	Decimal
0000 0000	00	00	0001 1111	1F	31
0000 0001	01	01	0010 0000	20	32
0000 0010	02	02			
0000 0011	03	03	0011 1111	3F	63
0000 0100	04	04	0100 0000	40	64
0000 0101	05	05			
0000 0110	06	06	0111 1111	7F	127
0000 0111	07	07			
0000 1000	08	08	1111 1111	FF	255[a]
0000 1001	09	09			
0000 1010	0A	10			
0000 1011	0B	11			
0000 1100	0C	12			
0000 1101	0D	13			
0000 1110	0E	14			
0000 1111	0F	15			
0001 0000	10	16			

[a] this last number is correct only if the byte is an 'unsigned' number.

Appendix 2. MIDI Commands

Channel Commands

Commands consist of a single status byte followed by either 1 or 2 bytes of data. All status bytes are identified by having the leftmost (most significant) bit set to 1.

Status Byte Format

The four least significant bits give the MIDI channel number. These are commonly referred to as channels 1 to 16, but are internally represented as channels 0 to 15 (i.e. '0000' to '1111' binary, '0' to 'F' hexadecimal).

The four most significant bits define the command itself:

Command code		No. of data bytes	Command
Binary	Hexadecimal		
1000 — — — — 8–		2	NOTE OFF
1001 — — — — 9–		2	NOTE ON
1010 — — — — A–		2	POLYPHONIC AFTER-TOUCH
1011 — — — — B–		2	CONTROL CHANGE; channel messages
1100 — — — — C–		1	PROGRAM CHANGE
1101 — — — — D–		1	CHANNEL AFTER-TOUCH
1110 — — — — E–		2	PITCH WHEEL CHANGE

Data Byte Format

For status codes 8– to A– (hexadecimal) the first byte gives the key number, in the range (decimal) 0 to 127; middle C = 60. The second byte gives the key velocity; a value of 0 gives NOTE OFF. Where an instrument is not velocity-sensitive a default value of 64 is sent.

For POLYPHONIC AFTER-TOUCH the second data byte gives the value in the range 0 to 127.

For CONTROL CHANGE the first byte gives the controller number in the range 0 to 121 (see next section), the second byte gives the control value.

For PROGRAM CHANGE the data byte gives the program (patch) number in the range 0 to 127. Individual instruments may represent patch numbers to the player quite differently. Details should be given in the implementation chart.

For CHANNEL AFTER-TOUCH the data byte gives the value in the range 0 to 127. This affects all notes currently sounding. Many instruments can respond to, but not transmit, pressure data.

For PITCH WHEEL CHANGE the two bytes give a fourteen-bit value, the least significant byte (LSB) being sent first. Centre position (no pitch-bend) is set at 2000 hexadecimal. The sensitivity of response to pitch-bend data is set at the receiver.

Control Change Codes: Data Bytes 1 and 2

Byte 1 (control no.)		Function	Byte 2 (value, decimal)
Decimal	Hexadecimal		
0–31	00–1F	Continuous controllers 0–31, MSB	0–127
32–63	20–3F	Continuous controllers 0–31 LSB	0–127
64–95	40–5F	Switches 0–31, status	0 = OFF, 127 = ON
96–121	60–79	Undefined	Undefined
122–127	7A–7F	Channel mode messages (see next section)	

In low resolution only the MSB is sent. In high resolution both MSB and LSB, in that order. If only the LSB changes value, it may be sent without resending the MSB.

Note: a number of controller numbers have been standardized. In particular: 1 (decimal) = modulation wheel, 2 = breath controller, 4 = foot pedal, 7 = volume.

Control Change: Mode Messages Data Bytes 1 and 2

Byte 1 (message)			Byte 2 (value, decimal)
Decimal	Hexadecimal		
122	7A	LOCAL CONTROL	0 = OFF, 127 = ON
123	7B	ALL NOTES OFF	0 (dummy value)
124	7C	OMNI OFF, [a] and ALL NOTES OFF	0 (dummy value)
125	7D	OMNI ON, and ALL NOTES OFF	0 (dummy value)
126	7E	MONO ON[b] (POLY OFF), and ALL NOTES OFF	1–16 (voices)
127	7F	POLY ON (MONO OFF), and ALL NOTES OFF	0 (dummy value)

[a] In OMNI OFF modes, the receiver is set to receive on any basic channel '*n*'.
[b] See note to table below.

Mode	Command	System response
1	OMNI ON/POLY	Voice messages on all channels are recognised and assigned polyphonically
2[a]	OMNI ON/MONO	Voice messages on all channels are recognised and assigned to one voice
3	OMNI OFF/POLY	Voice messages on channel n are recognized and assigned polyphonically
4[a]	OMNI OFF/MONO	Voice messages on channels n, $n + 1$, $n + 2$, etc., are assigned in sequence to the internal voices, up to the limit given in Byte 2 (see table above).

[a] Monophonic note priority is undefined by MIDI, so is dependent on the provision of each manufacturer. Where a choice is given it must either be set manually by the operator or, irregularly, by means of other uncommitted CONTROL CHANGE commands or System Exclusive messages.

System Commands

System Common

Status		Data (binary)	Function
Decimal	Hexadecimal		
241	F1	None	Undefined
242	F2	0 - - - - (LSB)	SONG POSITION POINTER
		0 - - - - (MSB)	
243	F3	0 - - - - (Song Number)	SONG SELECT
244	F4	None	Undefined
245	F5	None	Undefined
246	F6	None	TUNE REQUEST. Instructs analogue synthesizers to tune their oscillators.
247	F7	None	EOX (End of System Exclusive)

SONG POSITION POINTER tells a sequencer or drum machine at which point in a sequence, to a resolution of one MIDI beat (six MIDI clocks), it must start playing. Up to 16,384 MIDI beats can be counted.

SONG SELECT instructs a sequencer or drum machine to jump to a specified 'song' or sequence. Unless instructed otherwise by the Song Position Pointer, the instrument will jump to the start of the specified sequence, and start on receipt of a START command (see below).

System Real Time

Status		Function
Decimal	Hexadecimal	
248	F8	TIMING CLOCK (24 clocks per crotchet/quarter-note). Synchronizes all instruments
249	F9	Undefined
250	FA	START. Sequence starts immediately.
251	FB	CONTINUE. A previously stopped sequence continues immediately
252	FC	STOP SEQUENCE
253	FD	Undedined
254	FE	ACTIVE SENSING
255	FF	SYSTEM RESET

ACTIVE SENSING An optional command designed to prevent 'hung' notes if the MIDI connection is accidentally broken. The command is sent every 300 ms whenever there is no other activity. A receiver which responds to ACTIVE SENSING will, if the data stream suddenly stops, turn off all voices.

SYSTEM RESET A drastic command which instructs all instruments to revert to the state they are programmed to enter when switched on. The MIDI specification advises that the command should be used sparingly, preferably under manual control, and that in particular it should not be used automatically on powering up.

System Exclusive

Incorporating Universal System Exclusive (Sample Dump Standard)

Status		Data		Function
Decimal	Hexadecimal	Decimal	Hexadecimal	
240	F0	[ID]	[ID]	Manufacturer's unique SYSEX code, assigned by the MMA, followed by any number of data bytes. Any status byte except REAL TIME (see below), but properly EOX will terminate a System Exclusive message.
240	F0	126	7E	ID of Universal System Excusive, NON-REAL TIME (Sample Dump Standard)
240	F0	127	7F	ID of Universal System Exclusive, REAL TIME (MIDI time code)

Sample Dump Messages

(All numbers given in Hexadecimal only)

Code	Message
F0 7E cc 03 ss ss F7	DUMP REQUEST (cc = channel no., ss = samples no., LSB first.

Sample data is sent in 'packets' of 120 bytes, together with Header, Checksum, and EOX.

Handshake Messages

Code	Message
F0 7E cc **7C** pp F7	WAIT (pp = packet no., max. 127). Instructs sender to wait before sending the next packet. Used to allow time for tasks such as disk access.
F0 7E cc **7D** pp F7	CANCEL. Aborts dump, e.g. when memory is full.
F0 7E cc **7E** pp F7	NAK. Indicates a data error and asks sender to resend packet pp.
F0 7E cc **7F** pp F7	ACK. Acknowledges receipt of data packet.

Packet Header

F0 7E cc **02** pp [120 bytes data] cs F7   (cs = Checksum)

Dump Header

F0 7E cc **01** ss ss sf sp sp sp sl sl sl ls ls ls le le le lt F7

Key sf = sample format (word length, from 8 to 28 bits)
     sp = sample period (nanoseconds; = 1/sample rate)
     sl = sample length in words
     ls = loop start point (word no.)
     le = loop end point (word no.)
     lt = loop type (00 = forwards only, 01 = forwards/backwards)

All 3-byte data (sp, sl, ls, le) sent LSB first.

Appendix 3. Scale and Frequency Tables

Ratios of Ascending Chromatic Scale

Interval (from tonic)	Pythagorean Ratio	cents	Just[a] Ratio	cents[b]	Equally Temp cents
Semitone	256:243	90	16:15	112	100
Whole tone	9:8	204	9:8	204	200
Minor third	32:27	294	6:5	316	300
Major third	81:64	408	5:4	386	400
Perfect fourth	4:3	498	4:3	498	500
Augmented fourth	729:512	612	45:32	590	600
Diminished fifth	1,024:729	588	64:45	610	600
Perfect fifth	3:2	702	3:2	702	700
Minor sixth	128:81	792	8:5	814	800
Major sixth	27:16	906	5:3	884	900
Minor seventh	16:9	996	16:9	996	1,000
Major seventh	243:128	1,110	15:8	1,088	1,100
Octave	2	1,200	2	1,200	1,200

Notes:
[a] Just intonation offers alternatives for certain intervals:

Small semitone	= 135:128	= 92 cents
Small whole tone	= 10:9	= 182 cents
Harmonic seventh	= 7:4	= 969 cents
Large minor seventh	= 9:5	= 1,018 cents
Large major seventh	= 256:135	= 1,108 cents

[b] All calculations rounded to nearest cent.

Equally Tempered Scale

Frequencies		Multipliers (from tonic A)
A	220.000	1.000000
A#	233.082	1.059463
B	246.942	1.122462
C	261.626	1.189207 (Middle C)
C#	277.183	1.259921
D	293.665	1.334840
D#	311.127	1.414214
E	329.628	1.498307
F	349.226	1.587401
F#	369.994	1.681793
G	391.995	1.781797
G#	415.305	1.887749
A	440.000	2.000000

Index of Products and Manufacturers

Page references in bold denote a main entry.

Index of Names

General Index

Page references in bold denote a main entry.